MISGUIDED MORALITY

Misguided Morality presents a survey of how the Catholic moral programme has failed to make a decisive impact on the behaviour of the Church's members. Despite a cogent theology of human conduct, Michael M. Winter argues that its effectiveness is not impressive. This book analyses what has gone wrong in the transmission of the New Testament ideals. The book covers the whole field of morality, starting with the bible and tracing the historical and sociological factors which have effected the dilution of those ideals, frequently to the level of anodyne respectability. Having explored the causes of failure, Winter offers positive suggestions for improvement in each area where shortcomings have been revealed.

Combining loyalty to the Roman Catholic Church, with constructive criticism of shortcomings in implementing moral policies, this book is essential reading to those studying and participating in Catholic moral teaching in the contemporary Church.

Michael M. Winter is well known for his books on the challenges to the Church after Vatican II, including his books *Mission or Maintenance*, and *Whatever Happened to Vatican II*.

D1525182

Misguided Morality

Catholic moral teaching in the contemporary church

MICHAEL M. WINTER

Ashgate

© Michael M. Winter 2002

Published by
Ashgate Publishing Limited
Gower House
Croft Road
Aldershot
Hants GU11 3HR
England

Ashgate Publishing Company
131 Main Street
Burlington VT 05401-5600 USA

Ashgate website: http://www.ashgate.com

British Library Cataloguing in Publication Data
Winter, Michael, 1930–
   Misguided morality : Catholic moral teaching in the
   contemporary church
   1. Catholic Church – Doctrines 2. Christian ethics
   I. Title
   241'.042

Library of Congress Control Number: 2002103823

ISBN 0 7546 0741 0 (Hbk)
ISBN 0 7546 0742 9 (Pbk)

Typeset by Manton Typesetters, Louth, Lincolnshire, UK and printed and bound in Great Britain by MPG Books Ltd, Bodmin, Cornwall.

Contents

Acknowledgements

In the writing of this book I have been assisted by the advice of several scholars and the practical direction of a number of librarians. But I wish to signal my particular gratitude to two individuals and two libraries without whose help this modest volume would not have been completed.

In the first place I wish to express my gratitude to Professor James O'Connell of Bradford University, and to Canon John McNamara, for their kindness to me in reading the manuscript and for offering many important suggestions.

I wish to record my thanks also to the librarians at the Cambridge University Library, and in London University to the staff of Heythrop College Library. But for the priceless collections of periodicals and source materials in those two libraries, and others like them, books of this kind simply could not be written.

I also wish to express my gratitude to the America Press for permission to quote extracts from *The Documents of Vatican II*, 1966, ed. Walter M. Abbott SJ and to the Editor of *The Tablet* for his permission to reprint the article by Fr Ladislas Orsy SJ entitled 'The Vatican's Procedures against Suspect Theologians' (16 January 1999), and to the Editor of *Priests and People* for permission to reproduce the article 'A New Twist to the Celibacy Debate' (November 1996).

Abbreviations

ACOD   Alberigo, J. (ed.) *Conciliorum Oecumenicorum Decreta*. Bologna, 1973

DS   Denzinger–Schönmetzer, *Enchiridion Symbolorum, Definitionum et Declarationum* Edition 33, Freiburg, 1965

DTC   *Dictionnaire de Théologie Catholique*, Paris

DV II   *The Documents of Vatican II* (English translation), ed. Walter M. Abbott, New York, 1966

MPG   Migne, *Patrologia Graeca*

MPL   Migne, *Patrologia Latina*

ST   St Thomas Aquinas, *Summa Theologica*

Introduction

As a broad generalization it is fair to maintain that the Catholic Church has failed to translate the moral ideals of the New Testament into the lives of most of its members. This failure has immediate practical consequences. Unless the Church can make its moral programme visibly effective, its mission will suffer and its right to exist will be called into question. For without this tangible benefit to offer to the human race, why should anyone wish to join? To put it in simple practical terms, if a non-believer says to me, 'Why should I become a Christian and embrace the RC Church?' I should be able to reply, 'Because it will give you a moral programme that will enhance your own life, and enable you to enrich the world as you go through it over the years.' Unfortunately I cannot offer any such assurance to an enquirer because recent history shows few signs of that enhancement of life within the Catholic community.

Admittedly I can assure the enquirer that this Church has preserved faithfully the doctrines of the Trinity, the Incarnation, and many others. But these refinements are appreciated by those already on the inside. Newcomers need to be persuaded by more tangible and practical benefits for joining.

The inability of the Church to activate the New Testament's moral programme on a large scale has been so widespread that one is led to suspect serious functional shortcomings in the organization. Admittedly it is difficult to generalize about the performance of a community which is so vast, so complex and so ancient. Moreover at all times in its history there have been examples of heroic virtue as well as good average performance. Yet in situations of real moral urgency (such as warfare and its concomitants) it is hard to discern any significant difference between the conduct of most Catholics and those who have no religious faith to inspire or guide them. This holds true in active badness, such as indiscriminate bombing of civilians in war, as well as tacit acquiescence to situations like anti-Semitism, apartheid, or the maintenance of the death penalty. This failure has been so widespread that one must make a critical examination of the Church's organization and policies for translating the New Testament's moral programme into everyday life. I am not making judgements about the lives of individuals, still less am I criticizing the gospels. In this book I am concerned with the pedestrian process of transmission, and how the Church's functioning has blocked the ideals that should have animated the lives of all its members.

Confining my attention for the moment to examples drawn from living memory, the conduct of Catholics faced with Hitler's anti-Semitic policy seems to have been indistinguishable from that of committed Nazi party activists, no matter what personal anguish they may have endured interiorly. In other words the impeccably correct theology of the Catholic Church appears to have had no significant influence on its members' behaviour in that instance of incomprehensible evil. That episode was not an isolated example, as I will demonstrate further on.

Since the New Testament cannot be at fault, and since the teachings of Jesus and St. Paul take account of human frailty, the obvious place to seek the causes of failure must be the sphere of ecclesiastical policies and organization. This leads us to ask about such matters as the moral education of the clergy and laity. Have the teachings of Jesus been watered down in practice? Also, how do decision-making processes function? How is power exercised within the Church? What avenues of communication and dialogue operate between rulers and the governed? It is in this general area that deficiencies exist, which may appear tolerable in theory, and in a period of tranquillity, but whose shortcomings are seen to be disastrous in times of crisis, such as the Nazi period in Germany. In that situation the Catholic Church was almost totally ineffectual, so little did it achieve in resisting the cruelties in which its members collaborated.

In short, the mechanisms for translating the Church's moral ideals into the lives of its members have failed in really crucial situations. If this contention seems to be an exaggeration, I am confident that the evidence presented in this book will show that my evaluation is correct.

Catholic moral teaching presents a paradox, insofar as official pronouncements are (for the most part) impeccably correct, yet their application in the pedestrian realities of life is woefully inadequate. In simple matters, such as truthfulness and the practice of daily prayer, the Church has inculcated a reasonable standard of conduct into the lives of its adherents. Moreover the last few decades have witnessed authentic Christian heroism in the lives of such people as Mother Teresa of Calcutta and Archbishop Romero of El Salvador. In their different ways they have demonstrated heroic virtue that can compare with the moral excellence of any period of Christian history.

Furthermore, most readers, drawing on their own experience, will have enjoyed the acquaintance of self-effacing pastors of souls labouring devotedly for the spiritual welfare of their parishioners. In the same way many will have known devoted schoolteachers working heroically in inner-city areas to give their pupils some insight into the richness of Catholic faith, battling at times against impossible odds of poverty and deprivation. There is no denying the reality of all this moral effort. But the overall picture of the Church's ethical balance sheet presents a disturbing negative side, the effects of which are inescapably clear. In really crucial matters the Church's record is far from reassuring.

A few examples, drawn from recent history, will illustrate the point. I have already alluded to the Church's record during the Nazi period in

Germany. It warrants further reflection on account of the scale and gravity of the events. With very few exceptions the anti-Semitic policies that culminated in the extermination of millions met with only token opposition from German Catholics. Pope Pius XII has been blamed, perhaps somewhat unfairly, for his silence. Opposition should have come from the laity and clergy in Germany, but it did not. Apart from very rare and isolated instances, there was general acquiescence in the policy of exterminating the Jews, initially in Germany, and later in every area under the control of the German armies. Yet the Church in Germany at that period was extremely well organized. There was an adequate number of priests and religious in the parishes and other institutions. In the ideological sphere, faculties of Catholic theology were functioning in about half the state universities, and there was an abundance of Catholic newspapers and other journals. It is difficult to think of any other nation in the 1930s where institutional Catholicism was functioning so efficiently, albeit within its own terms of reference. Yet when the crisis point came, that superbly organized community failed to halt or alleviate the plight of the Jews, nor did it protest on their behalf in the name of justice.

A similar pattern was to be seen in the United States in the immediate post-war period and the 1950s. The civil rights movement for black people received very little support from the Catholic Church. Once again, as in Germany in the 1930s, the Catholics in the USA were extremely well organized. Even at that period they constituted the largest single Church in the whole nation. They had a comprehensive network of Catholic schools and universities. Priests and nuns were in plentiful supply. Thanks to the constitutional separation of Church and State, no other Church enjoyed a more privileged position. Yet in spite of all these advantages, the Catholics as a whole made scarcely any impact in the struggle to secure equality of treatment for black people. Clearly something serious had gone wrong, as in Germany, in implementing the simplest precept of Christian morality: to love our neighbours as ourselves.

Worse was to come in the 1970s in South America. Many countries in the subcontinent came under the control of military dictatorships. The crushing of legitimate political opposition and constitutional freedoms was carried out with total brutality. In Argentina, to cite but one example, thousands of people simply disappeared. When they vanished, it was generally supposed that they had been killed by government death squads. Years later it became clear that this was precisely what had happened. It also became clear that the Catholic Church had done virtually nothing to prevent such atrocities, either in its public stance or in the guidance given to individual Catholics serving in the armed forces and police. It was also alleged that the Papal Nuncio connived at the policy, something the Vatican of course denied.[1]

I will develop this theme in the course of the book, but the above examples illustrate my contention that on really serious matters the moral programme of the Catholic Church has failed to produce the results that could rightly have been expected of it.

There is no simple explanation nor is there a single cause for these failures: the reasons are diverse and for the most part historical in origin. The first major hazard arose when the Emperor Constantine made Christianity the religion of state in the fourth century. This alliance of Church and State introduced the first distortion of gospel values. From then onwards obedience to the Christian emperor assumed too large a place in the religious programme. Moreover, the benefits conferred by Christian rulers were potentially dangerous. The policing of doctrine by the civil authorities, culminating in the execution of heretics, was disastrous for the proper assent of faith. With the wisdom of hindsight we can see that the military defence and expansion of European Christianity by orders such as the Teutonic knights was equally harmful to true religion. Equally damaging to the true interests of the Church's mission was the widespread practice whereby kings and lesser nobles acquired the right to nominate bishops and to influence other ecclesiastical appointments.

Clearly, many of these policies were adopted hundreds of years ago, and some of these were abandoned well before the modern period. In spite of that, their momentum has left an indelible imprint on ecclesiastical policy right up to the present. The list could be prolonged much further, as will be apparent in subsequent chapters. For the present I mention these factors briefly to indicate the general area in which the process of distortion occurred, and how the moral programme of the New Testament came to be applied so badly in the lives of Catholics, particularly at the level of corporate behaviour.

This is all the more serious at the present time since morality has entered centre stage whether we like it or not. All public or private decision-making entails a moral component. In wage bargaining, taxation, education, building a new factory, or military intervention, a moral choice is always integral to the decision-making process, although the decision-makers may not consciously advert to its specifically ethical character. Decisions about the allocation of resources and the prioritizing of conflicting claims always entail moral choices.

In recent years the moral component has become even more prominent. Early in the year 2000 the question arose about the patenting of genes. Public opinion quickly realized that an urgent moral issue was at stake if certain drug companies were trying to acquire a monopoly in the business of human and plant genetic development. Similarly the Gulf War and its aftermath forced people to face up to the morality of the arms trade, since weapons made in Britain were then aimed at British troops. It was not simply a matter of expediency but a much deeper moral issue about the export of military equipment. Equally challenging was the morality of the economic sanctions against Iraq, whose principal victims were children whose health suffered as a result of the lack of medicines. The list could be prolonged almost indefinitely.

If the selfish interests of individuals or powerful groups are not to prevail, then a strong ethical basis must determine decisions in politics, business, and social affairs generally. Even in matters of international commerce and economics, market forces are not a self-regulating system. Greed and deception too often determine the final outcome. In this context the moral programme of the New Testament has assumed a new relevance. Hans Küng has pointed out[2] that it is only religious groups and systems that can demand an unconditional moral decision. Purely rational ethics will frame moral demands in terms like this: if persons are to fulfil their potential as human beings, they must act in accordance with the requirements of human nature. Such an obligation is hypothetical, and implies a deeper obligation to the Creator who has fashioned our nature and set its goals. Without this deeper moral imperative, the purely humanistic appeal to natural fulfilment is defenceless against a whole class of challenges. For instance an individual may say: 'I do not wish to fulfil my human potential, and if I choose to wreck my body by a habit of drug-taking, then in the name of freedom, autonomy and human rights, I will do with my own body what I want.' Provided that this does not damage the environment or other people, it is difficult to answer such a proclamation of freedom and autonomy. Only a God-centred moral system can make unconditional stipulations.

Paradoxically, as we recognize the urgent need to apply Christian morality on a worldwide scale, the shortcomings of the Catholic presentation of it become equally clear. This has an immediate practical bearing on people's loyalty. Is it reasonable to expect high-minded people to maintain their allegiance to the Catholic Church if its moral guidance is seen to be irrelevant to urgent matters that ought to be central to its concerns?

My concern in this book is to examine the effectiveness of the programme of specifically Christian morality and its development in the Roman Catholic Church.

Confining our attention for the moment to this Church, we can say that few errors have been promulgated over the centuries in the presentation of its moral teaching. However, in practice much of its ethical agenda has been so lacking in balance that in some areas it has done more harm than good. To put it in other words, there has been a distortion of values whereby trivialities have occupied the attention of preachers to such an extent that the crucial moral issues facing the human race have been all but neglected.

An example of disproportionate exaggeration, as well as misdirected instruction, is the U-turn on masturbation in 1997. Hitherto, generations of young people and others had been terrorized by constant admonitions that it was sinful and indeed always a mortal sin. This meant that those who had the misfortune to die with such a sin unabsolved would spend the whole of eternity in hell. This was the message of the first edition of the modern *Catechism of the Catholic Church* published by the Vatican. It stated uncompromisingly that 'The magisterium of the Church in the course of a constant tradition, and the moral sense of the faithful, have been in no doubt and have firmly maintained, that masturbation is an intrinsically and gravely disordered action.'[3] The fourth edition of that catechism published in 1997 not only removed it from the category of mortal sins but hedged the whole activity around with such modifications and qualifications as to concede that it was blameless, or almost. Prior to this welcome reversal of a long-established attitude, generations of Catholics had been led to believe that masturbation was as bad as armed robbery, for instance, both of them being classified as mortal sins and therefore susceptible of eternal punishment in hell. In short, it was a tragic example of gross exaggeration, to say the least.

A further weakness in the Catholic practical agenda has been our inability to translate ideals into practice. The popes in the last hundred years have enunciated many fine sentiments on social and economic matters but a high proportion have never left the pages of the encyclicals. The appropriate environment for such matters is the marketplace and not the archives. Effective implementation has been blocked by a variety of influences, which will be discussed in ensuing chapters.

I am not suggesting that the Catholic Church has consciously planned a destructive moral policy, but the results have frequently been catastrophic. The human race has been deprived of the services of what could have been one of its most effective moral guides, while terrible cruelties and injustices have been perpetrated in Christian countries without any effective opposition or indeed protest from the official organs of the Catholic Church. I have in mind such evils as warfare, economic exploitation, political intimidation, racial discrimination, and so on.

The aim of Christian morality should be liberation, that is to say, a completely positive process by which individuals are progressively set free from the damaging limitations of their personal weaknesses and propensities to evil, as well as freeing them from the harm which outsiders might inflict on their lives. The process should be one of fulfilment and joy, rather like a good education. Ideally schools should not be places for compulsion and drudgery but communities in which pupils should enjoy the acquisition of culture.

The perceived failure of the Church to endow its members with a positive, joyful and enriching morality is one cause, I am sure, for the massive abandonment of religion by young people in the 1980s and 1990s. (The other major cause of the leakage is the Church's unwillingness to make structural changes to its institutions which still bear basically the same form as they received in the sixteenth century when the Catholic Church reorganized them, reacting to the Reformation)

In all fairness it must be noted that the large-scale abandonment of formal religious practice is not confined to the Catholic Church. Other Christian Churches are facing similar shrinking of effective membership, so too are the Jews. Undoubtedly each community has its own specific problems, but the general field of morality is a common feature of the alienation in all the aforementioned groups. Whereas Catholics have been obsessed by supposed sexual deviations, the inheritors of the Puritan tradition have been ill at ease with a whole gamut of pleasures (typified in Britain by the closure of theatres during Cromwell's rule). The Jews for their part have considerable problems living with the Mosaic law whose hundreds of attendant regulations do not easily translate into spiritual liberation. To preserve a sense of balance I wish to draw attention to the overall decline in religion, but as my immediate experience has been within the Catholic Church, I will confine my observations to that Church, of which I have been a member for more than sixty years.

If morality is viewed in the way described above, then it should empower individuals to make their own moral decisions on the basis of an informed conscience, and also give the strength to implement them. This may entail great efforts such as when an alcoholic has to say No to his desire for another whisky or when one ought to say Yes to yet another disaster appeal. It may require courage too when what is needed is a refusal to one's commanding officer when ordered to commit an act of indiscriminate cruelty in time of war.

On the question of how individuals make their moral decisions the Church's practice has also been defective in the modern period. Briefly, our conscience makes a practical decision on the basis of the relevant facts and the perceived obligations. The obligations are known either from natural law or from biblical revelation. This is something of an oversimplification, but it will suffice for the present. The response to the requirements of natural law is a purely rational decision, and the response to revealed morality is an exercise of faith. The two sources are not always in watertight compartments, but I have expressed it in this way to emphasize the role of faith, which is frequently neglected in Catholic teaching.

Although primacy of conscience has been upheld at the theoretical level in the Catholic tradition, in practice it has not always been allowed its proper scope. One factor in this limitation was the apparently similar contention of Luther about private judgement in matters of doctrine. Having repudiated the authority of popes, councils, and all organs of the ecclesiastical teaching authority, Luther encouraged his followers to make their own decisions about doctrine in the light of their own reading of the scriptures. Although moral decisions and doctrinal understanding are quite distinct, the Catholic authorities at that period seem to have been opposed to anything Luther had championed.

It is difficult now to appreciate the shock and bitterness felt by Catholics in the aftermath of Luther's initial success. Within a decade of his excommunication in 1521 almost half of Germany had abandoned Catholicism in favour of Lutheranism. The speed and completeness of the Catholic collapse may perhaps account for the reluctance to countenance anything Luther had advocated, even where his policies were closer to those of the primitive Church than were those of late medieval Christendom. For example, at the Diet of Augsburg in 1548 the Emperor Charles V suggested a serious compromise to conciliate the Lutherans. It was agreed in the document, known as the Interim of Augsburg, that until the Council of Trent should settle the matters, clerical marriage should be allowed, so too should the giving of the chalice to the laity at the eucharist. The Catholic Church repudiated both suggestions.

One is left with the uneasy feeling that anything advocated by Luther would be rejected by the Catholic authorities. This may account for the reluctance on the part of the Catholic Church to allow the individual conscience to have its proper scope. In the aftermath of the Reformation, Catholic Church leaders were uneasy about any exercise of personal autonomy in religion and tended more and more to exact from their members obedience to external norms, dictated of course by those same authorities.

This orientation of moral guidance has had a deleterious effect upon the moral education of individuals within the Catholic Church. Clearly the process does require some measure of direction from the elders during the apprenticeship stages, when the child is taught basically to conform. It is rather like learning a musical instrument. Instruction is necessary and practising scales is boring but it must be persevered with if one is to acquire the expertise to enjoy playing Beethoven's sonatas. What is important to authentic morality is that adults do not remain in the state of pupillage all their lives, but this is what has happened to all too many Catholics.

The search for a corrective for these damaging but unnecessary distortions of the moral ideals of the New Testament will constitute the substance of this book.

To bring order and coherence to so large a quantity of material, I have decided to use the classification consecrated by Aquinas, and deal with the subjects within the categories of the three theological virtues of faith, hope, and charity, followed by the moral virtues of prudence, justice, fortitude, and temperance.

To keep the compass of the book within reasonable bounds, I have also decided to omit any detailed consideration of the workings of grace. I am well aware that it is indispensable for the Christian moral life, but its operations have been analysed so well in countless books that it would be superfluous for me to add to the literature. The same applies to the effects of Original Sin and the exercise of conscience. As with grace itself, they have been analysed and explained in all the standard textbooks of moral theology. In the pages that follow, I shall confine my exposition to matters on which other books have so far been silent, namely to the way in which moral obligations come to be perceived and how they are implemented. For it is at this practical level that the Church's mostly admirable agenda has failed in so many areas. The results have been a betrayal of the expectations engendered by the moral ideals and orientation of the New Testament.

Notes

1 *The Tablet*, 6 May 1995.
2 Kung, H. *Global Responsibility*, London, 1990, pp. 52,53.
3 *Catechism of the Catholic Church*, English translation, London, 1994, item 2352, on p. 503.

Chapter 1

Getting Started

Faith as the Foundation of Morality

The moral programme presented by the New Testament is positive, creative, generous, and indeed heroic. Believers who have made a definitive life commitment to the person of Jesus are led directly to express this commitment in the twofold injunction to love God and their neighbour. This orientation of life, which is the unfolding of the basic loyalty of belief, is disarmingly simple, perhaps alarmingly so.

However it lacks the detailed precision of the Old Testament's laws and the legal codes of the secular world. So, from an early stage in the Church's history, Christians were searching for something a little more precise to guide their conduct, over and above the general moral orientation that they took up when they pledged faith in Jesus. Over the course of centuries they have found supplementary guidance in two areas concerned with human behaviour, namely natural law, and Roman law.[1]

The Influence of Natural Law

In the first few centuries Christians turned to natural law in the context of the broadly based intellectual movement by which they interpreted the Christian revelation in the categories of Greek philosophy. The more obvious area of application was in doctrine where the theologians used classical metaphysics to throw light upon doctrines like the Trinity and Incarnation. Morality too benefited from the influence of the Greek thinkers. The ethical systems of Plato and Aristotle lent considerable support to the Christian programme of human behaviour. So too did the teachings of the Stoics. Their perception of an ordered universe operating purposefully was seen as a natural ally of the Christian doctrine of a benevolent Creator directing the universe according to his wisdom. The Stoic doctrine that man must collaborate with this order harmonized closely with the Christian moral endeavour. Thus Christians found guidance for life by examining human nature and the intrinsic demands which it displayed for the fulfilment of humanity's potential. The fundamental presupposition of natural law is that a rational examination of human nature will show what kind of behaviour will promote its well-being, development, and hence its proper conduct.

At the simplest level of this paradigm a consideration of the biological requirements of the body will indicate some basic obligations, such as that habitual drunkenness is damaging to the body and hence immoral. The refinements of ethics take us much further than that! Even at this basic level it is important to remember that with the passage of time and the alteration of historical circumstances the obligations can change as mankind's understanding of human nature evolves. As is widely known, Aristotle considered slavery natural, not a view that commands any confidence now. In the opinion of A.P. d'Entrèves, even Aquinas considered that the natural law could change.[2]

Modern psychology has made it clear that human nature cannot be considered in terms of the biological functioning of the body alone. We must take account of the person in his or her totality. This principle has been accepted generally by moral theologians.[3] Briefly it entails taking account of the network of relationships surrounding the person, without which human life as such is inconceivable. In practical terms, it means that moral choices have to take account of how that network of relationships will be affected.

To evaluate the enhancement or damaging of those relationships a threefold system of guidelines, namely Function, Solidarity, and Aesthetics, has been proposed by a modern writer.[4] The promotion of these three guidelines will enhance the common good without which we, as social beings, cannot achieve moral progress. The inclusion of aesthetics may seem unusual, but it is far more influential than we normally realize. For example, it has been a powerful motive in our instinctive revulsion about cannibalism. It was also the underpinning of the former Catholic prohibition against cremation, presented as a matter of natural law. In fact one French philosopher stressed its influence in the words, 'That which is beautiful seems to be a simpler route to the divine than that which is true.'[5] One is reminded of the anecdote reported about Albert Einstein. Having heard the youthful Yehudi Menuhin play one of Bach's violin sonatas, he is alleged to have said 'Now I know that God exists'.

Lest the considerations studied in the previous paragraph may seem somewhat imprecise, it is reassuring to remember that the moral obligations in social relationships have been given the most rigorous intellectual underpinning by Kant. His categorical imperative regulates the conduct of all interpersonal activity. It can be expressed thus: 'I ought never to act except in such a way that I can also will that my maxim should become a universal law.'[6] A homely example that makes it clear is the hosepipe ban. In a time of drought when the use of garden hoses has been forbidden, a keen gardener is sorely tempted to water his patiently cultivated roses shortly before the local flower show. Even though his garden is secluded from the prying eyes of his neighbours (and competitors), he realizes that if everyone were to water their gardens the water supply would dry up. He acts altruistically in a way which everyone should act.[7] Lest it be objected that the categorical imperative seems to be either enlightened self-interest or concerned mainly with the consequences of our actions, it should be remembered that the results of our moral choices are integral to morality. This follows from the realization that the moral requirements of human nature extend to the network of relationships which support the individual. For example, if lying were to become generally used instead of truth, then education, social life, and commerce would simply become impossible. To describe the categorical imperative as the extrapolation of individual conduct to the universal scene makes perfect sense in the light of that example.

Mary Warnock has pointed out that for all its merits Kant's work neglects all other components of the human personality, except the purely rational.[8] It was to the credit of David Hume that he included the emotional factors in his treatment of ethics. To quote his own words, 'What is honourable, what is fair, what is becoming, what is noble, what is generous, takes possession of the heart, and animates us to embrace and maintain it.'[9] Moral decision-making is not simply a rational process, it also engages the emotions when it is faced with practical choices. These are not shallow, transient or flippant sentiments, but profound and generous attitudes like sympathy and altruism.[10] Indeed one could say that the emotions must come into play in order to effect the transition from 'I ought' to 'I must'.

For all its rational cogency, we must remember that the natural law has undeniable limitations. In the first place the very word *law* is misleading. A system of rational ethics cannot give the detail and precision for human conduct that comes from positive law. Pure reason will indicate to me that driving fast in congested streets is immoral because it is potentially dangerous to human life but it requires legal machinery for the government to fix the limit at 30 mph.

Allied to this limitation is the logical problem of deducing particular courses of action from general principles. The health of the body and what promotes it is deducible from considerations of human nature's requirements. But I cannot strictly deduce therefrom that Mr X must have open-heart surgery here and now.[11]

Some of the victims of the misguided quest for unachievably specific certainty have been modern popes who have tried desperately to give universal rules on a variety of matters, allegedly deduced from the basic principles of natural law. At times the exercise is somewhat artificial, and at other times the claim is stretched beyond the point of credibility. A rather sad example of this was Pius XI's condemnation of co-education. Although it was enunciated with amazing confidence as if it were self-evident, the statement now displays a rather pathetic delusion. The significant paragraph reads as follows:

> That system of education of adolescents which is commonly called co-education, is fallacious and inimical to Christian upbringing. ... The two sexes have been constituted by the wisdom of God so that in the family and in society they should complement each other mutually and form a suitable unit. The distinc-

tions of body and soul by which they are differentiated are to be upheld in
upbringing and education, and indeed those distinctions are to be fostered and
fortified by appropriate differences and separation, suitable to their ages and
circumstances, ... these precepts are to be observed not only in all schools,
particularly in the perilous years of adolescence, ... but also in gymnastic games
and exercises.[12]

The third and most serious weakness is that the whole system of rational
ethics presupposes (implicitly at least) the hypothesis that a Supreme Being
has willed the fulfilment of human nature. To revert once again to the
example which I cited in the Introduction, if a heroin addict has no dependents
and makes no demands on the health service or anyone else, it is difficult to
disprove his claim that in the name of human freedom and autonomy he can
choose to end his life by drug addiction. If he is an atheist and admits no
allegiance to a Creator who wills the perfection of his human nature, it is
difficult to argue convincingly against his self-destructive practices.

In fact the classical exponents of natural law have always claimed that
they were elaborating their ethical systems in the context of a Higher Power
who had set the agenda. The underlying presuppositions were expressed
beautifully by Cicero in his *Republic*.

> True Law is right reason in agreement with Nature; it is of universal application,
> unchanging and everlasting; it summons to duty by its commands, and averts
> from wrong-doing by its prohibitions. And it does not lay its commands or
> prohibitions upon good men in vain, though neither have any effect on the
> wicked. It is a sin to try to alter this law, nor is it allowable to attempt to repeal
> any part of it, and it is impossible to abolish it entirely. We cannot be freed from
> its obligations by Senate or People, and we need not look outside ourselves for
> an expounder or interpreter of it. And there will not be different laws at Rome
> and at Athens, or different laws now and in the future, but one eternal and
> unchangeable law will be valid for all nations and for all times, and there will be
> one master and one ruler, that is God, over us all, for He is the author of this law,
> its promulgator and its enforcing judge.[13]

Paradoxically it is this theoretical weakness of natural law which has
commended most strongly its adoption by Christian writers. With full confidence in the Creator's implanting guidelines in his creatures' nature, Christian moralists have made use of the natural law to throw light on those areas
of human conduct upon which the New Testament is silent. It was their faith
in God which prompted them to treat natural law with such reverence and
confidence. As is well known, Aquinas regarded it as a participation in the
divine law. It was the underpinning of the moral force of human legislation,
to such an extent that if human laws did not conform to the underlying
rationale of natural law, they were no laws at all, merely an abuse, and
carrying no moral obligation for obedience.[14]

Thus it was that from early in the Church's history up to the present day,
natural law has been employed as an ancillary source of moral guidance,

providing a rational supplement to the New Testament's exhortations. Whereas the demands of rational ethics invite a corresponding rational response, the biblical norms require of the Christian a response motivated by faith. On the genesis and development of faith I will have more to say at a later stage in this chapter. For the present, I wish to clarify the supplementary guidance supplied by natural law. In the last two centuries the popes have made considerable use of it to give directives in areas where the New Testament is silent.

For the same reasons, moral theologians too have made extensive use of natural law in their studies, precisely because over vast areas of human conduct the New Testament is literally silent. A relevant example is the book entitled *New Directions in Sexual Ethics*.[15] In its 213 pages of text there is not a single argument drawn from the New Testament. This is not surprising, since the book deals with moral problems that have arisen since the Aids epidemic.

A more subtle limitation of natural law is the extent to which its proponents have been influenced, perhaps subconsciously, by the customs, laws, religion, and general culture of the societies in which they grew up. A number of moral imperatives have been advanced by ethical thinkers as if they were the fruits of pure reason. More recent history and a more critical outlook has shown them to be far from reasonable. As I noted above, Aristotle considered that slavery was natural. Until quite recently most societies considered the death penalty morally correct, and at an earlier date torture of suspects was generally acceptable. None of these examples can stand up to rigorous questioning in the modern intellectual climate, engendered by the Enlightenment of the eighteenth century.

Similar to the preceding limitations is the tendency seen in many textbooks of moral theology to make a subconscious equation between artificiality and immorality. It entails a line of reasoning which is something like this. If an action is artificial it is unnatural, and if it is unnatural it is immoral. This kind of argument was used frequently in the older textbooks to condemn activities such as artificial insemination. One suspects that there was a latent bias against sexual matters since it was never applied to other areas like modern surgery. For example, open-heart surgery has never been frowned upon even by conservative moralists. It entails disconnecting the blood supply, pumping blood through the body with an electrical pump for several hours during the operation. The lungs likewise are kept going by mechanical ventilators. And when the lengthy operation is over, the new heart is literally kick-started into action by administering an electric shock. It is difficult to imagine anything more artificial but it has never received any moral censure. That has been reserved for artificialities in the area of sex.

Needless to say, the observance of the natural law as such is not necessary for salvation, in spite of what some Christian fundamentalists maintain. Nevertheless a committed Christian will not fall below its demands, but for other reasons, as I will demonstrate later in the chapter. By the same token, the observance of the Code Napoléon or any other legal system is not necessary for salvation. Yet once again a committed Christian is unlikely to fall below its requirements on such matters as fraud or kidnapping.

The observation in the preceding paragraph is useful to bear in mind when considering a further limitation on natural law. It is not susceptible of irreformable definition by the Church's magisterium. It is clear from a simple reading of the statement of papal infallibility in the First Vatican Council that the Church's competence to make irreformable pronouncements is coterminous with revelation. The definition of 1870 was very circumspect in its wording, which is in harmony with the constant practice of General Councils. Their decrees have always been framed so as to secure the minimum basis which is necessary to exclude error. They have never been formulated so as to guarantee every aspect of the doctrine under consideration. The kernel of the relevant declaration is worded thus:

> We define as revealed dogma that the Roman Pontiff when he speaks ex cathedra, that is to say, when exercising the office of pastor and teacher of all Christians, and when he defines on his supreme Apostolic authority a doctrine of faith and morals to be held by the whole Church, … he exercises that infallibility which the Divine Redeemer willed his Church to have in defining doctrine of faith and morals: such definitions of the Roman Pontiff are irreformable of themselves not by reason of the consent of the Church.

Just what is meant by 'faith and morals' was indicated in a previous paragraph of the same document: 'The Holy Spirit was not promised to Peter and his successors so that they should disclose new doctrine by his revelation, but with his assistance they should piously guard and faithfully expound the revelation or deposit of faith handed on by the apostles.'[16] In other words, the power of making such definitions is confined to the interpretation of what has been revealed by God and not to that which has been devised by human reasoning.

The well known phrase 'faith and morals' has a more complex history than its simple terms would suggest.[17] In the present context I am concerned with its meaning in the text of the First Vatican Council. A study of the debates in the Council makes it clear that the bishops faced up to a complex question, and that their interpretation of it was to limit the phrase to morality as revealed in the Bible. The elucidation given by Bishop Gasser in the course of the Council is recognized as being crucial to the interpretation of the Council's decree. In the course of a lengthy speech, he explained why the drafting committee had decided to retain the well known phrase 'faith and morals' in preference to others which had been suggested, such as 'matters of faith and principles of morals'. His crucial words are as follows:

> But the Deputation for the Faith cannot admit even this emendation, partly because that word would be entirely novel, whereas the term 'matters of faith

and morals' and 'doctrine of faith and morals' is extremely well known, and every theologian knows what is to be understood by these words. Moreover, some 'principles of morals' can be merely philosophical principles of natural goodness, which do not belong in every respect to the deposit of faith.[18]

The same interpretation was supplied by Cardinal Franzelin, who had been one of the principal architects of the definition:

> The term 'faith' considered as the object of faith, is understood as revealed teaching which is of itself primarily theoretical and to be believed with subjective faith, but many moral obligations follow from it. The term 'morals' here means revealed teaching which is practical, which is, of course, also to be believed with faith, but which also has been provided to command and prohibit acts of morals.[19]

It is clear that the First Vatican Council clarified what had been the Church's habitual practice, namely the scope of infallibility is coterminous with revelation. It does not cover matters of moral philosophy which are the constructs of human reason.

A moment's reflection will reveal the irrational consequences of conceding that the Church could define matters of ethics. Since ethics is a branch of philosophy, why not define other areas of philosophy, the whole corpus of metaphysics, for a start? Large parts of it are closely interwoven with the elucidation of the doctrines of the Trinity and Incarnation. And why stop at philosophy? Should not psychology come within the scope of infallibility, since it is concerned with human behaviour, and therefore moral issues? If psychology were to be included within the ambit of infallibility because it is concerned with human behaviour, then why not take in economics as well, and for basically the same reasons? Such suggestions are patently absurd. We assent to revealed doctrine by faith, and if revelation is unclear the magisterium can clarify it, sometimes drawing on its endowment of infallibility.

If there might have been any lingering doubts about the limits of infallibility, the Second Vatican Council clarified the matter beyond any reasonable doubt. *The Constitution on the Church* stated the matter in these words: 'This infallibility with which the Divine Redeemer willed His Church to be endowed in defining a doctrine of faith and morals, extends as far as extends the deposit of divine revelation, which must be religiously guarded and faithfully expounded'. (Section 25)

The Church for its part has been consistent in its practice on this matter. Actually very few matters of morality have been defined by General Councils. A rare example is that of usury, the lending of money at unjustly high rates of interest. A number of General Councils in the mediaeval period condemned the practice and always based their condemnation on the revealed Scriptures, not on philosophical ethics. For example the Second Lateran Council of 1139 delivered its judgement in the following words: 'We condemn the detestable and insatiable rapacity of the money lenders, which is condemned by divine and human laws, and repudiated by Scripture in the Old and New Testaments, ... we deny them all consolations of the Church, ... unless they repent, they are to be denied Christian burial.' This condemnation was repeated in slightly different words in the Third and Fourth Lateran Councils, the First and Second Councils of Lyons, the Council of Vienne, and the Fifth Lateran Council.[20] The biblical authorities to which they were alluding were most probably Exodus 22:25, Deuteronomy 23:19, and Matthew 5:42. There was never any suggestion that they were defining matters of natural law, investigated by rational elaboration.

The Influence of Roman Law

The second source of supplementary moral guidance for Christians has been Roman law. In the twelfth century it was effectively rediscovered in the universities of Europe and became extremely influential, since it served as the inspiration, idiom, and terms of reference for Church law. From that time onwards, the study and practice of canon law developed prodigiously in the universities, in the Church courts and in the administrative activities of the Roman Curia. Since it was concerned with one area of human conduct, it is not surprising that it began to influence moral theology, and dogmatic theology too.

An example of the latter area is the fact that the validity of sacraments came to be judged according to the same kind of rules as the validity of contracts and other legal transactions. From that period onwards, the sacrament of matrimony was defined as a contract, whose principal substance was the right to sexual intercourse between the spouses. It is superfluous to remark on what an impoverished notion of marriage is implied therein, but it is unmistakably framed in a totally legalistic idiom.

The legal influence on moral theology was pervasive, mostly on account of its clarity, and its apparent ability to supply gratifyingly clear rules for conduct. Whether this meant accepting a measure of artificiality is a consideration which must be borne in mind. In the mediaeval period it was scarcely alluded to. Most writers were seduced by the precision and clarity of the categories as applied to the solutions of moral problems.

The seventeenth century saw a prodigious advance in the development of this kind of moral reasoning under the influence of scholars, like Suárez and Vittoria, who combined competence in theology and law. As the latter can be regarded as the father of international law, it is not surprising that his moral theology should have been developed in legalistic categories. The moralists of that epoch were responding to the increasingly complicated pattern of life. The discovery of America, the expansion of world trade, the process of colonization all brought with them a host of complex moral issues. So too did the proliferation of other Christian Churches in the wake of the Reformation, as well as advances in science. Furthermore the Renaissance had effectively broken out of a whole framework of psychological limitations inherited from the Middle Ages. In short, life had become far more enriched, diversified and complicated.

It was in response to this sophistication that the science of casuistry was developed. The moral procedures known as probabilism, tutiorism and epicheia were fashioned to enable the exactitude of moral laws to be applied validly to widely differing circumstances. Epicheia is perhaps the most interesting of the procedures. This principle teaches that an individual may act in a way which is to some extent at variance with the law, if the literal observance of the precept would lead to a result which was contrary to what the legislator had intended. A modern example is the Principle of Totality, which states that the good of the part may be sacrificed for the good of the whole. It has been invoked frequently in matters of medical ethics, in operations which entail amputations. It has been criticized for being so vague that it cannot really support the weight of argument which has been laid on it.[21]

The whole process takes for granted that the Divine Lawgiver has provided a comprehensive set of rules for every contingency in every human life. It is this presupposition which most perplexes the modern enquirer. In fact reality is much too complex for such detailed regulation, and theology gives no warrant to suppose that such a collection of directives has been instituted for Christians. A system which was eminently suitable for dealing with a mass of human legislation at the national or imperial level cannot presume to apply itself to God's dealings with individual human beings.

The legalistic orientation of moral theology has persisted, in some quarters, right up to the modern period. We still see a tendency to seek if not comprehensive rules then at least comprehensive systems of interrelated principles which can be applied unerringly to all areas of human moral choices. For example, Professor L. Janssens elaborated what he termed 'person centred morality' on the basis of eight interlocking principles. When a human being is considered as the centre of moral choices, he must be envisaged as:

1   A subject.
2   An embodied object.
3   Part of the material world.
4   Interrelational with other people.
5   An independent social being.
6   Historical.
7   Equal but unique.
8   Called to know and worship God.

Armed with this battery of principles, goodness or badness can be discerned, in the words of the author: 'Whatever promotes or violates the good of the human person considered in this comprehensive way is respectively right or wrong.'[22] One could perhaps be forgiven for thinking that the scheme might be a little too complicated and artificial for the banalities and tragedies of everyday life.

In fact St Thomas Aquinas had undermined the whole process, although this was not appreciated at the time. In recent years Professor Mahoney has drawn attention to this much neglected part of St Thomas's moral theology. To quote Mahoney's own words,

> It is possible to conceive of moral initiative as proceeding from obligation and compulsion laid upon man from outside, as it were, in the way of which law is a typical expression. But it can also be conceived as impulsion, as a movement welling up from within man to seek expression in behaviour, as in the experience of the artist or the prophet responding to stimuli or situations. ... the artistic urge of the poet, or composer, or painter is experienced as an inarticulate force welling up within, and as an impelling urge which is not just an 'I ought', but an 'I must', in terms of external expression. This, interestingly, is rather how Aquinas completes his systematic treatise on law in analysing the ' Law of the Gospel', a vital section of his Summa which subsequent moral theology was to ignore in its concentration on Aquinas the moral philosopher, and perhaps also in its concern to give nothing away to Protestant individualism and private judgement. After having established the essence of law in general and considered in turn the eternal law, the natural law, human law, and the Mosaic Law, Aquinas came finally, in a totally original treatment, to what he termed the 'evangelical law, which is called the New Law'. In this new law he posited a fundamental and radical distinction between what he called its primary and secondary elements. The secondary element comprises all the teaching of Scripture, the documents of faith, and the precepts which put order into human reactions and human behaviour ... all of which have one simple function, either to dispose man to receive the primary element of the new law or to help man express that primary element. And the primary element of the Gospel law is nothing other than the presence of the Holy Spirit within man.[23]

It is impossible to overemphasize the importance of that profound insight into the understanding of human conduct.

The same conclusion had been presented by St Luke in his description of the festival of Pentecost in the Acts of the Apostles. At the time of Jesus, the feast of Pentecost in the Jewish calendar was a celebration of the giving of the Mosaic Law on Mount Sinai fifty days after the Exodus from Egypt (which had been celebrated at Passover). It is no accident that St Luke recorded the bestowal of the Holy Spirit on that occasion. Although the connection may not seem obvious to the modern reader, for St Luke's readership and in the literary conventions of the period it was the most effective way of delivering a clear message. Namely, what the Mosaic Law had done for the Jews, the Holy Spirit would do for the Christians. Whereas the Jews had been given detailed rules for almost every eventuality in life, the Christians were given, not a more elevated law, but a totally different source of moral guidance, a person. They were being taught that the Holy Spirit would guide their choices and actions in a way somewhat similar to, but vastly more sensitive than, the laws in the Pentateuch.

Needless to say, such a momentous change of the terms of reference was not adopted without problems. Of all systems of law which one might envisage, that of Moses had the most powerful appeal. It was promulgated visibly by God, and it contained rules for every area of life. The nature of Israelite society was such that there was no distinction between public law and private morality, nor between criminal law and liturgical regulations. Private, public, political and liturgical rules were all catered for on the same basis. The divine authority gave reliable guidance for every area of life. Needless to say, some measure of the legislation pre-dated the covenant on Sinai. The similarities between Israelite laws and those of other ancient near-Eastern societies leaves this in no doubt. Furthermore, the Israelite people would not have been living in a legal and moral vacuum until the events of Sinai. Many of the dietary regulations, procedures for personal injury, and limitations of consanguinity for marriage must have been observed before the events of Sinai.

What was important to the Jews was that all of their traditional law was taken up into the Covenant and enjoyed the divine guarantees, authority, and sanctions. Even when this impressive body of legislation evolved over the centuries, the whole corpus enjoyed the divine authority as an integral part of the Covenant. In the days of Jesus, rabbinic tradition had systematized it into 613 regulations, many of which were clearly human elaborations. However they functioned in the shadow of the divine Covenant and carried quasi-divine authority. Their status and influence was the cause of many well-documented disputes between Jesus and the Pharisees.

It should cause no surprise that this body of sacred legislation should have been held in the utmost reverence, so that its abandonment was greeted with dismay. The fact that the Christians were being called to a more exacting, generous, and heroic pattern of conduct did not immediately wean its erstwhile supporters from the desire to retain it within Christianity. The task of educating the early Christians to the demands of the new morality, and persuading them to break out of the straitjacket of the Old Covenant was possibly the most serious problem which St Paul had to contend with during the whole of his apostolic mission.

The experience of two communities, the Galatians and the Corinthians, indicates the extremes to which the new converts might turn and from which he had to turn them back. The Galatians, in spite of their being a Gentile community, seem to have adopted the whole of the Jewish Law, whereas the Corinthians had come dangerously close to throwing off all moral restraint. To the former, St Paul wrote with severity pointing out their errors. With the Corinthians he patiently talked through each problem. Both groups, and indeed the whole Church, had to learn how to pursue a high standard of conduct without a set of rules which claimed to cover every eventuality, by making the correct moral choices in whatever circumstances the individuals found themselves.

Such a programme is terrifying in the amount of responsibility that it places upon the individual, and the degree of freedom which it presupposes. As Dostoevsky observed in *The Brothers Karamazov*, human beings are ill at ease with freedom and prefer security, even if that should mean various forms of slavery, whether physical or intellectual. For that reason theologians and popes have misguidedly sought to provide the faithful with something clearer, simpler, and more exact. This was precisely the attraction of the idiom and thought patterns of Roman law.

The Role of Faith as the Basis of Morality

Up to the middle of the twentieth century, the basis of Catholic morality was presented as obedience. That is to say a committed member of the Church was expected to direct his or her conduct in life upon obedience to the rules and regulations presented by the ecclesiastical institution acting in the name of Christ. In practice this meant obedience to priests, teachers, bishops and pope, in what they presented as God's will, lasting from childhood to the grave. In the same period the majority of Catholic theology textbooks presented the virtue of faith as the intellectual assent to theological propositions about the nature of God, which were presented to us for our acceptance on the authority of Christ and the Church.

At the time of Vatican II a more satisfactory understanding of both faith and the basis of morality gained currency. Namely faith is an act of commitment to the person of Jesus, in love and loyalty. Assent to the intellectual content of Christian revelation is indeed present, but as a subordinate element. The principal practical consequence of faith is the willingness of the believer to base his conduct on the perceived will of God. This is the authentic foundation of morality. Its implementation is more complex than appears at first sight, but this need not worry us. A well known moral theologian has expressed it in these words:

> The New Testament writers' appeal to Jesus ... led to a fundamental attitude both toward the individual and toward the community ... this ethos which was based on faith ... is distinctive, not because its individual normative statements are exclusive, but because it has a total attitude that is based on and justified by faith and provides an entirely new sphere of understanding which gives a definite status and value to the various behavioural norms.[24]

In analysing St Paul's understanding of morality, Professor Murphy-O'Connor has shown that with the command to love God and neighbour, the believer is presented with a pair of objectives which are positive and creative. In the achievement of them he is sustained by positive motivation, invisible grace, and a visible community engaged upon the same pursuit. He is not given a new set of rules, similar to those in the Pentateuch. That system became obsolete after the redemptive work of Jesus had been accomplished, leaving his followers with the obligation to act in such a way as to build up the Kingdom of God. More precisely this meant strengthening the community of the Church, which is the sign and embodiment of the Kingdom in this present world. I will elaborate this notion later in the chapter.

Once the act of faith has been made, and nurtured, one can begin to plan the moral development of the young Christian (or neophyte). Its genesis can be most easily described in negative terms (as I stated above), namely that for a Christian there is nothing similar to the Mosaic Law in ancient Judaism. The shaking off of that system of morality was the most difficult task for the infant Church. It haunted St Paul for the whole of his career as a Christian missionary and occasioned the most passionate passages in his letters. Basically one sentence in Galatians epitomizes his outlook perfectly: 'If the Law could save us, then the death of Christ was in vain'. (Gal. 2:21)

The psychological effect on converts from Judaism seems to have been traumatic. They felt as if they were in a moral vacuum, and many of them sought security by going back to the Pentateuchal laws and combining them with Christianity. That was bad enough, but for St Paul the worst aspect of the situation was that they wanted to bring the erstwhile pagans with them. In that context St Paul formulated his moral programme, basically in Galatians and more elaborately in Romans, to the effect that the Mosaic Law had been abolished and what replaced it was the simple ideal to love God and one's neighbour. This ideal is so comprehensive that it warrants careful elucidation.

There are two decisive differences between moral systems based on the New Testament revelation and all others, be they from Judaism or natural law. The first is that the New Testament writers take a realistic view of humanity weakened by original sin. Its effects entail that human behaviour is far worse than the philosophers contemplated in their theoretical treatises on how human beings could or should behave. The second is the insight, taken from the Book of Genesis, that man is fashioned in the image and likeness of God. This means that like God, he must act creatively (it has been described as 'creative freedom'),[25] in relation to other human beings, and in his use of material things.

Original sin shows itself in the moral challenge or choice presented to Christians to resist the allurements and pressures of human society which is permeated with sin. It is disorientated and provides the corroding pollution of a corrupt environment.[26] Sin, in this sense, is the inexorable pressure of a false value system which permeates society. In this environment human beings are manipulated like puppets. Their freedom remains merely theoretical. In practice they cannot act consistently in a virtuous manner. To regain authentic freedom we need the invisible grace of God and the psychological support of the Christian community, which acts as an alternative environment.[27] The community which St Paul has in mind is not the universal Church, nor the large conglomerations which constitute most modern parishes, but small communities whose size and structure ensured that all the individuals knew one another personally and could provide mutual moral support.

Being strengthened in this way Christians are able to acquire real freedom from the pernicious influences of a depraved environment. Having acquired this degree of poise they are free to act in a manner which is authentically human. What exactly does this consist of? It is not a return to the Mosaic law and the 613 elucidatory precepts of St Paul's Jewish contemporaries. Nor is it a different and perhaps more elevated system of rules.[28] Basically it consists of a new orientation of the personality. Having committed their life to Christ in a decisive relationship of loyalty, believers turn to the outside world and relate to the material creation and fellow human beings with relationships which are essentially constructive and not exploitative. This is deceptively simple. It is not a quick method of bypassing complicated rules, but a profound and careful process for choosing the creative and constructive response to an indefinite number of varying situations, all requiring a moral choice before acting.

In relation to all created things, the Christian can and will act in such a way that he is never enslaved to them. This would not be to act creatively, since the individual would have put himself under the power of the object. The same principle applies to rules of conduct which could also enslave an individual and remove his freedom, that essential prerequisite of authentic moral behaviour.[29]

In relation to other human beings, the Christian acts in such a way as to express generous love, which means enabling the other in his or her turn to act creatively. The opposite of this is behaviour which expresses itself in exploitative relationships.

Superficially St Paul's moral theology might appear to be nothing other than a form of situation ethics. It is not. There are four overarching principles which govern the whole field of human moral conduct. Firstly there is the injunction to love God and our neighbour, secondly there is the obligation to act creatively in relation to material things, thirdly we are bound to pursue non-exploitative relationships with other people, and fourthly our conduct must be conducive to the building up of the Christian community. To this end, individual fulfilment must give way to the edification (literally) of the Church.[30]

In reality this kind of moral reasoning has been employed consistently in the pastoral theology of the Church, but its workings were designated by another label, namely the interaction of universal rules. The kind of moral dilemma which used to be discussed in the textbooks was something like the following artificially constructed example. A wounded man runs into my house and begs to be hidden from armed criminals. A few minutes later two men with guns approach and ask if I have seen a man streaming with blood because they want to finish him off. Rules of strict truth would require me to say 'He is hiding in the cupboard in the kitchen', and upon receipt of that information they would assassinate him before my eyes. The traditional moralists used to argue that in such a case the criminals had no right to know the truth, and that I was entitled to conceal the whereabouts of their victim. This is mere sophistry. On the traditional legalistic principles the end did not justify the means. In reality they had been using the more nuanced criterion of applying the requirements of the love of God and neighbour, without acknowledging it.

One minor difficulty remains to be addressed. It is the apparent frequency of the summons to obedience in St Paul's writings. Admittedly the word *obedience* occurs quite often in his letters, and there are many lists of sins which are to be avoided. It is important to remember that for St Paul *obedience* means *faith*.[31] The lists of sins are presented for educational reasons. They provide examples of the kind of conduct which will be avoided, if Christians are living up to their vocation authentically.[32] The same applies to the moral exhortations of Jesus as recorded in the gospels. He provides many examples to illustrate how the love of God and neighbour works out in practice. They are not specific rules in a negative sense, nor does the avoidance of murder, adultery and the rest constitute the normative standard for Christian behaviour. These must be understood as benchmarks and not as regulations. The letters of St Paul do not contain any specific norms or rules.[33] This insight is important because it has proved all too easy for the lists of sins to be used as standards above which the mediocre Christian will not trouble to rise.

In this context it is important to clarify what I have noted once before, that the observance of the natural law as such is not necessary for salvation. Admittedly a devoted Christian, guiding his life by the love of God and neighbour, will not infringe the principles of natural law, like avoiding theft and telling the truth. But he has not been given the natural law as such for his rule of life.

The moral teaching of St Paul is fundamentally the same as that of Jesus, which should not surprise us. The basic summaries are the Sermon on the Mount and the parable about the Last Judgement in Matthew 25. They are both expansions of the simple principles of love of God and neighbour. In the interests of sound pedagogy, Jesus spelt out large numbers of illustrations as to what that comprehensive ideal would entail. His discourses contain dozens of exhortations, examples, applications and appeals to generous conduct, illuminating the positive orientation of the love of God and neighbour. He taught his followers to disregard human precepts that were at variance with that love, like not healing on the Sabbath, and he indicated that the Law of Moses was about to come to fulfilment. He did not propose an alternative system of rules.

The teaching of Jesus also makes provision for the complexities of moral choices for which there are no universal rules. In some instances Jesus appears to have given contradictory advice, that is two opposite ways of reacting to the same problem. One example will illustrate this. Whereas Jesus exhorted his followers to remain faithful to the point of martyrdom, when they were dragged before kings and governors, (Matt. 10:17-20, Luke 21:12), he also made provision for the opposite course of action. 'When they persecute you in one city fly to the next' (Matt. 10:23). St Athanasius did exactly that and had to defend himself against the accusation of cowardice. After the Council of Nicaea and when the Arian party had gained power throughout the Empire, Athanasius was the principal defender of orthodox belief as defined by that Council. He spent nearly twenty years in hiding and literally on the run, avoiding his persecutors, and writing a constant stream of books, letters and pamphlets to uphold the true faith of Nicaea. In his personal statement, the famous *Apologia pro Fuga Sua* (The Justification for his Flight), he defended his decision to evade imprisonment and possibly a martyr's death by appealing to the words of Jesus. No one simple rule has been given for the conduct of the Church's champions in the face of persecution.

One further aspect of St Paul's moral programme deserves comment, namely the similarity with the consensus of modern developmental psychology on the moral progress of children. Small children are intellectually incapable of working out a pattern of right conduct. It is beyond their rational and emotional capabilities. Naturally their parents and teachers give and enforce rules to live by, to ensure that they do not harm themselves physically, nor exploit other people in the ways in which they interact with them. In that simple context children gradually acquire the practices of telling the truth, sharing, being considerate to others, and all the other components of the moral life.

Initially a great deal of it depends upon obedience but it is important that obedience does not become an end in itself. It is equally important that good behaviour is not imposed by fear of punishment, particularly corporal punishment. For example, children may well ask why they are being required to act in a given way. 'Why must I go to bed at eight o'clock?' says the child, and the parent ought to reply 'Because your health and school work require that you get enough sleep.' And not 'Because I say so'. As children grow up, they will begin to make their own moral choices and if parents continue to exact obedience from them in adult years, it means that moral education has failed. The rules and their corresponding obedience are a temporary scaffolding for the developing child, destined to be outgrown and dispensed with.

In the context of the Church's life, it is sad to think that many Catholics never outgrow an infantile dependence on the clergy and the rules which the priests hand out. Until quite recently, bishops and parish priests used to talk about safeguarding the innocence of the simple faithful. It has been one of the basic causes of so much unchristian conduct, like the rounding up of Jews in the Nazi period when scarcely any Christian soldiers refused orders from their superiors. Their priests and pastors had never encouraged nor trusted them to make their own moral decisions, so when a ready-made solution commanded by the parish priest was not at hand, they did not know how to act and collaborated in the immoral practice of genocide. Admittedly that example is an extreme case but it is a pattern of conduct for which countless other examples could be adduced, and they are indicators of the gigantic failure of the Catholic moral programme.

The neglect of the role of conscience among Catholic teachers may well have something to do with Lutheranism, as I noted in the Introduction. It has been a constant principle of Catholic moral theology that the individual's conscience is the proximate guide, and one must never act against its dictates. The education of conscience is somewhat different, being distinct from the practical moral choices to be acted upon. Luther invoked private judgement in another area, maintaining that in matters of doctrine the Christian believer should arrive at his own judgement on the basis of his own interpretation of the bible. Although it is quite different from the moral decisions of conscience, there was enough superficial similarity between the two operations for timid Catholics to group the two together and outlaw both. For the short-sighted and small-minded among the clergy, it seemed safer to leave all decisions to the priest. The falsity of the position becomes apparent after a few moments of reflection.

Faith and its Origin in the Individual

Taking our stand on the fact that faith is the basis of Christian morality we must face the question, how does faith arrive in the life of the individual Christian? It is a particular problem for all Churches that give baptism to infants. Catholics, Orthodox, Anglicans and others whose normal practice is to give baptism in infancy all agree that faith is a gift from God, yet they all skate over the necessity for each individual to make an explicit personal commitment of belief at some time early in his or her life. In other words, when, and in what circumstances does the baptized infant make an explicit act of faith? The decision is either ignored or masked by a plethora of rules. Catholicism has had the worst manifestation of this on account of the rules regulating marriage, children, and schools. The baptized infant's development in faith, which ought to be free, is surrounded by strict regulations and commands. In the Code of Canon Law of 1918 it was expressly forbidden for Catholics to marry non-Catholics of any persuasion. Parents were under a serious obligation to baptize and bring up all children as Catholics (even if a dispensation had been given to marry a non-Catholic). All the children had to be sent to Catholic schools. The first injunction infringes the basic liberty to choose one's spouse freely. The commands about education are at variance with parental responsibilities and rights, which the English bishops have used in another context. That is to say, in negotiating with the British government to obtain money for Catholic schools from the taxed revenue, the bishops invoked the principle of natural law that parents had a right to choose for their children that kind of education which they, the parents, wanted for their offspring. Having got the government to underwrite the major part of the schools' funding, the same bishops commanded the parents to send their children to Catholic schools. In recent years many parents have ignored these rules, and the ecclesiastical authorities have proved powerless to persuade them otherwise. Persuasion does not come easily to a regime that has relied on obedient and unquestioning compliance on the part of subordinates.

The maintenance of a Catholic school system has constituted an important element of the life of the Church in the modern period. Its organization has varied from nation to nation, and for the sake of brevity I must confine myself here to the system in England,[34] although the underlying theological principles apply to other countries too. The schools in question have set themselves the tasks of consolidating their pupils' loyalty to the Catholic Church and its teaching, together with imparting to them the best possible secular education so that attendance at a Catholic school would not prejudice a pupil's ordinary career prospects. It was, and still is, an admirable programme, but one element had not been thought out clearly, namely the freedom of the act of faith. I will return to this problem a little further on in this chapter.

Prior to 1870, when the government assumed responsibility for educating the whole nation, the main Churches in England had already set up their own networks of schools. For Catholics this had been an exceedingly difficult task because of the poverty of most Church members. In spite of this disability, and thanks to immense efforts and generosity, a network of Catholic schools was functioning reasonably well by 1870. In that year the government belatedly took up the responsibility of providing free elementary education for all children, while recognizing that some were already in Church schools and others were being educated in a variety of privately run fee-paying establishments. The religious bodies negotiated a reasonable working arrangement with the government whereby the state provided most of the money, and the Churches controlled the appointment of teachers, as well as sharing part of the financial burden. On reflection one can perceive that it was an admirable solution for a pluralist society, all parties having made reasonable compromises.

By the year 1900, roughly, all Catholic parishes in England, except the most rurally isolated, had their own elementary schools. Quite apart from theology and education, they were powerful factors in maintaining the sense of community in a body that still felt itself to be a persecuted minority. For the next half-century they operated with a reasonable measure of success, and engendered in many of their pupils a strong sense of loyalty to the Catholic Church. It is difficult to estimate how much of this was genuine faith and how much was the purely cultural phenomenon of sociological cohesion to a community which was composed mostly of Irish immigrants who had a sense of bitter resentment against the British government. After the First World War the Church's influence on the working class became seriously weakened, but that was due to a variety of sociological factors, and the schools need not bear the total responsibility for the lapsing of many of their former pupils.

During the Second World War, the Education Act of 1944 brought about large-scale reorganization of education, mainly in the area of secondary schooling. Catholic schools responded admirably and took full advantage of the new situation. The proportion of pupils who went to university and thence on to brilliant careers is one of the success stories of the whole system.

Towards the end of World War Two the phenomenon of lapsing became recognized and indeed was inescapable. Hitherto the collection of statistics in the Catholic community had been lacking in scientific exactitude. During the war though, every serviceman who was not a self-declared agnostic had to state which denomination he belonged to. These identifications were passed on to the military chaplains, who became aware that the Catholics in that age range constituted approximately 10 per cent of the armed forces. This was a perfect sample of the total population, so it became apparent that for young adults at least, Catholics constituted a tenth of the population. This was much higher than anyone had expected and vastly exceeded any correlation to mass attendance, where numbers had been recorded. Hence there arose the awareness that large numbers were falling away from the Church of their baptism, in other words lapsing from the Church's practice. Clearly this had implications for the educational programme of Catholic schools.

As the post-war period developed, a subtle but profound change came over the whole religious ethos of schools. Educational methods were changing, society was losing its cohesion, and spiritual values were in decline. As far as Catholic schools were concerned, the regional secondary schools no longer had strong links with the local parish, and since they were effectively taking pupils out of their home parishes, they tended to weaken the sense of community of those very parishes.

The precise point at which modern educational methods made their most important impact on the religious ethos of the schools was the new orientation in teaching. Basically it has consisted in a generally critical approach that could broadly be called investigation, and it extends to all branches of learning. It has a strong presumption in its favour insofar as it embodies drawing out knowledge from experience, which is the basic meaning of the word *education* as opposed to *inculcation*. Children have been taught to question everything. This has had obvious repercussions on the freedom of the act of faith.

Conferring baptism in infancy always carried with it the assumption that the child would complement the sacrament with a deliberate act of faith. It has never been clear when and in what circumstances that decision should be made. This is perhaps the most crucial problem for pastoral theology, but even in the twenty-first century it still lacks a practical solution which is universally implemented. At the institutional level there has not been custom, ceremony, nor any formality to provide the occasion for eliciting the decisive commitment to Christ. This all-important step in religion and morality has simply been left without any guidance in the lives of the laity. Priests gave no specific advice. The catechism was silent on the matter as was the code of Canon Law. In short, all the normal sources for the comprehensive guidance of the Catholics' moral life were silent on the crucial starting point of the individual child's deliberate commitment to Christ. It is difficult to exaggerate the seriousness of this lacuna at the very start of a child's spiritual pilgrimage through life. All the rest of the disciplinary superstructure, moral obligations, doctrinal instruction, prayer, and worship lack a coherent foundation.

The initial lacuna has been compounded by the fact that the school system assumed that the definitive act of faith had been made. It was taken for granted that children who entered Catholic schools at five had made a deliberate decision about faith. From then onwards the obligations of a believer were imposed as a matter of discipline. At the age of six (usually) the class would be prepared for confession and Communion. The element of freedom was scarcely adverted to. In any case the psychological pressure of the group would ensure that it was impossible, in practice, for the parents of an individual child to opt out and ask for time to decide whether this was the appropriate occasion for their child to receive the sacrament. From that time onwards the child would be reminded of the obligation to go to confession frequently, and to attend mass every Sunday. That latter obligation was backed up by the threat that it was a mortal sin to miss Sunday mass and that meant hell for all eternity, should the child die in that state.

Every element in that scenario is open to serious questioning. First of all, there was no invitation to make an act of faith in Jesus. It was presupposed and represents the residual momentum from the era of mediaeval Europe when the total culture was Christian. In those days many people were content to go along with the crowd, accepting the Catholic programme on human authority, and being placed in a sociological situation where the contradictions in the arrangement were not apparent.

Confession prior to first Communion may have been a reasonable practice in the days when children received the Eucharist at about the age of fourteen. At the beginning of the twentieth century Pope Pius X commanded that Holy Communion should be given to children as soon as they attained the age of reason. Unthinkingly the old custom of its being preceded by confession was continued although the recipients of the Eucharist were then aged about six. For centuries there has been a well-established consensus among moral theologians that the only barrier to the reception of Communion is conscious mortal sin, and of that small children are incapable. It would have been better for them to be given the Eucharist first and then confession several years later. Moves in that direction were initiated in the immediate aftermath of Vatican II, but during the pontificate of John Paul II the policy was reversed and the Church was directed back to the old pattern.

Attendance at Sunday mass is another problem for small children since it bristles with what are, for them, anomalies. The language and underlying concepts are difficult even for adults. The symbolism is too difficult for children to understand, and as for remaining motionless and virtually silent for an hour, it is psychologically impossible. Admittedly, now that we have a vernacular liturgy the performance is not totally incomprehensible, nor totally silent, but of what value is it to a six-year-old child, to stand with the rest of the congregation and recite the Creed of Nicaea? Experience shows that conscientious parents often compel their children to come to mass with the family, in spite of their protests that they are bored. This activity continues until adolescence when the boring mass is one of the easiest targets for teenage rebellion. Sometime before the age of 20, the majority of those who were baptized as infants give up the practices of organized religion effortlessly. They should not be regarded as lapsed Catholics. They have not abandoned the faith: they never had it.

Doctrinal instruction in Catholic schools manifests the same contradictions because of the assumption that the definitive act of faith has been made by the child. The dogmas of the Church are explained, with scarcely a thought about the basic acceptance of the Church's teaching authority by the pupils. One sensitive and intelligent young man described, in later years, the attitude of a monk in a well-known public school. In the RE classes he would say 'We do believe this, boys, don't we?' In fact the young man in question did believe it, but he was sufficiently perceptive to resent the fact that the teacher presumed upon this consent of faith. If the definitive decision of faith has not been made by the child, neither the mass in a parish church nor instruction in a Catholic school will provide the appropriate setting for eliciting this all-important and sensitive choice.

I am not saying that a small child is incapable of faith. Many do arrive at belief in God by about the age of five or six. Somehow their parents have engendered it in them by example and by the transference to their children of their own deepest convictions. It is a process which cannot be charted methodically. It is normally connected with the parents' beliefs and the presuppositions of society as a whole. It cannot be presumed, predicted or planned, still less can it be commanded. My principal concern is that the Church makes no provision for its initial genesis in a child, yet presupposes its existence in education and the discipline of the sacraments.

So what exactly do we need for enabling faith to take root in the life of a child? Quite simply it must occur in the context of a community whose basic activity allows scope for believers to witness to their own faith and which enables a sensitive invitation to be offered to children to accept it too.

The Jews have got it right and so too did the infant Church. Following the instructions of Jesus they re-enacted the Passover supper every Sunday (by then they were commemorating the Resurrection rather than the Exodus). Of the three possible models available to him, Jesus had chosen the Passover supper as the paradigm for the Eucharist, not the liturgy of the synagogue nor that of the Temple. The Book of Exodus (12: 3–4) had specified approximately the numbers for this assembly, namely a group which was large enough to eat the year-old lamb. That would be roughly about a dozen people, which anchored the celebration naturally in an ordinary house and not in a larger public building like a synagogue. Once a year, on that solemn occasion, the youngest child would ask 'What is the meaning of this night?' and the head of the family would explain what it was all about. This is the perfect setting for the germination of faith. When stripped of the particular details it means that the initiative is placed upon the child, who can be carefully prepared for the occasion by his parents. On the solemn occasion it is the parent who explains the act of God intervening in history for the liberation of their ancestors and all their descendants. It is the ideal setting for parents to witness to their own convictions, since the celebration is clearly performed in the context of an important family reunion.

In its essentials the whole of that ceremony could be carried out by Christians at a Eucharist, specifically designed to invite a child to accept faith in Jesus. Something similar could also serve as the ideal setting for a child's first Communion.

The first few centuries of Christian life saw the Eucharist celebrated in basically this manner. Apart from the clear instructions of Jesus, they did not have the legal freedom to erect buildings of the size of synagogues, nor did they have the money to do so. These vibrant and intimate domestic liturgies were replaced by much larger assemblies in the fourth century after the conversion of Constantine, when converts flocked into the Church in their thousands. From then onwards there was a decisive change of tone. Vast numbers of people came to adopt Christianity, but one may have doubts about their motives and underlying conviction.

Another casualty of Constantine's promotion of Christianity was the decline of the catechumenate. This gathering of enquirers had served for the instruction of adult converts from paganism as well as for the children of Christian families. As is well known, Saint Augustine and Saint Ambrose were both catechumens in their early adult years, although both had at least one Christian parent. The early Church did not rush its younger adherents into full committed membership. They were allowed space and time to make their own deliberate decision. After the empire had embraced Christianity as the official religion of state, it seems that increasing numbers adopted it without too much deliberation. Eventually the citizens of Europe became Christians more or less as a matter of course. The conversion of England from the time of Augustine onwards illustrates the process in its simplest and most unsatisfactory form. As the Anglo-Saxon kings adopted the new religion so too did their subjects, seemingly as an act of corporate loyalty to their monarchs. After so many centuries it is difficult to speculate about how much authentic freedom was available to the populations of those primitive kingdoms, but it set the pattern which thereafter became permanent. All children were baptized in infancy and lived out the pattern of Christian discipline and worship, relying apparently on the support or pressure of uniform social cohesion and expectations. From the nature of that culture, society held them there with apparent harmony.

In that period the characteristic structures and institutions of the Catholic Church assumed their present form, notably parishes, religious orders, and schools. It is surprising that with the passage of centuries they have remained unchanged in their essentials, and in their implied presuppositions. The latter part of the twentieth century proved to be their undoing, on account of the extreme secularization and irreligious character of our society. In the latter part of that century vast numbers of young people abandoned religion, basically because they had never made a satisfactory act of faith. They are not guilty of infidelity. The institutional Church had not provided them with a satisfactory opportunity and context in which to make the all-important personal decision.

If we are to reverse the trend and convey Christianity to our children, as well as conducting a realistic missionary expansion, we must return to the structures of the infant Church. The most important of these is the basic eucharistic community, which must be a house church in essence. On account of its inherent flexibility, such a community could also function like the ancient catechumenate, providing for young people the psychological space and support for pondering the basic truths of Christianity. In that context they could approach Christian commitment in a reflective and non-pressurized manner. In the secularized and pluralistic society in which we now live, that structure has the greatest chance of engendering faith in children.

Disappointed Expectations

Over the centuries, the Church made extensive use of natural law and fashioned the science of moral theology also in the idiom, and under the influence, of the categories of Roman law. As an internally coherent intellectual system it was impressive. But its results, in the twentieth century at least, have shown its weaknesses. The simplicity of a moral programme based upon faith and its manifestations in conduct had been overlaid by a detailed system of rules and methods for regulating behaviour in a uniform manner. When Catholics were faced with the moral crises of the twentieth century, the system was shown to be defective.

The quest for a comprehensive moral programme based on rules and regulations has failed. Admittedly the textbooks presented comprehensive systems of laudable clarity and internal consistency, but their failure became apparent when they were applied to real life. The crucial areas of human conduct have been left without guidance because it is impossible to devise a theoretical system that will provide, in advance, a solution to every real-life situation. When the RAF adopted the policy of indiscriminate night bombing of civilian targets in February 1942, no Catholics are known to have protested. When the Germans launched their full-scale campaign to round up the Jews for extermination, how many Catholic soldiers and police refused? The list could be multiplied almost indefinitely. In short, the Catholic system has failed the members of the Church in many crucial areas, and I am convinced that it is one of the reasons for the massive abandonment of institutional Catholicism in the last decades of the twentieth century.

There are other factors, such as the general critical attitude of mind that is engendered in education from primary school upwards. One can also point to the decline in cultural Christianity. That form of religion is the acceptance of Christian principles on human authority, whereas faith entails the acceptance of them on the authority of God. Throughout the Middle Ages and beyond, much of our national life, morality, and ways of thought had been shaped by cultural Christianity as well as by the authentic faith. Since the latter part of the nineteenth century the cultural element therein has been seriously weakened.[35]

The decline in Church membership in the last decades of the twentieth century has been so widespread that it scarcely needs to be demonstrated. However a few statistics may illustrate just how far-reaching it has been among all Churches. Although I concentrate on Catholic failings, other Churches have suffered from a similar decline. All these bodies have two factors in common: retention of obsolete structures and inability to present their followers with satisfactory moral guidance.

A few representative statistics will illustrate the large scale abandonment of institutional religion. For example in the immediate post-war period, university chaplaincies were the most dynamic communities within organized religion. They also had the means of measuring religious affiliation with a fair degree of statistical accuracy. They are now experiencing sharp decline. In 1994 the Anglican and Catholic chaplains at Leicester University observed:

> Among the material sent to students about to start their first term is a white form concerning religious practice. In 1980 about 800 of the 1500 or so freshers returned forms filling in: Church of England. In 1989, only about 80 forms out of a considerably bigger first year intake were returned marked C of E. A similar trend, but not such a pronounced decline, occurred among Roman Catholic freshers, said Fr. Fabian Radcliffe, the university's full time RC chaplain. 'When I first came here in 1986, we used to receive 150 forms marked RC from an intake of about 2000. Now we get about 60 or 70 out of an intake of about 3000.[36]

Fr. Radcliffe became the national coordinator for Catholic chaplains, and three years on, his observations were even more pessimistic 'As the total number of undergraduates has doubled, numbers active in chaplaincies have at best remained the same'.[37]

In the nation as a whole, Catholicism remains the largest single denomination of regular church attenders, but between 1980 and 1994 it lost a large number of its active members. Their numbers fell from 2 million to 1.5 million in that period.[38] Within the Catholic community regular mass attendance (which is an indicator of committed membership) has also been declining steadily. Between 1988 and 1995 regular Sunday mass attendance shrunk by 200 000. If these trends continue it has been predicted by researchers at the University of Louvain that by the year 2005 regular mass attendance will be below 600 000.[39]

Whereas figures for mass attendance are collected in a somewhat informal fashion, other numbers are recorded with considerable care by Catholics. A professional survey published in 1999 showed that in the 30 or so years after the high point in 1964, the most accurately measurable pointers show a decline of 50 per cent or worse. Baptisms were down from 137 000 to 67 000, confirmations from 90 000 to 37 000, conversions from 12 000 to 5 000 and ordinations from 230 to 119.[40] (I have rounded off the figures to the nearest thousand, where applicable.)

Other Christian Churches have had similar losses. In 1994 the Presbyterian Church in Wales made the painful decision to close at least a third of their 4 000 chapels over the next 20 years. Figures for that year showed that their membership was down to 56 000 from a peak of over 300 000 at the beginning of the twentieth century.[41] All mainstream Churches have been on the decline during the last years of the twentieth century. Figures published in the *UK Christian Handbook* for 1995 showed that, if present trends continue, Anglicans, Methodists and Catholics will have lost about a third of their members by the year 2010, reducing the overall number of Christians in this country from 7.5 to 4.5 million.[42]

In order to preserve a sense of balance, it is relevant to bear in mind that this sort of decline has been experienced by the Jewish community as well. Between 1979 and 1994 the number of Jews in Britain dropped by 10 per cent to just over 300 000. More disturbing for the future of British Jewry is the fact that two-thirds of those born into the community are no longer marrying in a synagogue, which means that the drift is among young adults.[43]

These few indicators, cited above, confirm what is well known by all competent observers of the scene, namely that institutional religion is losing its grip on the loyalty of its traditional adherents and especially the younger members of those communities. All mainstream Christian denominations are plagued by obsolete structures and institutions, whose shortcomings have been criticized extensively in recent years. What they share with the Jews is irrelevant and misdirected programmes for the moral conduct of their adherents. I do not presume to offer advice to other Churches, so my observations in this book, and the suggested remedies, concern the Catholic

Church, but it is conceivable that other Christians may find something of value in these pages.

Faith and Prayer

In the early Middle Ages, Christians were divided into three social categories: those who tilled the land, those who fought (soldiers) and those who prayed (monks, nuns, and priests). There is an element of oversimplification in that scheme, but by and large it accounted for the pattern of life. St Francis de Sales was a far-sighted innovator with his book *The Introduction to the Devout Life*, in which he invited all conditions of men and women to seek spiritual perfection. The social composition of the Church and society were against him, but it had not been thus in the infant Church.

Prayer can be described as the articulation of faith. In this context I am using the term *faith* in its basic sense of a relationship with Christ entailing definitive personal commitment to him. From this it follows that all committed Christians should be engaged upon prayer seriously. (This is somewhat different from theology which is the intellectual elaboration of the content of faith, namely, what God reveals to the believer about Himself). In spite of the liturgical reforms of Vatican II, the prayer life in the average parish still leaves much to be desired.

There are several reasons for this. In one sense, the reforms of the Council demolished a great deal of the old-world pieties. This was not intentional but almost inevitable because their foundations were extremely fragile (such as the appalling poetry of the *Westminster Hymnal*). There were many other shortcomings which I will deal with shortly. As a result these old-world pieties could not withstand the critical appraisal which the Council occasioned. Another reason is that parochial clergy are now too few and generally too poorly educated to provide the necessary leadership and inspiration. This goes back to the seminaries of a previous generation and the shortcomings of the spiritual formation of the secular clergy. I can think of one seminary which in the 1950s did not have a resident spiritual director, where liturgy was not taught in the syllabus, nor was there any tuition which could be described as the theological basis of prayer. One cannot generalize from one bad example but I suspect that the seminary in question was not an isolated case. In the regime of that seminary the liturgy was an uncritical transference of some aspects of the prayer life of a monastery, with no thought about its future relevance to the spiritual life of the parishes in which the students would eventually be working. One symbolic indicator of the aridity of the system is the fact that the priests in any given presbytery do not usually pray together. In fact in the diocese which was served by that seminary I cannot recall one instance over a period of 30 years where the priests of a parish prayed any part of the daily Office together. It is all the more disappointing when one reflects that they lived under the same roof and were working as collaborators in the same locality.

A further problem which has affected the implementation of the Council's liturgical reforms in Great Britain was the lack of preparation beforehand. The contrast with mainland Europe is instructive and depressing. In France for example, several years before the Council, the Jesuit Père Gelineau set the Psalms to modern music, having first made a new translation of them which would convey something of the original rhythm. In Germany dialogue mass was initiated at the Abbey of Maria Laach in the 1930s. Austria and Belgium saw similar innovations and experiments, but in England there was absolutely no such research or experimentation. Actually the situation was even worse. Any attempt at innovation was repressed. One bishop in the south of England on the eve of the Council solemnly forbade dialogue mass, and the same bishop tried to suppress the Vernacular Society of Great Britain, which was a small pressure group advocating an English liturgy. Clearly this relates to the theological and pastoral expertise of the bishops. On this subject I will have more to say in the next chapter on hope. It is important to realize that the selection of bishops is a moral choice just as much as it is an administrative operation, and one hopes that papal nuncios and Vatican administrators realize the gravity of the decisions they make when appointing bishops.

Another factor working adversely on the prayer life of the Church was the effect of the Latin language. One has to accept the depressing fact that a considerable proportion of the clergy did not fully understand the hymns and other difficult parts of the language of the breviary. There was little or no instruction on the nature of the divine Office, other than instilling into seminary students that in major orders it was a serious daily obligation whose omission was a mortal sin. Small wonder then that the clergy did not really enjoy the solitary recitation of the breviary in Latin. Viewing it as a dry sort of duty like a penitential exercise was reinforced by the confessional practice which was then universal, namely of commanding the penitent to recite a given number of prayers as a penance. The long evolution of that sacrament over the centuries lies outside the scope of this book, but it is relevant to recall that over hundreds of years the practice of severe bodily penances was replaced by the recitation of prayers. One of the harmful effects of this process was that it gave rise to the unspoken assumption that prayer was not meant to be enjoyable. If a purely personal reminiscence is not out of place, I can recall what a profound change came over my own experience of the breviary when I was a student at Fribourg. Among my fellow students were a number of Benedictine monks who attached great importance to reciting together at least a part of the daily Office, and I used to join them. Actually it was not recited, but chanted in a monotone. For the first time I experienced the Office as a thoroughly satisfying experience.

The use of Latin in the public worship of the Catholic Church has been another problem for the laity. In antiquity the Church always used the vernacular, and as missionaries penetrated into new territories they translated the Bible and conducted the liturgy in the spoken languages of those regions, be it Ethiopic, Syriac, Armenian or any of the other languages where Christianity was being introduced. The retention of Latin in Western Europe was due to nothing more than a series of historical accidents. The evangelization of northern Europe from the sixth century onwards was done by Latin-speaking monks. Whereas their counterparts in Russia had invented an alphabet for the illiterate Slavs, no one in the West had the originality of mind to do something similar. Latin was used across the whole of western Europe.

An equally important factor was the slowness with which Latin evolved into the modern romance languages. At no period could the authorities observe the transformation within one lifetime. There was never an opportunity to observe that the younger generation no longer understood Latin, therefore an Italian or Spanish translation of the missal was necessary.

The man who realized immediately that vernacular bibles and liturgies were imperative for popular piety was Luther. The speed and success of his movement in Germany was, at least in part, due to the fact that he gave his followers a liturgy, which they understood. He also provided a vernacular Bible which was so well translated that it became the major factor in the development of High German as a literary language. The animosities of the Reformation period were such that Luther's espousal of the vernacular principle probably accounted for the Catholics' rejection of it.

In all fairness one must remember that animosity of that kind was not limited to the Catholics. It was the standard pattern in the Reformation period. For example when Pope Gregory XIII reformed the calendar in 1582, it was rejected by all Protestant nations in spite of its scientific merits. By that time the Julian calendar had accumulated an error of ten days. The Pope decreed that the day after October 4th in that year should reckoned as October 15th. Eventually the Protestant nations of Europe adopted it. England did so only in 1752 and the opposition calling on sentiment rather than science declared that the Pope was stealing ten days of their lives.

Of all the self-inflicted wounds from which the Catholic Church has suffered, the retention of Latin was one of the worst. It seems that the authorities were incapable of making a rational decision about the matter. However by the nineteenth century certain concessions were made to the vernacular in the form of public but non-liturgical prayers, like May devotions to Our Lady, October devotions, and the Stations of the Cross. These devotions illustrate the shortcomings of the Church's prayer life. The rosary and Stations of the Cross being essentially meditations were always unsuitable for use in public. Paradoxically Catholics never learnt to sing the psalms, which as part of the divinely inspired scriptures occupy a special place in the prayer life of the Church. In spite of the devotion to Mary the mother of Jesus, one would have been hard pressed to find any Catholic lay person who knew the Magnificat by heart.

The reanimation of the Church's prayer life requires basically two factors. The first is an increase in numbers and improvement in the theological formation of the clergy. The second is the need to take a serious look at the Church's practice in the third and fourth centuries to regain the dynamism of their spiritual life. Any increase in the number of aspirants to the secular clergy will have to wait until a pope is willing to set aside the condition of obligatory celibacy. This problem, and the whole question of vocations, will be dealt with in the chapter on justice, so I will not delay upon the matter here.

Deriving inspiration from the infant Church's practice could be undertaken without any delay.[44] Basically, in the fourth century, Christians had mass once a week and the laity sang the whole of the Office daily. That is an oversimplification but it highlights the essentials. For a long time mass was celebrated only on Sundays, and in each city it was celebrated just once, so that all the Christians of that city could assist at the same Eucharist. This was considered to be an important expression of unity and a causal factor in preserving it. Later on the increase in numbers required larger buildings, more of them, and eventually more Eucharistic celebrations.

Only at a later stage were masses celebrated on weekdays, initially to commemorate the deaths of martyrs. Obviously it is difficult to quantify the value of several masses. King Henry VIII used to attend several masses each day as a young man, but it would be unwise to generalize! But some attention ought to be given to the glaring contrast between today's practice and that of the early Church. Now we are in the situation where there is daily mass in every parish and several on a Sunday, but there is scarcely any other form of public liturgical prayer. The unfounded assumption that the Office is the province of priests and monks leads me to consider the second main element of the early Church's prayer life, namely the Office. In the third and fourth centuries this public prayer was undertaken jointly by the whole community. Several times during the day and night the bishop, priests, deacons and laity would meet in the church to sing psalms and read the scriptures in a pattern which has evolved into the monastic Office and the breviary. Clearly obligations of work, domestic duties and the care of young children would have made it impossible for every member of the community to attend all the hours. However, that did not detract from the principle that it was the whole community which had the obligation of regular public prayer, and this ideal was still upheld even if only a representative group was present, and not the totality of the Christians in that city.

In the fourth century two developments took place which were destined to modify the simple beauty of the ancient pattern. Firstly the creation of monasteries hived off enthusiasts who developed a more sophisticated form of the basic scheme of daily prayer. However it must be remembered that originally they brought to their monasteries the pattern of prayer which the bishop's lay community had evolved and not the other way round. The second development was the multiplication of parishes, and indeed rural parishes, which was necessitated by the increase in the numbers of Christians. In spite of these potentially divisive factors the old ideal of a unified praying community was not lost sight of. The new parishes which were not presided over by a bishop undertook part of the office, vespers perhaps, and they also assisted at the bishop's celebration when possible.

For the modern Church to return to the pattern of the fourth century's prayer life would entail considerable thought, planning, and organization, but it is by no means impossible. Many people today have considerable amounts of leisure time. The relaxations about times of masses and the eucharistic fast have had remarkable results in some areas. If the times of masses are chosen with care, some parishes have substantial numbers of people attending daily mass. Psychologically the laity who are deeply committed to their faith do not restrict their worship to Sundays only. It is eminently desirable that the divine Office should be reintroduced as the normal public prayer of the average parish. The principal reason for optimism about a satisfactory outcome of such a move is the fact that no element of it is at variance with ecclesiastical law. The breviary exists in the vernacular and the prayers could be led by nuns or lay people if no priest is available.

Once the divine Office is in place as the acknowledged central public prayer of the local community, the other forms of piety can be encouraged on a less structured basis. This does not mean that they should be left to random experiment. Some parameters must be set. For example people should be discouraged from the public recitation of the rosary immediately after mass.

As to the guidance of lay people in contemplative prayer, little need be said because this is an area to which religious orders have given a great deal of attention since the Council. Concurrently with rediscovering their authentic charisms and rewriting their constitutions, many religious orders have resumed the detailed cultivation of the interior life by courses and retreats at specialist centres. One cannot but praise the work that is undertaken at these centres. It has succeeded so much better than the kind of school retreats and parish missions which by the 1960s had come to the end of their usefulness.

The preceding pages contain in germ what I consider to be necessary for engendering and strengthening the virtue of faith if it is to be the authentic foundation of Christian morality.

Notes

1   I am indebted to Professor J. O'Connell for his kindness in allowing me to read his manuscript on *Natural Law and Morality*, prior to publication. It has inspired this section.
2   ST I–II, q.94, a.5, commented on by A.P. d'Entrèves, *Natural Law*, London 1970, 46.
3   Curran, Charles, E. *The Catholic Moral Tradition Today, A Synthesis*. Washington, 1999, 73.
4   O'Connell, J. 'The Discernment of Morality, Distinguishing Grounds, Guidelines and Laws', in *Theology*, May-June 2001, 175.

5   Nédoncelle, M. *La Réciprocité des Consciences*, Paris, 1946, 219.
6   The wording comes from H.J. Paton's *The Moral Law* (which is a commentary and translation of Kant's *Groundwork of the Metaphysic of Morals*), London, 1951, 67.
7   Warnock, Mary *An Intelligent Person's Guide to Ethics*. London, 2001, 117.
8   Warnock, 119.
9   Hume, D. *An Enquiry Concerning the Principles of Morals*. Book 1, section 1, para. 136, quoted in Warnock , 120.
10 Warnock, 125, 127.
11 Hughes, G. in *Christian Ethics, An Introduction*, ed. Bernard Hoose, London, 1998, 54.
12 Encyclical Letter, *Divini Illius Magistri*. Section 71, DS 3698.
13 Cicero, *De Republica*. III, xxii, 33, quoted in A.P. d'Entrèves, 25.
14 Aquinas, ST I–II, q.95, a.2, and II–II, q.104, a.6, quoted in A.P. d'Entrèves, 46.
15 Kelly, K. *New Directions in Sexual Ethics*. London, 1998.
16 First Vatican Council, decree *Pastor Aeternus*. July 1870, DS 3074, 3070.
17 The matter is discussed at length in the indispensable study of the history of moral theology by J. Mahoney, *The Making of Moral Theology*, Oxford, 1987, 120–35.
18 Mansi, *Amplissima Collectio Conciliorum*, Arnhem & Leipzig, 1927, vol. 52, col. 1224.
19 Mahoney, 155. This restriction of infallibility to matters of revelation is to be found in all standard authors on the matter, cf. Fessler, J. *Die wahre und falsche Unfehlbarkeit der Papste*, Vienna, 1871, 22 and 24. Dublanchy. E. 'Infallibilité du Pape', *DTC* Paris, 1922, vol.7, cols. 1699–1702.
20 II Lateran of 1139, canon 13 (ACOD 200), III Lateran of 1179, canon 25 (ACOD 223), IV Lateran of 1215, chapter 67 (ACOD 265), I Lyons of 1245, part 2, section 1 (ACOD 293), II Lyons of 1274, canon 26 (ACOD 328), Council of Vienne of 1311, canon 29 (ACOD 384), V Lateran 1512–1517 session 10 (ACOD 626).
21 Hughes, G.J. 'Totality, Principle of' in *New Dictionary of Christian Ethics*. eds J.F. Childress and J. McQuarrie, London, 1986, 629.
22 Quoted in Kelly, K. *New Directions in Moral Theology*, London, 1992, 30.
23 Mahoney, 254, 255, referring to Aquinas, ST I–II, q.106.
24 von Böckle, F. *Fundamental Moral Theology*, Dublin 1980, 227.
25 Auer, A. 'Christianity's Dilemma', in *Concilium*, April 1978, 52.
26 Murphy-O'Connor, J. *Becoming Human Together*, Dublin 1978, 89.
27 Murphy-O'Connor, 84, 95, 169, 170.
28 Murphy-O'Connor, 215; *Paul: A Critical Biography*, Oxford,1997, 205.
29 Murphy-O'Connor, *Becoming Human Together*, 105, 116.
30 Murphy-O'Connor, 229.
31 Murphy-O'Connor, 216, 217.
32 Murphy-O'Connor, 221, 222.
33 von Böckle, F. 176.
34 The literature on this subject is vast. A reliable guide is M.P. Hornsby-Smith, *Catholic Education: The Unobtrusive Partner.* London, 1978.
35 The matter is discussed in the perceptive study by O. Chadwick, *The Secularisation of the European Mind in the Nineteenth Century.* Cambridge, 1975.
36 *The Guardian*, Educational Supplement, 28 June 1994.
37 *The Guardian*, 25 November 1997.
38 *The Guardian*, 2 October 1995.
39 *The Guardian*, 30 January 1996.
40 *The Tablet*, 19 June 1999.
41 *The Guardian*, 6 July 1994.
42 *The Guardian*, 2 October 1995.
43 *The Guardian*, 7 June 1994.
44 For this section I am greatly indebted to Dom Pierre Salmon's seminal study *L'Office Divin*, Paris, 1959.

Chapter 2

How to Keep Going

The Virtue of Hope

Hope is perhaps the most distorted of the virtues in the popular mind, probably because the secular meaning has overtaken the New Testament concept. Every week several million citizens hope to win the lottery and buy a ticket accordingly. If one were to analyse their attitude, it would consist of an awareness that winning a prize was a mere possibility, and well-informed players would realize that the chance of doing so is about one in fourteen million.

In contrast to this trivialization of the concept, the theological virtue of hope underpins the whole of the moral enterprise. Though designated now with the same name, the theological virtue of hope has a very different meaning. In this context the prize has already been won, and it is only a question of the circumstances in which we will receive it. The prize in question is the ultimate victory of good over evil that has been achieved by the redemptive work of Christ. The extent of His achievement will become apparent at the end of time with His return in glory (the parousia, in theological language), when He will gather to Himself all the people who have accepted His gift of salvation. As individuals they attain it finally for themselves after death. All that is required of us is to cooperate with God's will in the conduct of our lives. The lifelong struggle against evil in all its forms is sustained by theological hope, lest the individual should be discouraged and abandon the quest. Unlike the lottery, there is no element of chance. Admittedly we could throw away the prize, but that would be by our own deliberate decision: it would not be the result of fate, nor something unpredictable like the random behaviour of balls in the lottery machine.

Hope is a virtue whose psychological manifestation is optimism. In the moral life of the Christian, its importance is to protect us against discouragement. This is no idle fear. In two perspectives human beings need massive injections of encouragement if they are even to embark upon the moral life and the quest for union with God.

At the theoretical level, one is entitled to speculate about the improbability that an infinite deity would or could have any interest in individual creatures who are so insignificant in comparison with his greatness. This problem was enunciated succinctly by an English philosopher who respects religion, although she is not a believer. Mary Midgley stated 'There are plenty of theologians who believe that God made creatures so that they could know and love him; but that is plainly false'.[1] The problem for those who subscribe to that opinion is basically a lack of confidence. They simply cannot conceive how an infinite God could really be interested in such relatively insignificant creatures as ourselves. Admittedly it is a staggering claim on the part of believers, and in practice it can be sustained only by the confidence which is engendered by hope in its strict theological meaning. There is a rather sad parallel with the case of unloved children. If the initiative has not come from affectionate parents, these children grow up feeling that they are unloved and indeed unlovable. From then onwards they lack the confidence to bestow love on others and are incapable of deep and lasting relationships.

The second perspective arises out of the prevalence of evil. The record of human history is so permeated by badness that a purely rational appreciation of our situation might well lead anyone to despair. Following St Paul, Christians ascribe it to original sin, and the overall picture accords closely with the experience of many shrewd observers of the human condition. The famous parliamentarian Edmund Burke declared that if evil were to prevail it was merely necessary for good men to do nothing. In other words, left to its own devices, human nature tends to evil, in the main by greed, violence, and deception.

In the 1970s the Quakers, after careful research, published an illustration in the *New Internationalist*, which later became a well-known poster. It depicted a skull in a military helmet, and bore a brief text: 'The money required to provide adequate food, water, education, health and housing for every one in the world has been estimated at $17 billion a year. It is a huge sum of money ... about as much as the world spends on arms every two weeks.' In 1981 the situation was even worse. *The Times* put the annual figure for the arms trade at £250 000 millions, which at the current rates of exchange was about $20 billion dollars each fortnight.[2] This kind of wickedness has been so constant in human experience that we are deceived in regarding it as normal (rather like the high incidence of infant mortality in the days before scientific medicine). It is necessary to study glaring paradoxes like arms expenditure to make us realize just how abnormal and immoral the situation is.

Examples of greed and violence could be multiplied almost without limit. In 1991 Hans Küng put together a striking and equally depressing set of statistics:

Every *minute* the nations of the world spend 1.8 millions of US dollars on military armaments; every *hour* 1 500 children die of hunger-related causes; every *day* a species becomes extinct; every *week* during the 1980s more people were detained, tortured, assassinated, made refugees, or in other ways violated by acts of repressive regimes than at any other time in history except World War II; every *month* the world's economic system adds over 7.5 billions of US dollars to the catastrophically unbearable debt burden of more than $1 500 billions now resting on the shoulders of Third World peoples; every *year* an area of tropical forest three-quarters the size of Korea is destroyed and lost.[3]

Examples like the list above could be multiplied almost indefinitely. Without the virtue of hope, the average person might well abandon the quest for goodness, being overwhelmed by a sense of helplessness in the face of so much evil.

A thorough investigation of the scriptural basis of hope was provided by Jürgen Moltmann in his important book *Theology of Hope*. At the collective level, he situated hope in the context of eschatology. That is to say, human history is not simply moving forward aimlessly, but progressing purposefully towards its culmination, namely the second coming of Christ.[4] In this perspective, individual Christians work towards the improvement of human society which is the establishing of the Kingdom of God here on earth. We are motivated and sustained in this daunting enterprise by the confidence engendered by the resurrection of Jesus.[5] In this task, the resurrection shows that the ultimate victory of good over evil is assured, and indeed that it has already begun.

Not surprisingly this understanding of hope has been taken up by Liberation theologians, since it is central to their quest for social justice based on gospel values. Bishop Casaldaliga expressed it quite briefly: 'The Passover of Jesus Christ, who is "our Passover" is the real reason for my hope. I hope because he is risen, and is "the resurrection and the life".'[6] Leonardo Boff spelt it out in somewhat more detail: 'Total Liberation, generated by full freedom, constitutes the essence of the reign of the eschatological goodness of God. History is en route to this goal. Our task is to hasten that process. God's reign has an essentially future dimension that is unattainable by human practices; it is the object of eschatological hope.'[7]

Hope is closely allied to the moral virtue of 'patient endurance', which is perhaps the best translation for *hupomone* which St Paul mentions frequently in his letters. It is a practical orientation of the personality by which the individual is encouraged to sustain any reversal or hardship without abandoning the pursuit of a moral goal. It is exemplified in the sufferings of the martyrs who would endure any amount of injustice, torture and even death, but would not renounce their loyalty to Christ and His Church. It is also to be seen in the work of social reformers like William Wilberforce who endured years of frustration, threats, and the wrecking of his political career in the pursuit of the anti-slavery campaign. Although St Paul's term is sometimes translated as 'patience', I trust that the examples cited will indicate that there is nothing passive in the concept. The modern usage of the word 'patience' is too negative and cannot now do justice to what St Paul had in mind when writing about *hupomone*. In his indispensable study of New Testament morality, Ceslaus Spicq has claimed that this virtue is the only unique moral virtue in the New Testament; the other four – prudence, justice, fortitude, and temperance – were known to the ancient Greek ethical systems.[8]

There is another component or complementary part to the virtue of hope; it could be called trustfulness. Whereas hope is the confidence which we repose in God and His dealings with us, trust is the confidence which we place in human beings. In one way it applies to our equals or subordinates, while hope it directed above us to the Supreme Being. It has its parallel in the moral and psychological development of children. If they are to develop properly, they must be entrusted with ever-increasing responsibilities. It all begins with simple things like trusting my infant son to carry a plate and cup from the table to the kitchen sink without dropping them. Obviously the parent can do the task with greater speed and reliability, but if children are not entrusted with small and increasingly demanding tasks their personalities will not develop properly. This applies to emotional as well as to moral development. A story is recounted by a traveller in Mexico, who was entertained in the house of a family who had three adolescent daughters. The three of them slept in one bedroom which could be entered only by going through the parents' bedroom which was adjacent to it. So little did they trust their daughters' virtue! The story is probably apocryphal but it serves to illustrate the importance of trust.

The existence of trust has important repercussions on the behaviour of communities. It can be seen in well-run commercial enterprises. Its absence from other organizations has a lot to do with poor industrial relations, frequent strikes, general disruption and inefficiency in the work place.

Its role in the life of the Church is crucial. St Paul displayed it on his missionary journeys. After spending about one-and-a-half or two years with a newly founded community, he would move on, and leave the infant community to run itself.[9]

In modern times the progress of the Church has been hampered because trust does not arise naturally between clergy and laity. I am not saying that the two parties are always at loggerheads, but the framework of parish and diocese, as enshrined in current canon law, does not facilitate trust because it does not allow lay people any real responsibility. For them to be asked their advice by the clergy is not a real demonstration of trust; they must be allowed to assume responsibility, to share in the decision-making process, and have the freedom to make mistakes too. The absence of trust is also sadly apparent in the way in which the Pope and Vatican treat local bishops.

This is particularly disappointing because it was Pope Pius XI who gave to the world a sociological tool of remarkable originality enshrining the concept of trust, namely the Principle of Subsidiarity. As first published in 1931 in the encyclical *Quadragesimo Anno*,[10] he declared:

> Just as it is wrong to withdraw from the individual and commit to the community at large what private enterprise and endeavour can accomplish, so it is likewise unjust and a gravely harmful disturbance of right order to turn over to a greater society of higher rank functions and services which can be performed by the lesser bodies on a lower plane.

In other words autonomy and decision-making should take place at the lowest possible level and not be monopolized by higher levels. The context was the pope's fear of fascism, socialism and communism. Mussolini's government was taking over many small commercial enterprises. Worse still was the collectivization of agriculture in the Soviet Union. The peasants had been deprived of their small farms which were amalgamated into much larger units and controlled ultimately by a ministry in Moscow. History vindicated the rightfulness of the pope's principle because the collective farms proved to be hopelessly inefficient. On the eve of the collapse of the Soviet system, concessions had been made allowing the peasants to culti-vate small plots on their own initiative. It had been estimated that these plots accounted for no more the 3 per cent of the country's cultivated land, but produced about 50 per cent of the nation's food.

The principle was quoted by Pope John XXIII in his encyclical letter *Mater et Magistra*, and it was reaffirmed explicitly in Vatican II in the document on *The Church in the Modern World*.[11]

If this principle, and the trust that it implies, were applied properly to the organization of the Church, it would mean that any decision which could be reached at parish level should not be reserved to the diocese. Similarly matters which could be dealt with at diocesan level should not be decided by the Roman Curia. Sadly experience shows just the opposite because count-less matters which could be arranged at diocesan or national level are routinely decided in Rome. One example was the granting of permission, from Rome, for girls to act as altar servers. It is an almost trivial matter (since altar servers are not necessary to the liturgy and perhaps not even desirable), but the fact that local bishops were not allowed to settle the question is a blatant reversal of the principle of subsidiarity.

A more serious example is the process for the laicization of priests. If a priest wishes to leave the active ministry, usually to marry, permission has to be sought initially from his own bishop. In fact the process and the decisions have been withdrawn to the Roman Curia who grant or withhold the authorization which allows the man to contract a Church marriage. It is hard to see why this decision could not be made at diocesan level. It would be perfectly reasonable for the Vatican to lay down universal guidelines such as a two-year period of reflection. The individual decision must de-pend upon knowledge of the individual priest's situation and personality. Is he making a serious decision or is it just a trivial crisis in his life? Personal acquaintance with the applicant can be presupposed in his home diocese. Equally it can be presumed that the officials in the Roman Curia will not know him personally. Does it indicate a craving for power and control by Rome? It is hard to say. But there is no doubt that it infringes the principle of subsidiarity.

Another serious disregard for the principle of subsidiarity is the modern practice for the appointment of bishops. Over the course of history a variety of methods have been employed in selecting bishops. In antiquity the local community elected its own bishop after the death of the previous incumbent, and the laity took part in the election. In the Middle Ages that admirable custom fell into disuse and increasingly kings and other politicians acquired control of appointments. For a long time a token of local choice remained in the cathedral chapters whose members voted on candidates but without the assurance that their decision would be adhered to. In 1832 the Italian theologian Rosmini wrote his famous book, *The Five Wounds of the Church*. One of the wounds was the way in which bishops were appointed, and he lamented particularly the control which secular rulers exercised in the matter.

At the time of his writing there were 646 ordinary bishops in the Church of whom 555 were appointed by civil governments, kings, noble families, or some form of lay patronage; 67 were elected by cathedral chapters; and a mere 24 were nominated directly by the pope.[12] (I will have occasion to refer to these figures at a later stage because they are so important. Here it is necessary to study them in relation to the principle of subsidiarity.) In less than a century various historical accidents and the centralizing theology of the papacy after the First Vatican Council thrust more and more of the appointments into the hands of the pope. The reunification of Italy in 1870 gathered into the hands of King Victor Emmanuel's government the patronage of all the Italian dioceses which had hitherto been divided among about half a dozen royal houses. That government had no wish to control episcopal appointments and literally dumped the responsibility on the pope. He tacitly accepted the opportunity in what was known as the 'unspoken compromise', and thenceforward nominated all the bishops of Italy. In 1905 the separation of Church and State in France was decreed and the French government renounced its competence to nominate bishops, acquired in the concordat between Napoleon and the Vatican. The Code of Canon Law was promulgated in 1918 and in view of the two important precedents, together with the defining of papal supremacy in the First Vatican Council, it is not surprising that the Code restricted to the papacy all episcopal appointments in the entire Church. Because of the modern expansion of the Church, the pope now controls the appointments of about 3 000 bishops throughout the world. Even allowing for the advice which he might receive (or ignore) from his staff, it is surely asking too much of one man to control so large an operation: it is certainly at variance with the principle of subsidiarity.

In antiquity, episcopal appointments were governed by simple principles enunciated by early popes and councils, later incorporated into mediaeval canon law. They are: 'On no account is anyone to be a bishop who has not been chosen by the clergy, desired by the people, and consecrated by the bishops of the province with the authority of the metropolitan' (Pope Leo the Great). And 'No bishop is to be imposed on unwilling subjects, but the consent and wishes of clergy and people are to be consulted' (Pope St Celestine). The same principle was enunciated by a sixth-century council at Orleans: 'No one is to be consecrated a bishop unless the clergy and people of the diocese have been called together and have given their consent.'[13] They reflect the almost universal custom in antiquity of electing bishops by the clergy and laity of the diocese. Pope Celestine's statement echoes the situation in the region geographically close to Rome in which the pope made the appointment.

After the papacy had acquired the effective right in the modern period to appoint all bishops, it was almost inevitable that safe men would be selected, whose principal characteristic would have to be loyalty and obedience to the pope. This is indeed what happened and the selection of these safe men is a manifestation of lack of trust. It suggests that the Vatican was uneasy about appointing really talented men lest they should prove difficult to control.

During the pontificate of Pope John Paul II there has been an even stronger tendency throughout the world to appoint bishops who are theologically conservative, known to be totally uncritical of Vatican policy, and unswervingly obedient to the pope. It is not in the best interests of the Church. History shows all too often how absolute rulers do not welcome independent minds around them. Ultimately it is unhealthy for societies to be controlled by men whose principal characteristic is subservience to the absolute ruler. In the context of this chapter it is doubly regrettable because it goes against the principal of subsidiarity and the virtue of trust.

Notes

1 *The Guardian*, Saturday Review. 13 January 2001.
2 *The Times*, 4 June 1981.
3 Küng, H. *Global Responsibility*, London 1990, 2.
4 Moltmann, J. *Theology of Hope*. English translation of the 5th German edition, London, 1967, 224–9.
5 Moltmann, 190–97.
6 Casaldaliga, Pedro *I Believe in Justice and Hope*. Indiana, 1978, 229.
7 Boff, Leonardo, *The Path to Hope*. New York, 1993, 94.
8 Spicq, C. *La Théologie Morale du Nouveau Testament*. Paris, 1965, vol. I, 353, 354.
9 Murphy-O'Connor, J. *Paul: A Critical Biography*, Oxford, 1997, 127.
10 DS 3738.
11 DV II, 300. Also cited there are references to the quotations of the principle in other papal encyclicals.
12 The numbers were researched originally by G. Sweeney, and were published in the symposium *Bishops and Writers*, ed. A. Hastings, Hertfordshire, 1977, 207.
13 These principles were incorporated into mediaeval canon law, in Ivo of Chartres's *Decretum*, V, 61, 65, 66. MPL vol. 84, cols. 347–9. They were also incorporated into Gratian's *Concordantia* C 13, D LXI.

Chapter 3

The Mainstream

The Virtue of Charity

The popularity of Mother Teresa of Calcutta in the 1980s and 1990s was an acknowledgement of the centrality of charity in the Christian moral programme. In her work she had added another dimension to this well-known virtue. Focusing her attention on the absolutely destitute people who were literally dying in the gutters, she brought them into simple but clean hospitals where they could spend the last few days of the lives in a measure of dignity. And where, to use her own words, many of them died beautiful deaths. Her worldwide reputation served as an inspiration to many who could not live up to her heroic generosity.

At this point in an analysis of the Catholic Church's moral programme, I feel that it is right to acknowledge the innumerable works of charity performed by religious orders right up to the modern period. Prior to the establishment of national welfare policies in education, healthcare and unemployment provision, practically all welfare work was performed by religious orders. Their efforts were most visible in Catholic nations like nineteenth-century France where almost all nursing and education of the poor was done by nuns and brothers. In modern times governments have accepted responsibility initially for education and then for other areas of welfare. One must applaud the actions of such modern governments but also realize the enormous debt of gratitude that many societies owe to the devoted work of so many religious organizations. This situation lasted up to the twentieth century when an increasing number of governments accepted the responsibility for the social welfare of their citizens.

It is a truism to repeat that the driving force of Christian morality is the virtue of charity, which is the love of God and one's neighbour. On this all are agreed, but complications arise because the concept is so rich and the applications are so diverse. How is it to be translated into action?

Various unconvincing attempts have been made by moral theologians to clarify the obligation by clear rules. For example, it has been suggested, with reference to Old Testament tithes, that a Christian should give one-tenth of his income to charitable causes, or was it one-tenth of his surplus income? In which case what constituted surplus, and who should decide it anyway? All such attempts have failed. Love cannot be organized in that fashion.

The New Testament accords a central place to charity, and the teaching of Jesus and St Paul indicates some of the main orientations for its application,

by a variety of examples and exhortations to generosity, but not with specific rules. The basic principle of the love of God and neighbour is found in
the Old Testament (Lev. 19:18 and Deut. 6:4), but it was smothered among
so many other rules and regulations that it did not emerge as the dominating
spiritual ideal. Jesus gave it overwhelming priority, disentangling it from a
mass of irrelevant legislation, and thereby incurring the permanent hostility
of the Pharisees. He gave one or two clarifications to the word 'neighbour'.
The ancient Israelites considered that fellow Israelites were their neighbours. The parable of the Good Samaritan (Luke 10:33) taught that the
designation was not limited to any race but that love must be shown to all
kinds of people. The parable also emphasized, by implication, the harmful
effects of man-made rules. Luke states that the robbers left the man 'for
dead'. The Levite and the priest, being on the way to Jerusalem for religious
duties, did not wish to incur ritual impurity by contact with a dead body,
because it was forbidden in the Pentateuch. Jesus also extended the concept
of love of neighbour to the love of our enemies and this is perhaps the most
original and generous moral ideal which has ever been proposed to the
human race (Matt. 5:44).

As is well known, the Sermon on the Mount and the discourse about the
Last Judgement in Matthew 25 give comprehensive examples of how to
practise the love of neighbour. This ideal has been adhered to, with varying
degrees of success, by all of the Christian Church, even at times when other
members of the same Church have been contravening it in ways which I will
discuss later.

The exercise of this virtue has varied over the centuries according to the
various social contexts in which the Church has found itself. In the first few
generations it was very simple. In his first *Apologia* written shortly after 148
AD, St Justin depicted the lives of the Christians of the early second century.
He described the celebration of the Eucharist, and the way in which each
Sunday money was collected and stored in a chest for the assistance of the
poor.[1]

Centuries later, St Vincent de Paul organized the operations on a scale
which would have been inconceivable to St Justin. He founded religious
orders and lay confraternities, purchased land, built hospitals, administered
vast sums of money and negotiated with the king and with nobles. I mention
this because the two practices of the same virtue illustrate how different are
the applications of the love of neighbour. The work of St Vincent shows that
charity and efficient organization are not incompatible. Christians have
never been advised to close their eyes, fold their hands and expect the Holy
Spirit to relieve poverty. In fact the New Testament does not urge us to pray
for the poor: practical generosity is what is required. It is the practical
expression of this task that has changed over the years, and some of these
practical steps have appeared dangerous to the conservative-minded members of the Church.

Case Study: The Abolition of Slavery

The famous rationalist, Lecky, declared that the abolition of slavery was one of the few achievements of which the human race could rightly be proud. (There are a couple more which are worthy of note, namely the replacement of blood feuds by the processes of law courts, which occurred about 3 000 years ago, and more recently the emancipation of women in the Western cultural ambit; which, admittedly occurred after Lecky's death.) However the abolition of slavery is a useful case study for examining the virtue of charity.

In the circumstances of the modern world, four kinds of operation are necessary for the practice of charity in the crusade against deprivation, namely: amelioration, enablement, protest, and structural change. They are clearly illustrated in the long campaign against slavery.

The eradication of slavery was one of the most daunting tasks which high-minded reformers could have undertaken. It was thoroughly embedded in European society as it had been in the ancient near-eastern societies from which mediaeval Europe derived its culture. In Greek and Latin the same word denotes both a slave and a servant, an indicator of how the ancient peoples thought of the institution. With the spectacular development of overseas trade in the sixteenth century the slave trade received a new impetus. This was principally because the white colonizers found it too difficult to do heavy work, like agriculture and mining, in the climate of the Caribbean and neighbouring parts of the mainland.

The facts are now well known. The bulk of the trade took place in a triangular route starting from Europe (mainly from the western seaboard, but most nations were involved to some degree, even Sweden and Denmark). They brought cheap manufactured goods from Europe and traded them with various rulers on the West African coast for prisoners of war. Eventually the Europeans sent out their own raiding parties too. The captives were shipped across the Atlantic and sold mostly to the sugar planters of the Caribbean islands. On the return journey to Europe they brought sugar which they sold for vast profits, as Europeans were becoming increasingly dependent upon that product, which as yet they were unable to cultivate at home.

For the purposes of the present study it is paradoxical and sad that the Catholic nations had by far the largest share in the trade, with Portugal topping the list. According to the most recent research, between the years 1440 and 1870, Portugese ships made 30 000 journeys taking 4 650 000 slaves from Africa to America.[2] In the same period the ships of Spain and France made approximately 4 000 voyages each, carrying a total of nearly 3 000 000 slaves. By the middle of the eighteenth century England had become the major actor in the business, and in one decade, 1740–50 British ships transported more than 200 000 slaves.[3] Another indicator of the scale of the trade and the economy which it supported is the fact that the French-occupied island of St Dominique had an estimated 200 000 slaves in 1765. To maintain that labour force they needed to import 15 000 slaves each year.[4] Throughout the whole of the period 1440 to 1870 it has been calculated that European ships undertook 54 200 voyages transporting to America approximately 11 000 000 slaves.[5]

The sufferings of the slaves were intense, but even without those hardships, the loss of liberty and the fact that legally they were merchandise was the essence of the evil. At the very end of the period, a number of slave owners in America were quite benevolent in the treatment of their slaves. This did not justify the institution morally. In fact G.K. Chesterton said of them that they were the worst enemies of justice because they disguised the intrinsic evils of the system.

However it was the sufferings of the imported slaves which sparked off the basic Christian response, traditionally known as the corporal works of mercy, as displayed in the life of St Peter Claver. He was born at Verdu in Catalonia in 1581 and educated in Barcelona by the Jesuits, whose society he entered in 1601. Nine years later he sailed to Colombia, was ordained priest in 1615, and worked in the city of Cartagena until his death in 1654. The whole of that period was devoted to the spiritual and material care of slaves. When the ships arrived, he tended the wounds and illnesses of the new arrivals and cared for their every need, including that of accompanying condemned men to the gallows. His reputation was such that, at his death, the Jesuit house was invaded by hundreds of his devotees, desperate for just one more glimpse of their hero. He was canonized by popular acclamation.

His lifelong work of charity was literally heroic but, without being ungenerous, one has to reflect upon its limitations. The cruel trade continued unabated: the evil had not been eradicated.

Eradication came a stage closer to realization with the next stage in the campaign against slavery, that of enablement. The principle has been stated succinctly by a South American bishop: 'If I give a fish to a hungry man, he will be fed for that day. If I give him a fishing rod he can feed himself for the rest of his life.' Admittedly that example is something of an oversimplification, but its basic insight is correct.

For the slave trade this principle was illustrated in the eighteenth century by the life and work of the American Quaker, John Woolman. He was born at Ranconas in New Jersey, the fourth child in a family of 13. As a young man he tried his hand at a variety of jobs, being at one time or another a tailor, shopkeeper, surveyor, and schoolteacher. Eventually he gave up work in order to free himself from the quest for money. His spiritual gifts were manifest and at the age of 23 the local Quaker community acknowledged in him the gift of 'vocal ministry'. He became an itinerant preacher speaking out against slavery. With this message he toured the English-speaking colonies of North America. In 1754 he published a book entitled *Considerations on the Keeping of Negroes*. Seventeen fifty-eight marked a decisive achievement in his work for he persuaded the Quaker community of Philadelphia to liberate all their slaves. Many other Quaker meetings were persuaded to do the same. He came to England with the same message but died in York in 1772. The publication of his journal two years later caused a considerable stir and continued the dissemination of his ideas.

At this period, the latter part of the eighteenth century, it is worth noting that Christian philanthropists were being supported by influences coming from the largely French-inspired Enlightenment. The ideas about human rights and equality associated with Voltaire and Rousseau which ultimately generated the French Revolution also influenced people's attitude to slavery. After the Revolution and during the long war with France, there was antipathy in England for any influences emanating from that country. As a result, it is difficult to estimate how much impetus these principles contributed to Christian initiatives in England.

The third stage in the Christian practice of charity is that of protest. The term speaks for itself and it is a legitimate and perhaps necessary stand to be taken if an evil cannot be remedied by practical means. It is the opposite of acquiescence, which is a form of sinful collaboration by passive alliance with wickedness. Protest is one manifestation of Christian witness to truth, whose highest expression has traditionally been martyrdom, the ultimate witness to the truths about God and his dealings with humanity. By enduring their sufferings, the martyrs have protested silently or vocally against the cruelty of persecutors when there was no practical possibility of converting them or inducing them to desist from their policies. Even when they were not being threatened with physical sufferings, the advocates of social reform manifested the same integrity by continuing to protest against other forms of oppression at times when any practical achievements were impossible for them.

During the period when the slave trade flourished, disquiet about it was expressed by various Church leaders. For the most part it was ineffectual, and did not quite add up to the ideal of Christian protest, as I will show shortly. The first such criticism came from the Spanish Dominican theologian de Soto, who wrote a book against slavery in 1557.[6] In 1569 another Dominican, Tomas de Mercado published a book against it, drawing on his own experiences in Mexico. In 1639 Pope Urban VIII wrote an encyclical letter against slavery, and in the following century Pope Benedict XV also condemned it.[7] None of these protests were backed up by any kind of practical action.

A different kind of protest, authentic Christian protest, is to be seen in the life of the famous Dominican Bartolomé de las Casas.[8] His contact with the slave trade extended back to the very beginnings of the colonization of America. He was born in Seville in 1484 and a few years later his father and one of his uncles accompanied Columbus on his second voyage to the Caribbean. In 1502 Bartolomé himself went to Haiti as a soldier. He served in the invasion of Cuba and, like so many other soldiers, he was rewarded with a grant of land in what was known as the *encomienda* system. The natives who were on the land were obliged to work for their Spanish masters without payment. It was not the total form of slavery since they were not reduced to the state of merchandise, but their loss of freedom and compulsory unpaid labour constituted a serious injustice. Bartolomé was ordained a priest, incidentally the first in the New World, and in 1514 he freed his own Indians and determined to end the system.

To this end he returned to Spain in 1515 and spent the next six years writing and lobbying the King and his ministers in an attempt to have the system changed. In 1516 he published his *Memorial de Remedios* in which he advocated the abolition of the *encomienda* system. In its place he advocated that the Indians should be paid wages, should not be allowed to work for Spanish masters for more than two months a year, and this work should not be too far from their homes. It is interesting to note that at this stage of his career, he supported the use of black slaves as labourers because he believed that they were all condemned criminals. At that time enlightened opinion tolerated and even advocated such treatment for criminals. In *Utopia*, Thomas More envisages that convicts would be put to useful public work rather than remain incarcerated in prison and therefore idle. In the navies of the Christian nations round the Mediterranean, the galleys were rowed by convicts.

In 1524 Bartolomé returned to America and entered the Dominican order in Haiti. After missionary work in Nicaragua and Mexico, he returned to Spain again in 1540. Two years later he wrote his famous *Brevissima Relacion de las Destrucion de las Indias*. This and his persistent lobbying had the effect of changing the Spanish legislation for the colonies. The New Laws required that the Indian labourers be freed from the *encomienda* system and paid wages. In reality those laws proved to be unenforceable by the Spanish government, which was simply too far away from the scene of action.

Back in Mexico in 1543 Bartolomé refused the sacraments to those colonists who did not liberate the Indians. It was this practical step which differentiated his protest from the other ineffectual statements made by the ecclesiastics cited above. Since he carried it through to action, where it was possible for him, his protest has the quality of authentic Christian witness to the truth. In 1552 Bartolomé journeyed to Spain yet again to continue his work of protest. It is interesting to note that at this late stage in his life, he also condemned the trade in slaves from Africa. He died at Valladolid in 1556 without ever seeing the end of the system against which he had protested for most of his adult life. Nevertheless his life and work were an authentic embodiment of Christian charity.

The fourth stage in the implementation of the virtue of charity is that of structural change, that is to say changing institutions or the legal basis of societies if necessary so that they no longer create injustices. It is the most complete service to the poor since it removes the causes that produce their poverty. Within the present case study, the work of Thomas Clarkson and William Wilberforce illustrates this stage in the practice of charity.

The two men were almost contemporaries, Wilberforce being born in 1759 and Clarkson a year later. Wilberforce was rich and brilliant, so much so that he was confidently expected to attain high office after his election to parliament in 1780, perhaps even the premiership. Clarkson was the son of a rural clergyman who was also headmaster of Wisbech Grammar School in Cambridgeshire. Like Wilberforce he studied at Cambridge where he gained a First in mathematics. More significant for his future labours was his winning of a university prize for an essay entitled 'Is It Right To Enslave Men Against Their Will?'. On the way to London in 1785 to arrange for the publication of the essay, he underwent a transforming spiritual experience. He abandoned his original intention of following his father into the ranks of the clergy and resolved to devote his life to the abolition of slavery. Wilberforce had a similar religious conversion while on holiday in France, also in 1785. Thereafter he changed his manner of life, devoting the early hours of each morning to prayer and study, and consciously looking for a good cause to which he could devote his life. Providentially the opening was provided for him when the Committee for the Effecting of the Abolition of the Slave Trade invited him to be their parliamentary representative.

The combination of disinterested love and hard-headed realism is to be seen in the work of both men. Clarkson toured the seaports of England collecting evidence from the seamen working on slave ships. Eventually he interviewed a total of 20 000 sailors. Wilberforce made the all-important practical decision of pursuing a limited objective. He realized that the eradication of slavery as such was too diffuse an operation. So he persuaded his collaborators to aim for the abolition of the trade. Once this had been achieved, he argued, the rest of the practice would inevitably collapse.

Needless to say the campaign stirred up powerful opposition from many influential people who had vested interests in the profits from the trade itself and the indirect benefits. It is surprising how many good people had taken it for granted, and only under pressure did they relinquish their support for the trade. Among them, for example, was the family of the future prime minister William Gladstone.

In 1789 Wilberforce put before parliament a bill for the abolition of the slave trade. It failed. Opposition came from many quarters. For example in 1791, Colonel Tarleton, one of the MPs for Liverpool, stated in Parliament that the abolition of the trade would bring an end to the work of 5 500 sailors and 160 ships bringing in imports with an annual value of six million pounds (at values then current). Even allowing for a measure of hyperbole, one can see how the vested interests felt threatened. Threats of another kind were aimed at Wilberforce and his supporters, who for nearly twenty years were obliged to endure vilification, hostility of all kinds, death threats, and for Wilberforce himself, the loss of any hope of the promotion of his political career. The historian Trevelyan was of the opinion that 'Wilberforce could probably have been Pitt's successor as prime minister if he had preferred party to mankind'.[9] The conduct of those campaigners illustrates the virtue of patient endurance (*hupomone*) of which I spoke in the previous chapter. After several unsuccessful attempts, a bill to abolish the slave trade was passed by Parliament in 1807. Slavery as such was outlawed in Britain and its colonies in 1833.

Needless to say the value of the Christian element in the campaign has been disputed. For example, Professor Eric Williams and others alleged that slavery collapsed in the early nineteenth century because it was no longer profitable financially. His views were disputed by Professor Anstey. These debates are only of academic interest. The unanswerable fact is that the trade continued until its operators were compelled to abandon it, as in Brazil and in the Southern States of the USA, right up to the time of the American Civil War. When the Northern States emerged victorious they compelled the Southern States to abolish slavery. The most recent and authoritative writer on the matter has stated unambiguously that moral conviction was the determining element in this chapter of English history.[10]

As I observed above, the roles of the Enlightenment and the French Revolution are problematical. Clearly slavery was at variance with the revolutionary ideals of Liberty, Equality, and Fraternity, and after the Revolution events move swiftly. In 1791 the National Assembly condemned slavery in principle, and in 1794 the Convention in Paris declared the universal emancipation of slaves.[11] It is questionable whether this helped or hindered the Christian-inspired movement in England. The revolution had caused such alarm in Britain that there was a reaction against anything that the French initiated. At this time the nascent Trade Union movement suffered severe setbacks since its opponents were able to liken its groups to revolutionary cells.

Whatever may have been the ancillary influence of the Enlightenment and the Revolution, there can be no doubt about the influence of practical charity practised by Christian politicians in England. It stands as a classical case study of structural change for human betterment inspired by the ideals of the New Testament.

Religion and Public Life

The interpenetration of religion and politics is a delicate business, particularly when a high-minded minority attempts to impose its views on the whole of society and makes use of the machinery of government to do so. The Prohibition legislation in the USA in the 1920s is a tragic example of how badly it can go wrong. The influence of the Catholic Church in the Irish Republic is another example. The teachings of the Church were prominent in the social legislation of the newly founded republic in the 1920s. Divorce was impossible under Irish law and contraceptives were legally unobtainable. The end of a marriage is clearly a tragic event, but it was unreasonable of the Irish government to deny the possibility of divorce to its Protestant or agnostic citizens. It certainly gave ammunition to Protestant zealots in the north, who in this instance had a serious grievance about being ruled by the Vatican if there should ever be a united Ireland. The sad fact is that the Catholic Church has perfectly adequate disciplinary and educational opportunities to impose its own discipline on its own members within the community of the Church. The utilization of the state's legal and coercive powers was unnecessary to say the least.

A rough and ready rule of thumb for utilizing the apparatus of government for a moral cause would seem to depend on whether the matter in question is one of natural law rather than particular doctrines of one individual Church. In such cases the course of conduct can be presumed in all people of goodwill. Such indeed was the situation of slavery and its abolition with the help of the law. It also explains why prohibition legislation in the USA was a failure. Serious-minded people were not convinced of the ethical case against the moderate consumption of alcohol.

Conservative-minded Church leaders have a tendency to fear social change. When soup kitchens distribute food to the hungry high ranking ecclesiastics do not feel threatened. But as Bishop Helder Camara once said, 'If I enquire into the causes of their poverty, people accuse me of being a communist'. Possibly it is the link with Marxism which causes the alarm. Marx himself has a pivotal role in the whole process of changing societies. In his *Theses on Feuerbach* he published his famous observation: 'The philosophers have been at pains to understand the world: the important thing is to change it.'[12] The world has never been quite the same since.

From the time of Marx onwards, roughly the middle of the nineteenth century, it has been possible to change the world to a degree that would have been inconceivable and impossible for our ancestors. Since that time, progress in science and technology, as well as psychology and the understanding of social systems, has enabled us to transform our societies. Christians should welcome this wonderful opportunity since it provides possibilities for the eradication of poverty and injustice, which would have been impossible for those who could practise charity only at the level of amelioration. In other words, soup kitchens and cottage hospitals are no longer adequate: we now need institutional changes like national health services and minimum-wage legislation.

Catholic bishops' conferences do not have a good record in this matter. In a variety of countries they have neither facilitated nor encouraged the establishment of national health services. In the 1990s, shortly after Bill Clinton had been elected as president of the United States, his wife Hilary made a determined attempt to establish a more satisfactory national health service for the USA. The move was frustrated by a combination of vested interests ranging from pharmaceutical companies to the insurance industry, both of whom foresaw that their profits would be diminished by such a scheme. The taxpayers too were hostile to even the slightest rise in taxes to pay for it. Those reactions were predictable, granted the human propensity to selfishness. What was really disappointing was the lack of support from the American Catholic community and its episcopal conference. Being by far the largest and best-organized Church in that nation, the wholehearted support of the Catholic bishops could have ensured the measure's success. As it is, millions of American citizens are still denied elementary medical care. The developments of scientific medicine have been so spectacular that it has become, almost inevitably, expensive. Drugs are costly to produce, and surgical techniques like heart bypass operations are so complex that they are intrinsically expensive. Poor people cannot have access to proper medical care unless the whole business is removed from the realm of private commerce and replaced by some kind of national health service. This will inevitably entail subsidizing medical care from public revenues, which means a small increase in taxes. The biblical injunction to visit the sick means just this in the modern world, and it is difficult to see how any committed Christian could object to it.

At the end of the Second World War, when the National Health Service was being started in Great Britain, Cardinal Griffin led the English bishops' negative stance. Their only real interest in the matter was to secure exemption from the scheme for hospitals conducted by Catholic religious orders. The government agreed, and the Catholic hospitals continued to work outside the NHS. This meant that the hospitals charged their patients for the care that they provided and a diminishing number of nuns gave their services free of charge. With the passage of time, the inevitable economic forces ensured that such hospitals catered mainly for the rich and many of them became wealthy institutions.

In 1995 small changes in the rules of the Charity Commission required registered charities to make known their accounts to the Commission which put the information into the public domain. This had some unexpected consequences. For example, information about relatively obscure religious orders' wealth became accessible to public knowledge. One fairly representative Congregation which had 89 sisters and half a dozen institutions in this country was obliged to declare an annual income of £27 million. Significantly, of the half-dozen institutions, three of them were private hospitals.[13]

I have refrained from naming the Congregation since I am sure that their situation is not unique, and many other religious orders are similarly wealthy but have hitherto concealed the fact from public knowledge. In 1999 a religious order in the south of England sold a property for £3.5 million to pay for the medical and other retirement expenses of its ageing communities. It had been leased to a diocese as a pastoral centre. When the property came on to the market the diocese in question could not afford such a sum and lost its pastoral centre. Admittedly the order in question did not have complete freedom of action. Being a registered charity they were required by English law to accept the highest offer.[14] One wonders if they were following the right law.

As the years went by it became sadly apparent that the NHS was providing adequate care for the poor and the hospitals of the religious orders were
providing special refined services for wealthy people. It was a complete
betrayal of the gospel injunction to care for the needy and of their founders'
intentions.

A few years after the establishment of the NHS in Britain, the Irish
government planned a national health service. The bishops in the Republic,
being much more influential than their British counterparts, were able effectively to stop the scheme. The reluctance of Church leaders to welcome such
a radical change in health care was the consequence of an innate conserva-
tism and timidity. They simply could not envisage the exercise of charity in
anything other than its traditional form. It also relates to the artificiality of
their way of life, about which I will deal in the final chapter. To put it
simply, the bishops have always been well provided for financially and
medically. They knew that if they should need medical care, they would
always be given priority treatment in nuns' hospitals. They never had to face
reality in its most tragic form, namely when a woman looks across to her
husband by the bedside of their sick child, and says the dreaded words, 'Can
we afford a doctor?'.

For Christians it is important to remember that such social changes are
authentic expressions of charity. The sufferings of the poor are alleviated,
and there is nothing unspiritual about structural changes and legal measures
which protect their rights. Such measures are basically the same as the
means adopted to abolish slavery in the nineteenth century.

Many people who react strongly against poverty and injustice turn
almost naturally towards socialism and communism as systems that offer
hope to them. A few examples will suffice. About twenty years ago a
group of students in a polytechnic in East Anglia were studying to become
social workers and probation officers. After about a year half of them
underwent a process analogous to religious conversion. They said to themselves: 'It is pointless to spend our lives supporting society's casualties.
Our efforts will be like water running into the sand. What we need to do is
to change society so that it will not produce casualties.' At that point many
of them became Marxists, seeing it as the system best orientated to changing society. That honour might well be attributed to the Church if its
support for charitable work was functioning properly and not timidly
resisting institutional changes.

The hostility on the part of Catholics to structured social reform is probably a short-sighted knee-jerk reaction against any imitation or influence
from communism and socialism. During the Cold War period one American
politician declared that it was his intention to fight communism wherever
and in whatever form it was to be found. It is a pity that the Vatican had to
be equally blinkered in its policies.

As far back as the 1930s, generous people who were really in touch with
poverty did not turn to Christianity but to the political left. For example a

retired nurse, by the name of Patience Edney, speaking towards the end of a long life, stated how she felt when confronted by poverty in London:

> I worked in University College Hospital, and in London in those days, before the National Health Service, women were coming in to die ... because they didn't have a shilling for the doctor or the nine pence for the medicine. There was nothing we could do for them. People could only get unemployment benefit after they had proved that they had sold everything. They were allowed to keep a table, a chair, a cup, saucer and teapot, but that was it. I didn't know what to do about that either. I decided to go to Spain because there they seemed to know how to do something about it.[15]

At that period the communist struggle in the Spanish Civil War was an inspiration to many on the political left.

Right-wing, and capitalist-inspired governments are naturally fearful of such changes. They perceive rightly that any major restructuring of society would shift vast sums of money from the privileged class into national schemes for education and medical care, which are intrinsically expensive.

The Catholic Church cannot act in a vacuum. Hostility to communism which worked wonderfully in Poland cannot simply be transposed to all other nations. The situation in Latin America, for example, is full of potential for progress or spiritual disaster for the Church. If it does not align itself fully with the preferential option for the poor, which was proclaimed at the meeting in Medellin in 1968, it will find itself inevitably in alliance with repressive right-wing dictatorships whose record on human rights is indefensible. For example, the Brazilian bishop, Dom Lucas Moreira, refused to speak out in public protest against the torturing of priests by the military, although he was quite willing to speak out against abortion and contraception. Unfortunately he was elected chairman of the Brazilian bishops' conference in 1995, an indication of how Pope John Paul II's policy of appointing conservative-orientated bishops is having a profound effect on national hierarchies. This in turn is turning the Church more and more towards right-wing regimes and away from the concerns of the poor.[16]

It seems that the Church authorities have not learnt the lessons of the Nazi period in Germany. I will deal with the Church's reaction to the Holocaust later in the book, but for the moment it is relevant to reflect, in the context of charity, upon the duty of solidarity with victims of oppression. Miklos Hammer, a Hungarian Jew, survived Birkenau, Auschwitz and Buchenwald. During the course of his captivity he met, among others, a converted Jew, and a half-Jew raised as a Catholic. Neither of them survived. The converted Jew had said to Hammer on one occasion, 'Not a single voice from my own Church spoke up for me when I was drafted.'[17]

To return to the theme of charity, it is clear that human behaviour, dominated by original sin, does not automatically lead towards social justice. Economic exploitation has been endemic and became the normal concomitant of modern industrialization in virtually all countries. Recent history contains

no lack of examples. The practices of the asbestos industry are a stark reminder of exploitation at its worst. The danger of contracting an incurable
lung disease (mesothelioma) was known in the 1950s and possibly earlier. In
that period the extensive asbestos mines in South Africa had the material
extracted without any thought to the protection of the workers. About a third
of those workers were children, some as young as seven, and their work
consisted of hammering the lumps of rock by hand. Vast quantities of asbestos
fragments and dust permeated the atmosphere, literally for miles around the
mines. The mine owners were totally frank about their reasons for employing
children. 'It would be most uneconomical for us to employ fully grown men
to do the work done by these minors.' Such was the unequivocal motivation of
the employers. In the 1990s a number of survivors were able to sue the
company via one of its British subsidiaries in the English courts. At that time
the disgraceful practices of the recent past became public knowledge.[18]

   If the poor are to be protected from exploitation, ameliorative charity is
not enough, they must be helped by charity which has produced structural
changes, such as trades unions or appropriate legislation. The statutory
minimum wage is a very good example.

Alliance with Society: The Harmful Pattern

Whereas the abolition of slavery illustrates a beneficent alliance between
Christianity and the state in the performance of charity, the history of the
Church has all too many examples of harmful liaisons. The Crusades, anti-
Semitism, and the burning of heretics are perhaps the worst examples of
misdirected morality, in which the Church leaders and their policies have
been not only partners in cruelty but have actually initiated and led those
policies. Basically they arose from a degree of interpenetration between
church and state, in which the Church took on the ethos of society, instead
of acting as the leaven which would transform the body politic according to
the ideals of the gospel.

   The first Crusade was proclaimed by Pope Urban II, on the 22nd of
November 1095 at the council of Clermont in France. As is well known, the
object of this and subsequent Crusades was to use military force to conquer
Palestine. In those days it seemed desperately important to keep in Christian
hands the land in which Jesus had lived and taught. With the wisdom of
hindsight we can see that the physical possession of land and buildings in
Palestine has little to do with the mission of the Church. It is dangerous to
criticize previous generations since it is so hard to enter into their psychological perspective, but it does seem difficult to justify the moral decisions
entailed in the Crusades. It was the biggest military operation of the Middle
Ages. Thousands of people, including children, were killed. It was all done
in the name of Jesus who had clearly and consistently repudiated any use of
political or military power to further his mission. That at least should have

been apparent to the Church leaders and theologians. Without exaggerating, one can say that the crusading movement is one of the worst examples of misdirected morality, and it is not surprising that it has soured relations with the whole Muslim world ever since. The year 1995 was the ninth centenary of the inception of the Crusades, but it passed without any repudiation of the movement.

Anti-Semitism is another collective betrayal of charity. The widespread influence of this attitude and its prevalence at the highest levels is a sobering and humbling fact that modern Christians must come to terms with and rectify. It cannot be denied that hostility to Jews was preached vehemently by some of the Church Fathers, among whom one has to include the saintly John Chrysostom. In the Middle Ages when the Church had so much control over the ideology and moral perspectives of all Europeans, attitudes hardened. Legal restrictions against Jews multiplied and these culminated in the influential Fourth Lateran Council of 1215. It was that council which decreed distinctive dress for the Jews, in these words:

> In some provinces Jews and Saracens are distinguished from Christians by their dress, but in others confusion can arise because no difference can be discerned. Whence it might happen by error that Christian men might have relationships with Jewish or Saracen women, or Jews and Saracens might have relationships with Christian women. Therefore lest this excess of reprehensible intermixing should become further widespread through the error of concealment, we decree that such persons of either sex, in all Christian provinces, at all times must be distinguished from other people by their manner of dress in public.[19]

This dress was a conical hat in German speaking lands and a yellow badge stitched on the clothing in Mediterranean regions. In England the badge stitched on the clothing consisted of two small tablets, reminiscent of the Decalogue.[20]

By the middle of the sixteenth century, Jews had been expelled from most of the nations of western Europe but by a tragic irony, anti-Semitism persisted. England presents a sad example. Jews were expelled in the reign of Edward I in 1290, and were not officially readmitted until 1656. However anti-Semitism was still strong, as can be seen for example in the works of some of our most famous writers. In Chaucer's *Canterbury Tales*, the Prioress recounts a legend about the murder of a Christian boy by the Jews in an Eastern city. The narrative is rounded off with by her likening it to the popular myth of the murder of young Hugh of Lincoln, also by the Jews. In the sixteenth century the greatest of the dramatists display the same prejudices. The anti-Semitism in Marlowe's *Jew of Malta* and Shakespeare's *Merchant of Venice* evidently pleased contemporary audiences. Human nature is all too prone to demonize those who are thought to be different from ourselves. It is the psychological background to racial prejudice.

Practically every nation in Europe has been guilty of anti–Semitism at some time in its history. In the modern period, the Dreyfus affair in France indicated a widespread attitude of venomous hostility towards Jews in general, and at a time when Catholicism claimed the allegiance of the majority of the population. A random indicator of the underlying bigotry was the subtitle of the Catholic newspaper *La Croix* which was owned and directed by a religious order, the Assumptionists. Up to 1907 it carried the subtitle: *Le Journal le plus anti-Semitique en France* (The most anti-Semitic newspaper in France).[21]

It is deeply regrettable that the long-term official attitude of the Catholic Church, expressed in its legislation on the matter, gave a semblance of legitimacy to this despicable trait in human nature. It is no exaggeration to say that it was the remote cause of that climate of anti-Semitism in Europe which culminated in the Nazis' Holocaust.

An attitude that has become so firmly entrenched as anti-Semitism cannot be eradicated quickly. One fears that it still lingers in the collective mentality of many Catholics. In Poland for example there have been disputes for years about erecting commemorative crosses on the site of Auschwitz and the building of a Carmelite convent there. All of this is clearly offensive to Jewish sensibilities, and in that particular place it behoves the Catholics to be generous.

There is also the mysterious suppression of the Feast of the Circumcision in 1969. From the sixth century at least until that date, the first of January had been celebrated as the festival of the Circumcision of Jesus. It was among the small group of feast days that are well supported by New Testament evidence. St Luke 2:21 records the rite as taking place eight days after Christ's birth in accordance with the Mosaic Law. The theological significance of that ceremony was that it explicitly made Jesus a member of the Israelite religion. His biological inclusion in the Israelite race was assured by having a Jewish mother. Theological incorporation into the faith of the Patriarchs was effected by the ceremony of circumcision. Nothing else could emphasize so strongly his Jewishness. Was it therefore a residual anti-Semitism which prompted the alteration of January 1st into the Solemnity of Holy Mary the Mother of God? Surely that aspect of Mary's role had been made clear at Christmas and the Annunciation, not to mention several other Marian festivals in the calendar? It is difficult to account for the alteration in 1969 by any other explanation.

The burning of heretics is the final example that I will mention. Somewhat surprisingly it had the support of Aquinas, who said: 'Heresy is a sin which merits not only excommunication but also death, for it is worse to corrupt the faith which is the life of the soul than to issue counterfeit coins which minister to the secular life. Since counterfeiters are justly killed by princes as enemies to the common good, so heretics also deserve the same punishment.'[22] In the mediaeval period, those who were condemned for heresy by the Church courts were handed over to the civil authorities to be killed by burning. Although the activities of the Spanish Inquisition have attracted most attention, it is worth remembering that it occurred in England too. In 1401, the Act *De Haeretico Comburendo*[23] became law, having been enacted to combat the national dissident movement known as the Lollards. Most probably the motivation behind it was the perception that since Church and state were so completely interpenetrated, anything which threatened to undermine the authority of the Church was considered to be equally dangerous for the state. Hence heretics received the same punishment as those who plotted against the Crown. Once again, even allowing for different historical perspectives, it is impossible to justify the Church's adoption of such a policy.

Even when things had not got out of hand, as with the Crusades, the alliance between Church and state in the mediaeval period was not healthy. The two organizations were too close. It is an oversimplification to speak of control, but generally the Church leaders had got themselves in a position where they could effectively influence the conduct of kings and princes with a view to ensuring that the law of the land enshrined the morality of the Church. By a series of unlikely historical accidents, it is the Church of England which still exhibits this sort of relationship. The presence of the Anglican bishops in the House of Lords illustrates the arrangement that mediaeval churchmen considered to be normal. Elsewhere in Europe such privileges were lost at the time of the French Revolution, and the revolutionary movements which followed it in the nineteenth century. The Catholic Church attempted to claw back influence by means of concordats with the governments of Catholic countries. They are not really effective for achieving Christian solutions to current problems, precisely because of the complexity of modern life and the fact that when the concordats were drawn up, their framers could not possibly foresee all the situations in which a Christian response would be needed.

The organization of confessional political parties suffers from the same problems. Moreover they carry with them the danger of creating false alliances and rivalries. If a government is debating about customs duties at the frontiers, it is unlikely that there will be a clear Christian solution. But if a confessional party espouses a 10 per cent tax on alcohol rather than 15 per cent, it could have the indirect effect of bringing loyal Christians (in other parties) into indirect opposition to the Church. Both from the theoretical and practical standpoint, something more flexible is needed.

Latin America has provided an admirable model with basic communities inspired by Liberation theology. Both the theology and the group are sufficiently small and flexible to enable them to provide a Christian response to the most diverse political situations which might arise, such as the arrest and torture of political activists or the allocation of farm land to landless peasants. In addition these small groups illustrate perfectly the Principle of Subsidiarity.

In recent years there have been several moves on the part of the Vatican to disassociate the Church from past excesses and to repudiate the evils. At one level, such admissions are welcome as a manifestation of truth, yet from other points of view they are unsatisfactory. Basically they remain little more than words. Admittedly it is impossible to repair the damage which was done centuries ago, but if the repudiations are sincere, there should be some sort of practical component in them to ensure that the same thing will not happen again. One looks in vain for such practicalities by the Church authorities. By contrast the record of the Federal German Republic is edifying since the Germans have paid out approximately £35 billion to former victims of Nazi atrocities. In addition to the national compensation the large industrial organization, Volkswagen, has made its own reparation. During the war when its factories were making armaments, they employed about 10 000 slave labourers – Russian prisoners of war, Poles, and Jews drawn from concentration camps. For the few survivors of that operation who are still alive, Volkswagen has set up a special fund to give them financial compensation.[24]

Pope John Paul II has publicly apologized to the Jews for their treatment in the past at the hands of the Catholic Church. In the year 2000 on March 12th he led a service in St Peter's Basilica, in which he apologized on behalf of the Church for the cruel treatment of Jews, heretics, and Muslims.[25] All these cruelties have one thing in common. They were gross violations of human rights. One could contemplate the apologies with a greater sense of reassurance if measures were taken to strengthen human rights within the Church. The publication of the new Code of Canon Law in 1983 provided a perfect opportunity, but neither then nor later has anything similar to the United Nations Declaration on Human Rights been incorporated into the legislation of the Catholic Church.

In view of the enormity of moral badness entailed in the evils that I have described, something more than a form of words is necessary for their repudiation. Words without practical expression does not add up to authentic Christian witness or protest, as I pointed out earlier in this chapter in the context of slavery, and the actions of Bartolomé de las Casas.

Notes

1 Justin *Apologia*, I, 67.
2 These figures are taken from the indispensable modern study by H. Thomas, *The Slave Trade*, London, 1996, 805.
3 Thomas, 244.
4 Thomas, 277.
5 Thomas, 805.
6 Thomas, 126.
7 Thomas, 146.
8 Gutiérrez, Gustavo *In Search of the Poor of Jesus Christ*, New York, 1993, is mainly about Bartolomé de las Casas. A summary of his life is to be found in Chapter 3 of David Brading's *The First America: The Spanish Monarchy, Creole Patriots and the Liberal State 1492–1867*, Cambridge, 1992.
9 Lean, G. *God's Politician*, London, 1980, 89.

10   Thomas, 494.
11   Thomas, 522.
12   'Theses on Feuerbach', number 11, in *Karl Marx and Frederick Engels: Collected Works*, London 1976, Vol. 5, p.5.
13   *The Guardian*, 28 March 1995.
14   *The Tablet*, 16 January 1999.
15   *The Guardian*, 15 July 1996.
16   *The Guardian*, 26 May 1995
17   *The Tablet*, 22 July 1995.
18   *The Guardian*, 4 June 2001.
19   IV Lateran Council, Constitution no.38, ACOD 266.
20   Wistrich, R.S. *Anti-Semitism*, London, 1991, 25. Litvinoff, B. *The Burning Bush: Anti-Semitism in World History*, London 1988, 165.
21   *The Tablet*,12 August 2000.
22   Aquinas, *Summa Theologica*, II–II, q. 11, a.3. cited in Southern, R.W. *Western Society and the Church in the Middle Ages*, London, 1970, 17.
23   2 Hen. IV, c. 15.
24   *The Guardian*, 8 July 1998.
25   *The Guardian*, 13 March 2000.

Chapter 4

Get Religion into Politics

Great achievements for human betterment, like the abolition of slavery and the establishment of National Health Services, could not have been realized without the intervention of political forces. Politics and morality cannot ignore each other, nor can they merge. The extent of their interpenetration and mutual independence has been one of the thorniest problems for politicians and political theorists. History is awash with failed experiments, from the closure of theatres in Cromwell's England, to the Prohibition legislation in the USA in the 1920s. Is it possible to devise a set of principles or even a simple rule of thumb by which the balance might be achieved? A few recent examples may serve to clarify the issues.

In 1926 Cardinal Bourne warned English Catholics that to take part in the General Strike would be sinful, declaring that it would be contrary to the obedience which was owing to the lawfully constituted government.[1] In 1938 the Austrian hierarchy led by Cardinal Innitzer welcomed the takeover by the Germans and assured the people of the excellence of Nazism.[2] On those two occasions the cardinals would have been well advised to stay out of politics. It seems that some bishops, like the Bourbons, have learnt and forgotten little with the passage of time. In the latter days of colonial rule in what was then Northern Rhodesia, a Catholic labour activist named Charles Mzingele was trying to start a trade union among the exploited black workers. The attitude of the local bishop was completely uncomprehending and he threatened to excommunicate him.[3]

However, other situations require that the Church should intervene, though by what segment of the Church's membership is not always clear. In 1989 an Ursuline sister, Dianna Ortiz, from the United States was arrested by the security forces in Guatemala where she was working as a missionary. She was raped and tortured by her captors in a most brutal manner, including beatings and being burned over 100 times on her back with cigarettes. She was lowered into a pit where injured women, children, and men writhed and moaned, and the dead decayed, under swarms of rats. Eventually she was released, and has spent the next nine years trying to obtain justice. All her attempts have been blocked by officials of the governments of Guatemala and the United States.[4] What were the Church authorities doing for her?

Examples of this kind can be multiplied dozens of times in the recent history of Latin America. For instance, in 1995 the writer Gore Vidal gave an account of his experiences in Guatemala in 1946. A local politician confided in him his worries that their government would not last much longer because it was necessary to raise the taxes and the only group wealthy enough to pay any was the American United Fruit Company. Their annual revenues were twice as much as those of the Guatemalan state, and their workers had recently gone on strike seeking a daily wage of $1.50 cents. 'What's going to stop you taxing them?' asked the 20-year old Gore Vidal. 'The American government,' was the reply.

Sure enough in 1954 a well-known American Senator, who was on the board of the United Fruit Company, denounced the popularly elected President Arbenz as a communist. The reason was that in 1952 he had expropriated some of the United Fruit Company's unused land, which he then gave to 100 000 Guatemalan families. The company had been compensated at what was a fair price, namely the evaluation of the land that the company had made for tax purposes. The CIA went into action. Guatemala City was attacked by land and air. President Arbenz resigned, and the American ambassador appointed the army's chief of staff as president. He handed him a list of 'communists' to be shot. The chief of staff declined and the American ambassador replaced him by another military man. Since then Guatemala has been a slaughter ground. Later it was discovered that President Arbenz had no communist connections. However the disinformation had been so thorough that few Americans knew to what extent they had been lied to, by a government that had put itself above the law.[5]

At a less dramatic level, but in its own way equally tragic, was the case of a priest in Northern Ireland. Four priests were living in the presbytery of a run-down parish in a working-class district of Belfast. The junior priest began to take an interest in the people's material welfare. He organized the occupants of the blocks of flats into residents' associations and encouraged them to put pressure on the local council over such matters as the regular emptying of dustbins. It might have been assumed that the other priests in the presbytery might have welcomed his solicitude for the poor but that was not to be. They accused him of 'going political', and ostracized him. Quite literally they did not speak to him, although they were living under the same roof. One of them actually beat him up when he (the aggressor) came in drunk one evening. Presumably the others felt threatened by his zeal which was an implicit criticism of their inactivity.

Clearly the problem hinges upon the deceptively simple question of when the Church should intervene in political and social matters and when it should remain silent. The related question is who should do the intervention, and who has the right to initiate action in the name of the Church. These questions are of profound importance and also extreme delicacy. They require carefully thought-out principles for their proper implementation.

To find a solution to those questions we could do worse than turn to what Aquinas has to say about the badly neglected virtue of prudence. In his more general treatment of the virtue Aquinas stated that it is necessary for humans, because 'a man must be rightly disposed by a habit (*habitus*) of reason to that which is suitably orientated towards his worthy purposes'.[6] In the more specific treatment of the virtue he is more precise,[7] where he is discussing Aristotle's classical definition of the virtue as *recta ratio agibilium*, which could be translated as 'the right plan for activity'.[8] In that context it is important to remember that the word *recta* (right) denotes that which is morally right, not just intellectually correct. He also describes it as 'wisdom in human affairs'.[9] He distinguishes it from intellectual virtues because it concerns activity in contingent affairs.[10] It also applies to the political field in what Aquinas rather quaintly calls *prudentia regnativa* (governmental prudence) because that is what kings employ to rule the kingdom or city.[11]

When we penetrate through the rather stilted style of the mediaeval Latin text, we see the presentation of a virtue which guides us to see the right moral course in matters which are both practical and, more particularly, in the public domain. The neglect of this virtue has meant that Christians either ignore the practical (social or political) matters, or else blunder in unthinkingly, as did Cardinals Bourne and Innitzer. Lest I may seem to be biased against cardinals, let me remind the reader that in the Dock Strike of 1889, Cardinal Manning did intervene, publicly supporting the right of the dockers to maintain their strike in the quest of a minimally adequate wage. The most obvious lesson to be drawn from the two English examples is that Manning's education at Oxford prepared him better for public affairs than did Bourne's at the seminary of St Sulpice in Paris.

Bearing in mind what Aquinas has to say about the amplitude of prudence, we could perhaps rephrase the translation of Aristotle's *recta ratio agibilium*, defining prudence as the virtue which guides us to the 'appropriate course of action'. It is obvious that everything hinges upon the word 'appropriate'. Its scope can best be appreciated by posing a number of questions. First of all we must ask, is there a moral or religious dimension to the matter, or is it simply a question of commercial reckoning, like deciding on the retail price of a bicycle? If there is a moral element in a human situation, the next question is: who is competent to make the decisions? In Cardinal Bourne's time, it would have seemed inconceivable that a layman should have an opinion on the matter, and still less that he should take any practical initiative about it. With the wisdom of hindsight, it seems obvious to us that in the circumstances of the General Strike an unemployed miner, facing a cut in the dole, would be the best-placed person to appreciate the reality of what was taking place. We live in the aftermath of Pius XII's teaching about the laity, what Vatican II had to say about them, and the vast output of theology on the subject since the Second World War. Bourne's outlook was limited to the simplistic ideas in the catechism about lay people's obedience to their pastors. For generations it had been customary for the priests to issue instructions to the laity without any dialogue or consultation.

As in other moral matters, the correct doctrine has been present all along in the New Testament and the classical theologians, but in practice it has been overlooked in the day-to-day conduct of affairs. As a result the Church's moral programme has frequently been misdirected in the practical arena.

Prudence governs the pivotal problem of discerning what is appropriate. It has been given clarity and prominence in recent years thanks to Liberation theology. The precise contribution has been the methodology called conscientization. Basically it is an educational tool for the raising of awareness. There are two levels at which it is employed. The first stage of discernment is to ask of any given problem: is it normal, natural, and inevitable, or is it a series of ghastly accidents which can be put right? For example in many parts of Africa, infant mortality is as high as it was in Europe in the middle of the nineteenth century. Conscientization of the people requires that they examine it in the light of experience, faith, and science. Is it one of life's inevitable hazards, like incurable illnesses which have to be tolerated and spiritualized by 'offering them up'? Clearly it is largely a matter of providing pure drinking water.

The second stage of conscientization is more specific. If it has become apparent that the problem is not inevitable, what are the appropriate means to solve it? In the context of Christian morality, this is to be understood as the morally appropriate course of action, and not simply the organizational measures that might be necessary to solve a practical problem. It is at this point that the relevance of prudence becomes apparent. For example, in industry, practical expediency will demand low production costs if the process is to be profitable. All too often this is achieved by low wages. Conscientization, in the context of moral prudence, will motivate workers and employers to seek efficiency and low production costs together with a just wage.

Complex problems usually contain a moral component for which a religiously inspired course of action will be necessary. For example in the 1970s a certain Swiss company made great efforts to sell powdered milk in Africa. Women who were deceived by the advertisements and gave up breastfeeding in favour of the more sophisticated method not infrequently saw their babies die of dysentery or other enteric poisonings. Without absolutely pure drinking water and the facility to sterilize the bottles, the use of powdered milk was literally lethal. The differences between Swiss kitchens and those in rural Africa should have been apparent to the manufacturers. With incredible callousness they had promoted their own commercial interests at the expense of the lives of children. That was a situation that merited, and received, strong moral protest. It is to the credit of many Christians and other people of integrity that large-scale pressure was put on that company in its home territory in Switzerland and the iniquity of its activities was exposed for all the world to see.

Similar situations have arisen in Africa and Latin America over wages, where multinational companies have counted upon the lack of education and experience of the indigenous workforces and have offered their employees wages which would never be tolerated in Europe or North America. The moral issues have not been lost on the Christian activists and it is to the credit of Liberation theology that it has provided the rationale in the quest for justice. I will have more to say on the matter in the next chapter. For the present it is instructive to observe the role of prudence in the discernment of the moral issues in the quest for a just wage. It is regrettable that the Church authorities have not always given the exploited peoples the support to which they were entitled. The hierarchies not infrequently took the view that it was a Christian duty to obey lawful governments. They did not enquire too closely into the legitimacy of those governments and the extent that they were compromised by the financial advantages which they derived from the commercial organizations in question. Here too is a whole area where Church leaders would do well to take up the practice of the virtue of prudence and apply the tools of conscientization to the activities of so-called lawful governments, and their links with powerful commercial organizations.

Latin America has been the scene of some of the worst human rights abuses in the 1970s and 1980s usually where military dictatorships were in power.[12] The tragic question of the *desaparacidos* (the people who disappeared) belongs properly to the next chapter, but I would like to mention it in the context of prudence. The silence of so many bishops' conferences and the suggestion that they could achieve more by quiet diplomacy with the brutal regimes could never have arisen if they had reflected on the realities in the light of prudence.

A final word on prudence is prompted by a practical problem nearer to home. Is there a moral issue at the heart of the English public school system? It is a distinguishing feature of our national life, and has so far influenced the religious orders who are dedicated to education that one well known Catholic school set out in the 1930s quite deliberately to imitate Eton. Concerning the system and its promotion of privilege, a highly respected journalist had the following to say about it:

> Even more corrosive than the calculus of economic inefficiency is the value system that supports it. To justify such structural inequality requires the elevation of the values of exclusion, opting-out and individualism, and the denigration of inclusion, opting in and co-operation. Yet these are not values that support a culture of production, or even at the limit of citizenship; they are the values of the deal-making apostles of apartheid. Thus the gradations in accent and deportment conferred by schooling and which still characterise English life … are less important than what this reveals about the way the products of private schools think about themselves and their relation to others. One example is the recent bout of extraordinary pay increases that senior executives have awarded to themselves – justified by a culture in which those at the top have no sense of belonging, or social obligation to the companies which they run.[13]

It is notoriously easy to see faults in the lives of other people and other societies. South Africa was understandably criticized and ostracized because of its apartheid policy. Perhaps we should ask ourselves if the public school system might perhaps be our own form of 'separate development'?

Compared with the *desaparacidos* of Latin America the problem is not dramatic, but it is a matter of considerable consequence to the health of this nation. Whether or not it has a moral component that requires a moral response can only be decided in the light of prudence, and the careful evaluation of the system by the tools of conscientization.

Notes

1   Oldmeadow, E. *Francis Cardinal Bourne*, London 1943, vol.2, 218; Hastings, A. *A History of English Christianity 1920–1985*, Oxford, 1986, 188.
2   Duffy, E. in *The Tablet*, 24 February 1990.
3   Lessing, Doris *Under My Skin*, London 1994, 305.
4   *The Tablet*, 4 July 1998.
5   *The Guardian*, 25 February 1995.
6   *ST* I–II, q. 57, a.5.
7   *ST* I–II , q.47, a.2.
8   *Ethics*, Book 6, chapter 5.
9   *ST* I–II, q. 47, art 2, ad 1.
10 *ST* I–II, q.47, a.5.
11 *ST* I–II, q.50, a.1.
12 Human rights activists estimate that the number of people who disappeared in Argentina alone was about 30 000. *The Guardian*, 7 July 1998.
13 Hutton, Will, writing in *The Guardian*, 17 May 1993.

Chapter 5

Justice in the World

Whereas most virtues concern an individual's moral obligations to others, justice is concerned also with those owed to him. To put it in slightly different words, justice can be defined as a relationship between myself and the outside world, which establishes the moral obligations on other people towards me, and the duties that I owe to them. For instance I may not take the wallet out of another man's pocket nor should I be put in prison without a proper trial. The recognition of the latter category owes a great deal to the Enlightenment and it still has not been embraced fully by the Catholic Church. Property rights have always been proclaimed adequately in the official documents of the Church. They are to be found in textbooks of theology, catechisms, papal encyclicals and the documents of General Councils.

In recent years the Catholic Church has had two theologies of justice: that of the papal encyclicals, and more recently Liberation theology.[1] Justice in the papal encyclicals is developed largely from rational considerations, an ethical system with embellishments from the New Testament. Liberation theology is firmly rooted in the Bible and derives intimately from the doctrine of the redemption.

It has been a consistent insight of Catholic spirituality, which sets it apart from some of the otherwise edifying Oriental religions, that human beings are not to be consoled with the promise of spiritual benefits here and hereafter while being left to live in material squalor or injustice. The emphasis on practical charity in the Bible leaves this in no doubt. The modern world has seen exploitation institutionalized by systematic organization that would have been impossible in antiquity. In order to alleviate it, something more than charity is required. The understanding of economics and technology that has made large-scale impoverishment a reality can also be harnessed to change the systems which keep people impoverished. However, before the social and economic planners can get to work, deciding on the re-allocation of resources, something more basic is required. A moral conversion is necessary if this reorganization is to get to the roots of the problem. Unless the redistribution of the world's wealth is perceived as an issue of justice, it will be vulnerable to market forces and the activities of greedy predators. It is in this context that Liberation theology was born.

About the time that the calling of Vatican II was announced, theologians all over Latin America were reflecting on the relationship between Christianity and the disparities of wealth and poverty. The movement took root in that region because the Catholic Church was well established, and the gap between rich and poor was worse than practically anywhere else in the world. A landmark in the new theology came in 1971 with the publication of *A Theology of Liberation* by Gustavo Gutiérrez.[2]

The choice of the word 'liberation' was fortunate since it does justice to the Greek and Hebrew biblical terms which have been debased by their earlier translation as 'salvation'. This word has now become too anodyne by overexposure in mediocre religious poetry and hymns. 'Are you saved, brother?' is something of a joke. Authentic liberation is a much more serious business. It takes place in three stages, and the spiritual and political cannot be separated. Firstly, man is set free from unjustly imposed poverty; secondly, he assumes conscious responsibility for his own destiny; and thirdly, Christianity sets him truly free, from the consequences of his own sins and other peoples.[3] Liberation theology has drawn inspiration from the biblical Exodus since it shows clearly God's interest in human freedom. The same power is seen at work in the return of the Israelites from captivity in Babylon. The same preoccupation with justice is also evident in many of the sayings of the prophets. The words of Amos (8:4–7) are well known, but deserve repetition on account of their importance:

> Listen to this you who trample on the needy
> and try to suppress the poor people of the country
> you who say, When will the New Moon be over
> so that we can sell our corn,
> and the sabbath, so that we can market our wheat?
> Then by lowering the bushel and raising the shekel,
> By swindling and tampering with the scales,
> We can buy up the poor for money,
> And the needy for a pair of sandals.
> And get a price even for the sweepings of the wheat.
> Yahweh swears it by the pride of Jacob,
> 'Never will I forget a single thing you have done'.

It is regrettable that Catholic, and indeed much general Christian spirituality, has neglected the practical aspect of the Exodus in favour of a spiritualized understanding of it. This interpretation would reduce the political slant to nothing more than a symbol of man's liberation from sin in this world in order to enter heaven after this life is ended. It is also the motivation for urging people to endure poverty and other sufferings in a spirit of penance, hoping thereby to be purified of sinful tendencies and better prepared to enter heaven. A few moments' reflection will indicate that this is a distortion of authentic Christianity. At every period of its history, the Church has striven to alleviate material hardship. It is only the methods that have changed in response to social circumstances and the different perceptions of reality.

Liberation theology is the newest method, born of the perception that the world's economic functioning can be changed. This received great encouragement from Vatican II. After the council its most satisfactory proclamation was made by the meeting of Latin American bishops at Medellin in 1968: 'It is the same God who in the fullness of time, sends his Son in the flesh, so that he might come to liberate all men from all slavery to which sin has subjected them: hunger, misery, oppression, and ignorance, in a word, that injustice and hatred which have their origin in human selfishness.'[4] Whereas the virtue of charity does not stop at the preaching level but when we write out cheques, Liberation theology does not stop at the textbook level but moves on straight away to find practical political and structural changes to society. That is why Rome took fright. For centuries the authorities in Rome have been apprehensive about all political change. For example, the establishment of democracy in the modern world was opposed as long as possible by the popes. The worst example was Pius IX's explicit command that the Catholics of Italy were not to take part in the elections or take office in the democratic government that was established in 1870.

In Latin America in the 1970s there was another alleged peril lurking in the shadows and causing alarm in Rome, namely Marxism. Pope Pius XII had adopted a policy of resistance to communism in Italy and Europe in general, and his successors, particularly John Paul II, had continued the hostility. The authorities in Rome simply could not understand how Catholics and Marxists in Latin America might become allies in championing the cause of the poor. In 1986 an extremely unsympathetic document came from Rome stressing the dangers which might arise from liberation theology.[5] Leonardo Boff, one of the foremost of the liberation theologians was subjected to a personal investigation. Two Brazilian cardinals accompanied him to Rome for the investigation, thereby witnessing to their support for the movement.

So, in the post-Conciliar period, the Church has been served by two theologies of justice, Liberation theology orientated immediately to practical matters, and the theology of the encyclicals more concerned with principles.

For all that, the theology of justice in the papal encyclicals and Conciliar documents should not be underestimated.[6] Papal interest in modern social matters was first demonstrated by Leo XIII's encyclical *Rerum Novarum* in 1891. The background was the plight of workers in the capitalist industrialized environment of the late nineteenth century. He enunciated very generalized principles of universal applicability about the rights of private property (against socialism), the right to a living wage (against the employers), and the concept of the common good. Trades unions were just about legitimized, although the pope envisaged that they would include employers as well as workers, and all of them would be Catholics.[7] With the wisdom of hindsight one can see the limitations of the document. For example 80 years were to elapse until another pope (John XXIII) declared that the common good took precedence over the rights of private property, thus providing a limitation on capitalism.[8] Leo XIII had taken for granted that capitalism was the normal background to economic life, and he tried to shame the wealthy into a compassionate exercise of their financial muscle.[9]

In 1931 Pius XI developed the ideas of social justice in his encyclical *Quadragesimo Anno*. He built on the principles of Leo XIII and made one innovation of extraordinary value, namely the Principle of Subsidiarity.[10] This principle has been discussed earlier but it is so important that I must return to it here. The pope's simple enunciation of the principle is as follows:

> Just as it is gravely wrong to take from individuals what they can accomplish by their own initiative and industry and give it to the community, so also it is an injustice and at the same time a grave evil and disturbance of right order to assign to a greater and higher association what lesser and subordinate organizations can do ... The supreme authority of the State ought, therefore, to let subordinate groups handle matters and concerns of lesser importance.[11]

At the level of planning it means that decisions should be taken at the lowest feasible level of command and not the highest. The pope had in mind the state-run corporations of Fascist Italy and the nationalization of every commercial enterprise in the Soviet Union but the principle is of much wider applicability. It was invoked by politicians in the 1990s in discussions about the European Union and what decisions should be taken at Brussels or in the national parliaments.

The intellectual basis of these early pronouncements was an appeal to natural law as perceived by human reason. The issues at stake were deemed to concern the whole of society, and the morality was assumed to be accessible to non-believers as well as Christians. Vatican II marked a change in that it appealed as much as possible to the Bible as the inspiration for the Church's stance on matters of social justice. In the immediate aftermath of the Council, papal encyclicals also invoked the New Testament. However in the latter years of Pope John Paul II there has been a reversion to natural law as the principal intellectual foundation of his pronouncements.[12]

The chapters on justice in Vatican II are genuinely edifying. The document entitled *Gaudium et Spes* (generally known as *The Church in the Modern World*) epitomizes much that was best in the Council, insofar as it was absolutely positive in its perception of the modern world and its potential for good. In this way the Council signalled an end to centuries of negative attitudes. From the time of the Reformation there had been a consistently negative attitude to the achievements of Protestantism (illustrated by the fact that it took 400 years for us to acknowledge that Luther had been right about a vernacular liturgy). It also marked the end of the negative attitude to the modern world's political advances which reached its most intense form when Pope Pius IX retreated into the Vatican after the loss of the Papal States.

Having shaken off all those pessimistic inhibitions, it is a joy to read in *Gaudium et Spes*, an explicit affirmation of the principle of human rights: 'Therefore, by virtue of the gospel committed to her, the Church proclaims the rights of man. She acknowledges and greatly esteems the dynamic movements of today by which these rights are everywhere fostered.'[13] In December 1998 the Bishops of England and Wales published an important document to mark the fiftieth anniversary of the United Nations Declaration of Human Rights. In this statement they upheld all that had been declared about human rights in Vatican II, and amplified the teaching with reference to papal encyclicals published since the Council.[14]

In addition to the Council's statement of human rights, a number of specific freedoms were enunciated, namely that of conscience, also the more general state of social freedom which a human being is entitled to expect, and finally religious freedom. Concerning conscience, the Council stated:

> Conscience is the most secret core and sanctuary of a man. There he is alone with God, whose voice echoes in his depths. In a wonderful manner conscience reveals that law which is fulfilled by love of God and neighbour. In fidelity to conscience, Christians are joined with the rest of men in the search for truth, and for the genuine solution to the numerous problems which arise in the life of individuals and from social relationships, ... Conscience frequently errs from invincible ignorance without losing its dignity.[15]

Concerning the more general scope of personal freedom the Council stated: 'Only in freedom can man direct himself towards goodness. Our contemporaries make much of this freedom and pursue it eagerly; and rightly so, to be sure.'[16]

The subject of religious freedom is so important that the Council devoted to it a whole document entitled *Dignitatis Humanae*. The core of its message is contained in a paragraph in section two:

> This Vatican Synod declares that the human person has a right to religious freedom. This freedom means that all men are to be immune from coercion on the part of individuals or of social groups and of any human power, in such wise that in matters religious no one is to be forced to act in a manner contrary to his own beliefs. ... The Synod further declares that the right to religious freedom has its foundation in the very dignity of the human person, as this dignity is known through the revealed Word of God and by reason itself.[17]

The concept of freedom is developed to include what would normally be called academic freedom, which in its constituent parts entails freedom of enquiry, investigation, and research. The Council expressed it as follows:

> If by the autonomy of earthly affairs we mean that created things and societies themselves enjoy their own laws and values which must be gradually deciphered, put to use, and regulated by men, then it is entirely right to demand that autonomy. Such is not merely required by modern man, but harmonizes also with the will of the Creator. For by the very circumstances of their having been

created, all things are endowed with their own stability, truth, goodness, proper laws, and order. Man must respect these as he isolates them by the appropriate methods of the individual sciences or arts. Therefore if methodical investigation within every branch of learning is carried out in a genuinely scientific manner and in accord with moral norms, it never truly conflicts with faith. For earthly matters and the concerns of faith derive from the same God. ... Consequently, we cannot but deplore certain habits of mind, sometimes found too among Christians, which do not sufficiently attend to the rightful independence of science.[18]

Turning from the familiar fields of scientific research, the Council also directed its attention to other areas of intellectual research.

Literature and the arts are also, in their own way, of great importance to the life of the Church. For they strive to probe the unique nature of man, his problems and his experiences as he struggles to know and perfect both himself and the world. They are preoccupied with revealing man's place in history and in the world, with illustrating his miseries and joys, his needs and strengths, and with the foreshadowing a better life for him. Thus they are able to elevate human life as it is expressed in manifold forms, depending on time and place. Efforts must therefore be made so that those who practise these arts can feel that the Church gives recognition to them in their activities, and so that, enjoying an orderly freedom, they can establish smoother relations with the Christian community.[19]

The complementary freedom without which the others can scarcely be realized is freedom of expression. Significantly this freedom is vindicated in the section where the Council expressed the hope that laypeople would take up the study of theology, and then added: 'In order that such persons may fulfil their proper function, let it be recognised that all the faithful, clerical and lay, possess a lawful freedom of inquiry and of thought, and the freedom to express their minds humbly and courageously about those matters in which they enjoy competence.'[20]

Excellent as are these principles, the Council offered an even stronger foundation for the basic human rights, paradoxically because the human person is destined for fulfilment not just in the visible world, but in heaven. Taking its stand on man's having been created in the likeness of God and destined for the vision of God in eternity, Christians ought to have an enhanced motive for ensuring that there shall be justice between individuals and societies in this world. This vision of humanity and its situation leads naturally to a consideration of the constant need to improve the conditions of society, and the Council expressed the desire in these words:

The social order and its development must unceasingly work to the benefit of the human person if the disposition of affairs is to be subordinate to the personal realm and not contrariwise, as the Lord indicated when he said that the Sabbath was made for man, not man for the Sabbath. This social order requires constant improvement. It must be founded on truth, built on justice, and animated by love; in freedom it should grow every day toward a more humane balance. An improvement in attitudes and widespread changes in society will have to take place if these objectives are to be gained. God's Spirit, who with a marvellous providence directs the unfolding of time and renews the face of the earth, is not absent from this development. The ferment of the gospel too, has aroused and continues to arouse in man's heart the irresistible requirements of his dignity.[21]

Further on in the same document, the Council expressed the connection between religious commitment and the quest for a better society in the following words: 'Christians, on pilgrimage towards the heavenly city, should seek and savour the things that are above. This duty in no way decreases, but rather increases the weight of their obligation to work with all men in constructing a more human world.'[22]

In practical terms, insights of this kind translated immediately into an unconditional condemnation of discrimination:

Since all men possess a rational soul and are created in God's likeness, since they have the same nature and origin, have been redeemed by Christ, and enjoy the same divine calling and destiny, the basic equality of all must receive increasingly greater recognition. ... with respect to the fundamental rights of the person, every type of discrimination, whether social or cultural, whether based on sex, race, colour, social condition, language or religion, is to be overcome and eradicated as contrary to God's intent.[23]

As far as the conditions of life are concerned, the document drew attention to the unprecedented wealth in the world, thanks to modern science and technology, but noted equally that there is still appalling poverty for countless people: 'Never has the human race enjoyed such an abundance of wealth, resources, and economic power. Yet a huge proportion of the world's citizens is still tormented by hunger and poverty, while countless numbers suffer from total illiteracy.'[24] In stating that all people have a right to a decent standard of living, the Council did not limit its observations to money but included in the normal expectations of a proper human life such benefits as education and medical care. Faced with inequalities in the distribution of this world's goods, both material and cultural, the Council insisted that these inequalities must be removed: 'If the demands of justice and equity are to be satisfied, vigorous efforts must be made, without violence to the rights of persons or to the natural characteristics of each country, to remove as far as possible the immense economic inequalities which now exist. In many cases, these are worsening and are connected with individual and group discrimination.'[25]

As a programme of ideals in the realm of social justice, the document could hardly be bettered. It stands as one of the landmarks of Christian achievement in the aim of improving the quality of life of the whole human race. All Catholics may justly be proud of a Council that had stated such principles so uncompromisingly. Having said that, it is no criticism of the document to draw attention to some limitations in its programme. From the nature of the case, the Council Fathers did not investigate the causes of world poverty nor did they spell out in detail how the principles were to be translated into practice. The former belongs to the realm of scholarship, and the latter must await the practical plans of local Christian communities working out solutions in the context of their immediate opportunities and circumstances.

In the years following the Council, the popes continued to issue encyclicals on social justice, advancing on the statements of Vatican II and becoming ever more explicit. One important idea made explicit in the post-Conciliar encyclicals was the concept of structured injustice. This is a situation where economic or political power has been institutionalized in such a way that wealth or freedom automatically move away from the poor and into the grasp of those who are already rich. Pope Paul VI first wrote about this in the context of capitalism where he declared that a just economic order could not be built on liberal capitalism.[26] It was highlighted too in John Paul II's *Sollicitudo Rei Socialis* of 1987.[27] The same pope was unambiguous in urging the cancellation of Third World debt in his 1994 encyclical *Tertio Millennio Adveniente*.[28]

Another area in which papal teaching has become more specific in the post-Conciliar period is that of the preferential option for the poor and its practical working out in Liberation theology. The foundation for the option for the poor was laid down in the first section of Vatican II's *Gaudium et Spes*. The notion became explicit with Paul VI's *Octagesima Adveniens*. Paul VI declared that working for liberation from injustice was integral to the gospel message, thus giving a powerful mark of approval to Liberation theology.[29]

In the post-Conciliar period, the statement of the Latin American bishops at Medellin in 1968 on the preferential option for the poor was a model of how a local Church ought to face up to its own problems and opportunities.

It would be foolish to pretend that the Church's social teaching, as expressed in the encyclicals and Vatican II, was perfect in all respects. There is very little analysis of the causes of collective injustices. The class struggle is not mentioned in these documents nor is the vexed question of the ownership of the means of production.[30] On the question of structural sin, Pope John Paul II declared that structures are shaped by people yet he fails to note that unjust structures powerfully influence people's actions, as for example under the apartheid regime in South Africa. [31]

Equally frustrating has been the reticence about the implementation of the ideals presented in these statements. For example, something as simple as the quest for a just wage is left, so to speak, hanging in the air. Was it to be achieved by appealing to the benevolence of the employer, by government legislation for a minimum wage, or by trade union activity? Although *Rerum Novarum* approved of trade unions, Pius XI condemned strikes, and Paul VI said that unions should not become involved in matters which are directly political.[32] Writing in 1971 he could not have foreseen the activities of the Polish Solidarity union whose activities have never received any measure of papal censure.

There are, moreover, a number of unacknowledged inconsistencies between the documents. The concept of human rights was condemned by Pope Pius VI in 1791. This included freedom of expression and freedom of religion which were also repudiated in Pius IX's blanket condemnation of liberalism in 1864.[33] It was not until Vatican II that human rights received the unequivocal blessing of the Church.

Finally it must be noted that capitalism is accorded rather more tolerance than it merits. Admittedly there is a constant repudiation of greed in the whole corpus of Catholic social teaching. This has been articulated admirably in the 1990s by strong statements by Pope John Paul II and other bishops calling for the cancellation of Third World debt. Indeed, one Catholic writer has pointed out that effective debt relief to the 20 most needy countries would cost less than the price of one Stealth bomber.[34] It is equally true that Pius XI followed by other popes declared that the right ordering of economic life cannot be left entirely to the free competition of forces.[35] Nevertheless, one looks in vain for the precise identification of the morally evil foundation of capitalism, which is the untrammelled quest for unlimited profit. From this premise spring the attendant evils of unrestricted competition, the uninhibited build-up of monopolies which corner and control whole markets, and the unchecked power of multinational companies whose activities are outside the control of individual national governments. Armed with this amount of economic power, the operators of the capitalist system can inflict intolerable injustices on whole sections of society and indeed upon whole nations.

In the aftermath of Vatican II, the period which saw the publication of some remarkable social encyclicals, the leaders of the Church had the opportunity to put into effect the social ideals which had been formulated. In spite of some admirable initiatives motivated by that Council the overall result has not lived up to the reasonable expectations which could have been hoped for in the wake of a General Council.

It must be acknowledged that during this period, the authorities in Rome showed a singular lack of vision in facilitating the implementation of the Council's ideals. In fact it looks as if the Curia was intent on blocking progress in that direction. The revision of the Code of Canon Law in 1983 provided a perfect opportunity to translate the Council's ideals on justice into the legal practice of the Catholic Church. It is a matter of bitter regret that the 1983 Code was little more than a cosmetic updating of the Code of 1918 rather than a total recasting of the legal system and its presuppositions. For example the concept of human rights has not been enshrined in the Code nor has the principle of the equality of all people before the law, nor does it accept the principle of the independence of the judiciary and the open form of judicial processes. I will develop these matters in the next chapter on justice within the Church. For the present I wish to point out that after the Second Vatican Council, the new Code of Canon Law should have been a total recasting of the legal system rather than a mere updating of the Code of 1918.

Although it was promulgated in 1983, this Code presupposes the political model of the absolute monarchies of the eighteenth century and the practice of systematic secrecy which evolved in the Italian political situation at that time as a means of ensuring the rulers' freedom from outside interference. It is worth remembering that the first session of Vatican II took place in secret. Journalists were excluded and given totally inadequate press releases as a sort of favour. Thus the sequel to Vatican II illustrated a weakness which has been seen all too often in the Church's moral programme, namely that the practice has not always lived up to the ideals. In some cases the failure to proclaim justice and witness to it in situations of gross injustice and cruelty has amounted to a betrayal of the gospel and exploited peoples.

This has been due to a series of historical accidents and institutional arrangements in Church structures. As I noted above, the framework of government in the Catholic Church resembles the absolute monarchies of the eighteenth century rather than any other model. Even at diocesan level the bishop is administrator, legislator, and judge. So is the pope, but at a more dangerous level, since there are no constitutional checks and balances placing any limits on his power. He is accountable to no one and unlike the bishops who retire at 75, the pope is entitled to stay in power until his death. At diocesan and papal level there is no such thing as the independence of the judiciary, nor are the operations of the Church courts or administrative offices open to public scrutiny. The ancient Anglo-Saxon principle that justice must be done and be seen to be done has no place in the administration of the Catholic Church.

In short, there is significant potential for injustice within the Church because it has not aligned itself with the enlightened social reforms of the nineteenth and twentieth centuries. The French Revolution, which gave the Church a severe shock, was repudiated by the senior clergy throughout the world, as were the reforms of the nineteenth century. The most obvious reactionary was Pope Pius IX whose liberal leanings were shattered by the revolutionary events of 1848. Worse was to come in 1870 with the seizure of the Papal States in the Reunification of Italy. After that, quite literally, he never set foot outside the Vatican, he forbade Italian Catholics to take part in the democratic processes of the new Kingdom of Italy, and consciously directed Church policies against the trend of what were then modern developments.

Pius IX showed a distrust of nearly all things modern, including democracy and trade unionism. As a result the worst injustices of the industrial revolution were perpetrated without any serious guidance or protest from the Church. By the time that Leo XIII began to reverse the policy at the end of the century, it was too late. A golden opportunity had been lost, the champions of workers' rights were the socialists and communists. Trade union recognition in law had already been achieved by the British parliament before Leo XIII accepted the principle in his encyclical *Rerum Novarum*.

The Code of Canon Law promulgated in 1918 made no mention of human rights. It embodied the older concept that rights accrue to property. In that legal system, for example, a parish priest had rights because of being the possessor of the benefice (that is, parish) which was his source of income. In that Code the parish is consistently referred to as a benefice and the care of souls recedes into the background, overshadowed by the concept of property that generated income. Consistent with that outlook was the fact that curates had no rights because they were not benefice (property) holders. The new Code of Canon Law, promulgated in 1983, does not rectify those underlying presuppositions. It was merely a cosmetic adaptation of the former Code and not a total recasting of the system and the juridical and ecclesiological bases upon which it reposed.

Case Studies: Justice Promoted by the Church

In spite of that inauspicious background, there have been some truly edifying efforts by the Catholic Church to secure justice among the most exploited peoples of the world, thanks to the influence of Liberation theology in the main. A few examples will make this clear. The Central American republic of El Salvador is one of the poorest countries of the world, and it witnessed the killing of 75 000 of its citizens during the period of military dictatorship between 1978 and 1993. Those people were killed by the Salvadorean security forces, aided and abetted by the United States, because in one way or another they had dared to question the status quo, that is to say, the endless misery brought about by poverty, disease, degradation and oppression.[36] Among the victims were four American nuns, six Jesuit priests assassinated together in one attack, and Archbishop Oscar Romero, who was shot while celebrating mass. At the time of his appointment as archbishop of the capital city of El Salvador he was a man of conservative outlook. After a few years in office his views underwent a dramatic change. He became acutely aware of the injustices of which the people were the victims and he supported the reformist efforts of clergy and lay activists. The most powerful motive for the change of his outlook was most probably the constant assassinations of priests and lay people who were actively involved in the quest for social justice.

In recent years the United Nations' Truth Commission has sought to establish the facts. It has concluded that the vast majority of those who were killed were the victims of the Salvadorean armed forces and not the FMLN guerillas. The Commission named army officers and government ministers as being responsible for the atrocities and also recommended the mass resignation of the members of the Supreme Court. In response to this,

President Alfredo Cristiani forced through the Legislative Assembly an amnesty for all those who had been accused. They have all gone free. So too have the American advisers. Throughout the 1980s the United States government subsidized the Salvadorean government to the tune of $6 billion, plus the services of the CIA and military advisers.

In a situation of such cruelty and institutionalized injustice, it is genuinely edifying to perceive that the Catholic Church has been in the forefront of the struggle to achieve justice. Equally important from the moral point of view was their witness to truth and justice, even if practical measures were blocked. However, one has to take note of the fact that the Vatican has distanced itself from the struggle. Moves to canonize Archbishop Romero have moved with unenthusiastic slowness, (although the founder of Opus Dei had his cause pushed through quickly and smoothly). When Pope John Paul II visited the country in 1996 he did not make a courtesy visit to the Jesuit house in San Salvador where the six Jesuits were murdered. It is baffling to try and understand what is going on, but the impression given is that the Church authorities are more concerned with courting the goodwill of the government, regardless of the moral issues at stake. It is a sad example of misdirected morality, and one cannot be surprised if high-minded people of independent spirit turn their backs on the institutional Church.

Another edifying chapter in the quest for justice is the record of the Catholic Church in East Timor. Shortly after Portugese colonial rule came to an end in 1975, East Timor was invaded by Indonesia. After that there has been a policy of genocide comparable to Stalin's assault on the kulaks or the Nazis' extermination of the Jews. Thousands of people simply disappeared and 200 000 died out of a total population of approximately 700 000. At one level the performance of the Catholic Church has been admirable. It emerged as the only coherent opposition to the tyranny. This should not surprise us, since the Church is international, well organized, and possessed of a coherent ideology about justice and the eradication of poverty. This explains why, as an organization, the Church has become so prominent in the economic and (inevitably) the political struggles of the poorest nations in the Third World. Most often there is no other credible organization that can speak out for the poor.

The hero in East Timor is Bishop Belo, who was awarded the Nobel Peace Prize in 1997. His policy has brought its own rewards at one level. In 1975 there were 250 000 Catholics in the nation, by 1983 after nearly a decade of terror there were 420 000, and in 1994 the total had reached 674 000 approximately 90 per cent of the population. In 1989 Pope John Paul II visited Indonesia, and came to East Timor as well. He celebrated mass in public but it was a disappointing occasion. He spoke in English not Portugese which is the language which the people all understand and he called on them to reconcile themselves with their oppressors. No rebuke for crimes against humanity was made.[37]

South East Asia provides another example of Church intervention in a difficult political situation. In 1986 at the end of the Marcos regime in the

Philippines, there was massive public discontent. Virtually the whole population had realized the extent to which they had been exploited by the outgoing president's family and political allies in a corrupt regime. It was clear that the nation's economy had been organized for the benefit of a number of wealthy individuals and commercial enterprises. There had been very little attempt to distribute wealth equitably and the majority of the people lived in grinding poverty. The streets of Manila were crowded with demonstrators and the situation could have developed into a bloodbath. However the presence of priests and nuns at the head of the crowds ensured that the protest remained non-violent. It lost none of its psychological force by being restrained, and in the event a peaceful transfer of power took place. In the delicate balance of religion entering the political arena, the Catholics in the Philippines acted with admirable prudence. No other organization was at hand to guide a turbulent situation, and they were able to guide popular feelings because it was recognized on all sides that they understood the frustrations of the people and were animated to obtain social justice and not for any personal political ambitions.

A further example of the Church's involvement with the cause of justice for the poorest peoples comes from Brazil, in this instance involving the land rights of the indigenous Indians. After years of stagnation Brazil's most northerly state, Roraima, was developing rapidly. The state capital, Boa Vista, was bustling with life, and the state governor, Brigadier Ottomar Pinto, wanted to construct an asphalt road to Venezuela and create a duty-free region. He was also keen to exploit the region's minerals: gold, tin, and diamonds. But there was a big obstacle. The Indians' lands cover almost half the state. The attitude of many of the aspiring developers was summed up by the sentiments of an old cattle rancher, 'We should be doing what my grandfather did in the south of Brazil. He alone drove off 3000 Indians from his land.'

Fortunately the Indians found allies in the Catholic Church. Following the meeting in Medellin in 1979 that proclaimed the preferential option for the poor, large numbers of lay workers and priests have been working for the betterment of the Indians' cause. They have the full backing of the Italian-born bishop, Dom Aldo Mogiano, who has been working in the region since 1978. The cattle ranchers and gold prospectors have not been idle. The bishop and his collaborators in this work have been subjected to numerous death threats. To demonstrate their solidarity with the 72-year-old bishop, a day of solidarity was organized, culminating in an open-air mass concelebrated by nine bishops and guarded by 150 armed military policemen. While 3000 faithful sang hymns calling for social justice, several hundred gold prospectors on the fringes shouted abuse and called for the bishop's removal from their town.[38]

The instances, which I have cited in the preceding paragraphs, show how the Church can and should work at the public and institutional level for the promotion of justice. It has been an edifying and in some cases heroic struggle in which not a few have lost their lives. What is depressing is that since about 1980, that kind of activity has been discouraged by the Vatican. In fact there has been a mounting hostility against Liberation theology and all that goes with it. The instances cited above show that, generally speaking, in situations of serious injustice and exploitation, the Church comes into conflict with ultra-right-wing governments, often military dictatorships, and the capitalist organizations which support them. In the same situations, the Church's allies have frequently been Marxists. This has not come about by deliberate choice but by an inevitable alignment of interests. Pope John Paul II has steadily weakened the quest for institutional reform of unjust structures by his practice of appointing politically and theologically conservative bishops. One cannot help reflecting on the extent to which his outlook may have been influenced by the recent history of his native Poland where the struggle against communism and the Soviet Union had been the defining factors for Polish Catholicism.

Case Studies: Justice Hampered by the Church

A particularly sad example of this is to be seen in the sequel to the heroic life and work of the Brazilian bishop Adriano Hypolito. He was born in the north-eastern province of Sergipe and was ordained priest at the age of 22 as a Franciscan. After serving as auxiliary bishop of São Salvador de Bahia and attending the Second Vatican council, he was appointed as bishop of Nova Iguacu in 1966. His enthusiasm for Liberation theology brought him into conflict with the conservative Catholic hierarchy of Brazil. Criticisms of the way in which he ran the diocese and obstructions from his archbishop did not deflect him from his beliefs and commitment to social justice. He was admired as a scholar, a gifted poet and musician, and always lived in true Franciscan simplicity with regard to material possessions. Inevitably he came into conflict with the government. When the authorities banned the publication of a book by one of his friends, Bishop Hypolito translated it into German so that it could be published in Europe. Thanks to that book, the world learned of the existence of the Brazilian death squads charged with eliminating opponents of the government.

For his action in making the translation Hipolyto was put on the hit list of the Department of Political and Social Order. In 1967 he was kidnapped, beaten, stripped naked, tied up and sprayed with red paint. He was then forced to drink a whole bottle of rum and was abandoned to die on a lonely road. Instead he survived though was not found until the following day. Eventually he recovered from his ill-treatment. Despite threats that other so-called communist bishops would receive the same treatment, Hipolyto continued working as before, particularly among those who lived in the notorious slum district of Baixada Fluminense, just outside Rio de Janiero. He retired at the age of 75 in 1993, and his successor, appointed by Pope John Paul II was a man of extremely conservative orientation, which caused Hipolyto great bitterness in his final years.[39]

Even better known is the career of the saintly Bishop of Recife, Helder Camara. Even before Vatican II, he was determined that the Church should serve those who were poor by changing the structures which institutionalized their poverty. As a young man, when auxiliary bishop in Rio de Janeiro, he had pioneered a major change in the Church's structure, persuading the nuncio, and the future Pope Paul VI, to authorize the world's first national episcopal conference in Brazil in 1952. In 1955 he also persuaded the authorities to authorize the Latin American Council of bishops (CELAM).[40] At Vatican II he was a tireless networker, not only helping to overthrow the Curia's theological agenda, but pressing world development on to the agenda of a still Eurocentric assembly.

He was one of the few bishops who was critical from the outset of the 1964 military coup in Brazil. For this he was made a non-person in his own country for nine years and all references to him were banned. As a result he travelled the world, warning of the links between poverty and violence and preaching brotherhood. A young priest, Henrique Pereira, was brutally murdered by the agents of the dictatorship, but it seems that those sent to kill the archbishop, disguised as beggars or taxi-drivers, could not bring themselves to do the deed but confessed and asked forgiveness of their intended victim.

After the Second Vatican Council Helder Camara was made Archbishop of Recife in a desperately poor region in the north-east of Brazil. His work there was a model of how best to implement the Council's vision, particularly in relation to an economically backward region. He avoided wearing the archbishop's purple sash and abandoned the palace in the pretentious suburbs. He chose to live in what was called the 'Church of the Frontiers', tucked away behind the city's inner ring road. He had his supper at the taxi-drivers' stall across the road and hitched lifts around the city instead of running an official car. Nor were these mere gestures. Camara gave away Church land to provide a settlement for landless peasants and set up a credit union. He took the students out of the seminary and put them in small communities in the parishes. He set up a theological institute in which future priests would study alongside laypeople and receive lectures from women too. When he reached the age of 75 he retired and much of his creative work has been undone by the bishop whom Pope John Paul II appointed to succeed him.

Examples such as those cited above demonstrate just how vast are the problems and challenges facing the Church in the Third World. The exploitation of the poor has been organized systematically by large and powerful commercial corporations, backed up by governments from whom they derive support or who are too frightened to oppose them. As with the exercise of charity described in Chapter Four, individual benevolence is not enough. These problems will only be eradicated by some form of structural change, frequently entailing political activity. As with charity in the abolition of slavery, such political action is not only permissible but is necessary if justice is to be established.

To illustrate this contention, I will draw attention to one further piece of evidence (out of many possible instances), that of transnational corporations. I quote from a letter published by Ian Linden, the Director of the Catholic Institute for International Relations in the context of the United Nations Social Development Summit:

> The United States and the European Union have managed to delete all reference of trans-national corporations (TNCs) from the draft text of the Social Development Summit (March 4th 1995). TNCs now control over 80 per cent of world trade and their international investment has reached $2.1 trillion, one third of which is controlled by the largest 100 TNCs. To hold a world summit on poverty, employment and social cohesion and ignore one of the most powerful actors in determining the economic and social future of our planet is like holding a summit on malaria and refusing to mention the word mosquito. The removal from the summit's agenda of the most vital issues for social development such as the regulation of TNCs, debt relief, and increased aid is a reflection of the short term, myopic interests of the powerful governments of the North, and those who benefit from the status quo. It is essential that discussion begins on how TNCs can be harnessed to become a motor for social development. This will demand international regulation to achieve transparency, and corporate behaviour which promotes social welfare rather than undermines it.[41]

Faced with problems of this magnitude, it is hard to see how anyone could object to the Church's involvement in exerting moral pressure to ensure structural change. It is inevitable that this will bring the Church into conflict with powerful commercial organizations and even the national governments that are allied to them. It is a regrettable but normal part of mission in a world where wickedness so profoundly permeates literally everything. A retreat to the sacristy would be a total betrayal of the Church's mission.

Of all the large-scale injustices that afflict the world, none has been as serious in the 1980s and 1990s as that of Third World debt. The salient facts are sufficiently well known so that they do not require more than summary repetition. The increase in oil prices, and hence revenues, in the 1970s meant that certain parts of the world were awash with money which was looking for an outlet. In an ideal world it could have been given to the poorest countries as a gift. This is not as unrealistic as it sounds because it is precisely what the USA did at the end of the Second World War, by giving money (called Marshall Aid) to the devastated countries of Europe so that they could rebuild everything. No such generosity was to be seen in the 1970s when the surplus money was invested as loans in Third World countries. Events, largely outside their control, have rendered them incapable of repaying their debts, and their problems have been compounded by their borrowing yet more money to service existing debts.

The situation deteriorated and became an international crisis in 1982 when Mexico threatened to stop paying. That might have had a domino effect and the world's banking system could have been at risk. To cope with that threat the debtor countries were offered packages for rescheduling their debts, deferring payment, lending further money to help with repayment, and controls on how the governments spent their money internally. (Usually this meant less being spent on education and health.)

A few figures will illustrate the extent of the crisis. In the decade 1983–93 Latin America paid $296 billion in interest, while its debt increased from $242 billion, to $429 billion.[42] In Africa between 1986 and 1990 the indebted countries were paying $10 billion a year to the West in debt and interest payments. In the 1980s soaring interest rates and a fall in the prices of exports pushed Africa's debt up from 28 to 109 per cent of Gross National Product. In more human terms this means that in Zambia, for example, every man, woman and child owed the nation's creditors $766 each, which was twice the average income.[43]

Statistics of this kind hardly do justice to the horror of the reality. Moreover people living in the comfortable countries of North America and Western Europe find it almost impossible to envisage the misery and suffering, particularly in sub-Saharan Africa. For those people it is not merely a question of hardship but of survival. Life itself has become precarious. In that region, in 1993, 4.2 million children were dying of malnutrition, another 30 million were underweight, and overall two-thirds of people in Africa do not have access to clean water for drinking and cooking.[44]

In 1989 UNICEF published an important report on the matter, stating, among other things:

> For almost 900 million people, approximately one sixth of mankind, the march of human progress has now become a retreat. In many nations, development is being thrown into reverse. After decades of steady economic advance, large areas of the world are sliding back into poverty. Throughout Africa and much of Latin America, average incomes have fallen by 10–25 per cent in the 1980s. The average weight-for-age of young children, a vital indicator of normal growth, is falling … In 37 poorest nations, spending per head on health has been reduced by 50 per cent, and on education by 25 per cent over the last few years.[45]

Towards the end of 1999 the British Government announced that it would write off the debts of a number of the poorest countries of the world. This gesture was followed by a few other nations.

It was a welcome gesture, but without being cynical it did not get to the root of the problem. It was a gesture of amelioration that left the capitalist system intact. Although the USA has strong legislation to control the power of monopolies, and in Britain and other nations the concept of the limited liability company protects the owners of bankrupt businesses, nothing similar operates at the international level. The poor countries of the world are still vulnerable to unlimited demands from those who lend them money. The tragedy could occur again in a few years, because the causes have not been removed.

The most callous repressive measure is that of death squads. In various parts of the world, poor families are obliged to drive away their own children whom they can no longer afford to feed. (Obviously this has a bearing on birth control, which I will discuss in a later chapter.) They roam the streets in search of food or employment of any kind. Their numbers are so large that they cannot be concealed or ignored by the authorities. Being unwilling to provide a humanitarian solution which would cost money, they are not infrequently killed. For example in 1990, 450 such killings were reported to Amnesty International in Brazil, in the cities of São Paolo, Rio, and Recife alone.[46]

Until such injustices and cruelties have been remedied, no honest person is entitled to remain silent and inactive. No Christian Church may ignore the problems under the pretext of upholding the authority of legitimate governments. Above all, the Catholic Church, being the largest and best-organized international Church, must work for the removal of these injustices if it is to be faithful to its mission in general, and more particularly to the recent declarations about the pursuit of justice in the Second Vatican Council.

Case Study: The *Desaparacidos* of Argentina

The death squads operating against political dissenters have been mentioned earlier in this chapter. The most shocking instance of this policy was in Argentina in the time of the military dictatorship which followed the collapse of Eva Peron's presidency. The reality of the abductions and the reaction of the bereaved became known worldwide on account of the courageous protests of the mothers. Wearing white scarves they paraded slowly round the central square in Buenos Aires.

During the crisis period in the mid-1970s thousands of people disappeared. Estimates of the precise number vary between 11 000 and 30 000. The figures were compiled, when the crisis was over, by the National Commission for the Disappeared. Their task was difficult because the military government had ordered the destruction of all relevant records.[47]

The situation arose out of the revolutionary activities of two left-wing guerilla organizations, the Ejercito Revolucionario del Pueblo (People's Revolutionary Army) and the Montoneros. In the late 1960s they killed approximately 2000 soldiers, politicians, and ordinary civilians. The government's reaction escalated to a liquidation of all opposition of any kind. It was an indiscriminate elimination of opposition politicians, journalists, trade union activists, student leaders, in short anyone who might be in a position to influence the population against the military junta.

The authorities in Argentina were careful to avoid the mistakes of Pinochet in Chile. Within a few days of seizing power he had ordered the killing of more than a thousand supporters of the former government. This brought widespread hostility from international public opinion. In contrast the authorities in Argentina worked in secret. Their victims were arrested with the minimum of fuss, frequently being simply kidnapped. After that they were never seen again. Their interrogation and subjection to torture were conducted in secret, as were their executions. The psychological effect of this insidious process of people simply disappearing was terrifying. About two million citizens emigrated during this period.[48]

When the crisis was over, a small number of the military and police who had taken part revealed what had happened. The victims were buried in unmarked mass graves or else dropped into the sea from helicopters. When it was all over a former navy captain, Adolfo Scilingo, indicated the ineffectuality of the military chaplains, who comforted the military personnel who took part in such atrocities.[49]

As a reaction to this policy of terror, one group of heroic women devised a method of protest. After the disappearance of their husbands, their sons or their daughters, the families initiated the usual enquiries with the police. They met with a wall of silence and never received any information about an arrest, detention, or death. It was as if their loved ones had been spirited away without trace. People were left to conjecture what their fate might have been. In Buenos Aires a group of women determined to find out what had happened to their sons who had disappeared without trace, by forcing the hand of the authorities. The first demonstration took place on 13 April 1977 involving only 14 women. Gradually their numbers increased and they assembled at five o'clock every Thursday evening in the Plaza de Mayo, in the centre of the city. Eventually their number increased to a weekly attendance of two or three hundred. They walked round the square slowly, wearing white headscarves, as a silent protest against the secret abduction of their loved ones.

In October 1977 several hundred of them demonstrated outside the Congress building and presented a petition bearing 24 000 signatures demanding an open investigation into the fate of the people who had disappeared. At this point the foreign press began to take an interest in the movement, and police intimidation increased. On 10 December of the same year, nine key members of the group were arrested on leaving the church of Santa Cruz where they had held a meeting. Along with the mothers, two French nuns were arrested for being present with the group and supporting them. In spite of protests from the French government nothing was heard of the nuns, and at the time of writing their book, Simpson and Bennett recorded complete silence about their fate.[50] Several years later, when the terror had ended, a former policeman disclosed to an Argentinian newspaper, *Perfil*, that the two nuns had been killed and their bodies had been put in a sealed drum which was dropped into a river.[51]

The Mothers of the Plaza de Mayo displayed the courage that comes from having lost so much that they were no longer afraid of death. Similar courage was not displayed by the institutional Church, although with the demise of free political activity, the Church was the one organization which could have exerted pressure on the government. The verdict of the authors Simpson and Bennett deserves to be quoted verbatim: 'The Church as a whole was noteworthy for its silence during the years of repression, – a silence which helped the military regime, even while individual priests and members of their congregations were being abducted and killed.'[52]

The record of the Church's activity during those years makes depressing reading. Cardinal Juan Carlos Aramburu, who was the head of the Argentinian Church, refused to receive relatives of people who had disappeared. When the Mothers of the Plaza de Mayo sought a meeting with the bishops' conference, they were shunted away from the front door of the building where the bishops were meeting, although they had stood waiting in the rain for a whole day.[53] In fact, they had to wait 20 years for a meeting with the bishops' conference. On that occasion they delivered a document protesting against the shameful participation of many priests during the military dictatorship. Unfortunately they were given no satisfactory reply. In 1984, when the terror had ceased, Archbishop Carlos Perez of Salta province opposed the exhumation of bodies from the anonymous mass graves, although it was the obvious first step in trying to find out what had happened to the disappeared people. Silent acquiescence was the overall stance of the Church in that terrible period.

There were a few isolated instances of heroic protest among the clergy. In the first eight months of military rule 30 priests were arrested. Four of them were deported, nine were released and the rest were held as prisoners, or simply disappeared. On 25 July 1974, two priests were killed by the police in the north-west province of La Rioja. The local bishop, Enrique Angelelli, protested strongly. Within two weeks he had died in a car crash which had all the marks of a deliberate killing. Not even this galvanized the hierarchy as a whole into making some sort of protest. The focus of concern for justice was not with the bishops' conference, but the organization known as the Ecumenical Movement for Human Rights led by Bishop Novak of the diocese of Quilmes. Their work was undermined by lack of support from the Catholic Church as a whole.[54]

Eventually in March 1977 the twelve archbishops of Argentina drew up an anodyne document about human rights in general, and presented it to the government. However at the insistence of the conservative wing in the episcopate, it was agreed that the document was not to be published.[55] It is difficult to envisage a clearer example of the betrayal of the duty of Christian witness to the truth. As has been indicated at various points in this book, Christians have a duty not only of abiding by the truth in their lives but of witnessing to it also. This entails some sort of public gesture and an element of confrontation with those who are denying the truth or perpetrating injustices in practice. It is simply not adequate for Church leaders to limit themselves to written statements that might remain unread on library shelves, in official archives, or in unpublished memoranda.

As a result of the hierarchy's conciliatory policy, in public perception the Church was viewed as a constant ally of the military regime. This perception was nourished by symbolic gestures such as President Videla leading the public prayers at the 1979 congress at Mendoza in honour of Mary the Mother of Jesus.[56] Years later, Bishop Miguel Hesayne of Viedma admitted the grave responsibilities of the Church during the period of the dirty war. He said that the Church authorities showed no scruple in dining with the torturers.[57] As is well known, the Papal Nuncio Archbishop Pio Laghi continued to play tennis with the commander-in-chief of the navy, although he did attempt to intercede for some of the prisoners.[58] These details may seem trivial but symbolic gestures are important even in normal conditions, and even more so in times of crisis.

The end of the regime of terror owed nothing to the Catholic Church. It was a combination of outside pressures beginning with the Carter Administration in the United States, and ending with General Galtieri's fall from favour after the Falklands War. The Church's role had all along been one of acquiescence, even in such details as blessing the weapons of the military.[59] This detail reminds one of Pius XI's unfortunate gesture of blessing the regimental flags of the Italian soldiers setting out for the invasion of Ethiopia.

The poor showing of the official Church in Argentina during the dirty war is one more example of the Church's failure to translate edifying moral ideals into practice. When confronted with a situation of terrible cruelty and injustice, the Church's overall response was one of tacit acquiescence. Once again, it should not surprise us if high-minded people, particularly those who are young and idealistic, should turn their backs on the institutional Church. It has forfeited their respect. By contrast the Mothers of the Plaza de Mayo have earned the respect of the whole world, and their heroism was rewarded on 13 December 1999 when UNESCO conferred on them the international Prize for the Promotion of Peace.

Subsequently the hierarchy of Argentina have attempted to make amends. On 11 May 1996 they issued a document stating their profound regret for the Church's failure to mitigate the tragedy. On 8 September 2000, Bishop Karlic of Parana, speaking in the name of the whole episcopate, made a plea for forgiveness at a National Eucharistic Congress in Cordoba attended by more than 100 000 people. It was an anodyne statement containing phrases such as a prayer that forgiveness would be given to those who had stayed silent as well as those who had effectively participated in torture. This kind of statement accords ill with the traditional Catholic doctrine on reconciliation. In the sacrament of penance, Catholics have been taught that their sins will be forgiven only if there is sincere self-accusation of specific sins, coupled with a firm purpose of amendment (which includes restitution if necessary). All these specific elements were lacking in the Argentinian bishops' prayer (as reported in *The Tablet*, 16 September 2000). No one accepted any specific responsibility for the silent complicity, no one has been punished, and there has been no mention of compensation. One is left wondering if it was more of a retrospective exoneration than an authentic act of repentance.

The Causes of Apathy

The widespread suppression of justice throughout the world, which reaches to so many departments of life, in so many societies, requires some sort of comprehensive explanation.

There are two minor and two major causes for this widespread tragedy. The lesser causes are inefficient management and corruption. The former is regrettable but not of devastating importance: every nation in the world has it to some extent. Corruption is less easily excused. The well-known celebrity Bianca Jagger traces her conversion to political activism to her first perceiving the extent of corruption. After the earthquake in Nicaragua in 1972, when she was 22 and just married, she came to the stricken country and discovered that Somoza, the Nicaraguan leader, had doubled his fortune by pocketing the money sent for the disaster victims. From that time onwards she changed her life from one of wealth and pleasure to being a tireless worker for Christian Aid in the quest for the relief of world poverty.[60]

Moving now to consider the major causes of the suppression of justice, there is the complex of forces latent in the quest for power. The pursuit of political power frequently leads to violence if there are no adequate constitutional constraints in place. This has been the tragic history of many of the fledgling democracies in post-colonial Africa during the latter part of the twentieth century. When uncontrolled power gets out of hand, truth, freedom, and justice are banished.

Paradoxically the fourth cause of the disappearance of justice is not when power gets out of hand, but when this particular kind of power is operating normally (normally that is, according to its own rules). I refer to the activities of international finance which operate in favour of those who are rich enough to make loans and whose activities are not controlled by any realistic limitations. So what is the remedy?

An interim solution, which must not be despised, is the work of various non-governmental aid agencies, like Oxfam, Christian Aid, CAFOD, Save the Children Fund, and dozens of others. For the most part they are motivated by Christian charity or humanitarian philanthropy, and they operate at the first three levels of charity, as discussed in Chapter Three. That is to say they provide amelioration, enablement, and protest. But for their financial help, educational projects, and self-help schemes, the plight of the Third World countries would be incomparably worse. However, they do not eradicate the causes of the problems. As with the abolition of slavery, a fourth level of action is needed, which is structural change.

The broad outlines of such measures are not difficult to envisage. At the national level, Great Britain for example, has for many years legitimized the concept of the limited liability company. If a commercial organization become bankrupt, the creditors take a limited amount of compensation from the wrecked enterprise. They do not strip the workers of their furniture nor the shareholders of their houses. That, in effect, is what the banks and other financial organizations are doing to the Third World in an arena where the concept of a limited liability simply does not exist. The institutions are organized on the quest for profit, which is quite literally unlimited.

To create some constraints, similar to the principle of the limited liability company, would entail international legislation which was enforceable. A self-regulating voluntary code of practice would be ignored. But it is not a great problem. The insurmountable difficulty is the moral issue of motivation. The political will is lacking. It is here that the Church comes into its own. Catholicism should be at the forefront of efforts to make international structural change in the rules of international commerce. Inevitably this will bring the Church into conflict with powerful vested interests. This struggle must be undertaken if justice is to be promoted. There is no other way, and if the Church tries to evade it, it will constitute a massive betrayal of the Church's vocation to promote morality.

Prophetic Office of the Church

A final consideration of justice which ties in with the virtue of truthfulness is that of prophetic witness. Since the time of Amos in the Old Testament, the prophets have spoken out in protest against injustices and cruelties that they could not remedy by practical measures. This is not the action of soured and disgruntled personalities but a genuine witness to the truth. The underlying truth which is at stake is the realization that injustices cannot be remedied by practical means, until the moral dimension and other psychological components of the situation are brought to the attention of those who have the power to remedy them.

Amos shouted his protests in the Temple to make sure that the king should hear them. This is very different from bland statements about justice in general published in arcane scholarly periodicals or the columns of the *Osservatore Romano*. The actions of the black sash movement in South Africa and the women in Buenos Aires are classical examples of how this is to be done. Regrettably the institutional Church has been notably absent from such activity. The silence that reigned in Germany during the Nazis' persecution of the Jews has been commented on frequently. The same absence of protest was all too common in South America in the 1980s and 1990s when the Church's maintaining of friendly relations with the military dictatorships amounted to complicity with their death squads.

Notes

1 For this distinction I am indebted to Professor J. O'Connell, who kindly allowed me to read his work on Justice and Morality prior to publication.
2 It was translated into English and published under that title by the SCM Press, London in 1979.
3 Ibid., 37.
4 Ibid., 37.
5 *De Libertate Christiana et Liberatione*, 22 March 1986, published in *Acta Apostolicae Sedis*, 1987, 554–99.
6 For much of what follows, I am indebted to *The New Politics: Catholic Social Teaching for the Twenty-First Century*, ed. Paul Vallely, London, 1998.
7 Walsh, M. in *The New Politics*, 32.
8 *Mater et Magistra*, section 43, noted by M.Walsh in *The New Politics*, 39.
9 Vallely, *The New Politics*, 4.
10 Walsh in *The New Politics*, 36.
11 *Quadragesimo Anno*, section 79, DS 3738.
12 Vallely, *The New Politics*, 11.
13 *Gaudium et Spes*, section 41, DVII 241.
14 The text was published in full in *The Tablet*, 12 December 1998.
15 *Gaudium et Spes*, section 16, DVII 214.
16 *Gaudium et Spes*, section 17, DVII 214.
17 *Dignitatis Humanae*, section 2, DVII, 678, 679.
18 *Gaudium et Spes*, section 36, DVII 234.
19 *Gaudium et Spes*, section 62, DVII 269.
20 *Gaudium et Spes*, section 62, DVII 270.
21 *Gaudium et Spes*, section 26, DVII 225.
22 *Gaudium et Spes*, section 57, DVII 262.
23 *Gaudium et Spes*, section 66, DVII 274.
24 *Gaudium et Spes*, section 4, DVII 202.
25 *Gaudium et Spes*, section 66, DVII 274.
26 *Populorum Progressio*, section 26, commented on by Julian Filochowski in *The New Politics*, 63, 66.
27 Noted by Clifford Longley in *The New Politics*, 101.
28 Cf. Vallely, *The New Politics*, 136.
29 Cf. *The New Politics*, 55, 67, 79, and 80.
30 Walsh, M. and Linden, I. in *The New Politics*, 31 and 91.
31 Linden, L. in *The New Politics*, 93.
32 *Quadragesimo Anno*, section 94, *Octagesima Adveniens*, section 14.
33 Walsh in *The New Politics*, 40.
34 Vallely, *The New Politics*, 167.
35 *Quadragesimo Anno*, section 88.
36 The facts in this section are taken from *The Observer*, 28 March 1993.
37 *The Observer*, 19 February 1994.
38 *The Guardian*, 19 April 1993.
39 *The Guardian*, 9 September 1996.
40 *The Tablet*, 13 February 1999.
41 *The Guardian*, 7 March 1995.
42 *The Guardian*, 8 February 1993.
43 *The Guardian*, 14 May 1993.
44 *The Guardian*, 14 May 1993.
45 UNICEF report entitled *The State of the World's Children*, quoted by Dr. D. Logie in the *British Medical Journal*, 30 May 1992, 1424.

46 Logie, 1423
47 John Simpson and Jana Bennett, *The Disappeared*, London, 1985, 3 and 78. The larger figure was published in *The Tablet*, 6 May 1995.
48 Simpson and Bennett, 126.
49 *The Tablet*, 6 May 1995.
50 Simpson and Bennett, 147.
51 *The Guardian*, 7 July 1998.
52 Simpson and Bennett, 159.
53 Simpson and Bennett, 160, and *The Tablet*, 6 May 1995.
54 Simpson and Bennett, 164.
55 Simpson and Bennett, 166.
56 Simpson and Bennett, 168.
57 *The Tablet*, 6 May 1995.
58 *The Tablet*, 1 July 1995.
59 Simpson and Bennett, 279.
60 *The Guardian*, 14 March 1996.

Chapter 6

Justice in the Church

Although the Catholic Church has proclaimed admirable principles of justice for the consumption of society at large, the implementation of those same principles within the community of the Church raises some disquieting questions.

Case Study: The Right to the Sacraments and the Absence of Priests

Very few rights are guaranteed for the members of the Church in the Code of Canon Law. One of these rare concessions is the statement in Canon 213 (of the current code) that the laity have the right to receive the sacraments. The implementation of this right is effectively denied to millions of Catholics because of the shortage of priests and the refusal of Pope John Paul II to remove the principal obstacle to increased numbers of clergy. I refer of course to the requirement of obligatory celibacy.

The problem has been debated so openly and fully over the last 30 years that a brief rehearsal of the facts will suffice. From apostolic times until the early Middle Ages, those who would now be described as the parochial clergy were married. Various sporadic attempts were made to curtail their sexual activities but they seem to have been ineffectual. In the early mediaeval period there was a growing tendency by the authorities to promote the celibate life for clergy. This was due to an enhanced respect for monastic life and a fear that clerical families might monopolize the property of an increasingly wealthy Church. This latter consideration seems to have been the motive for the legislation of Pope Benedict VIII at the Synod of Pavia in 1022.[1] There was also a pessimism about sex which the Western part of the Church had inherited from influential patristic writers notably St Augustine and St Jerome. It is worth noting that zealots of that era who advocated the celibate life for priests, like St Peter Damian and Chrodegang of Metz, were also supporters of community life for the clergy. Being compelled to live alone has nothing to commend it yet this has been the inevitable fate of the rural clergy from that period up to the present day.

The First and Second Lateran Councils of 1123 and 1139 enacted laws by which major orders became a nullifying impediment to marriage and marriage was a condition which invalidated ordination.[2] Although the canons of those two Councils have survived, the records of their deliberations have not. However the underlying motives for the legislation can be evaluated in the light of statements made at that period by high-ranking ecclesiastics. For example in 1054, Cardinal Humbert, the pope's representative at Constantinople, condemned the Eastern Churches for the conduct of their married priests: 'Young husbands, just now exhausted from carnal lust, serve the altar. And immediately afterwards they again embrace their wives with hands that have been hallowed by the immaculate Body of Christ. That is not the mark of the true faith, but an invention of Satan.'[3] In the following century, between those two general Councils in fact, Pope Innocent II, addressing the Synod of Clermont in 1130 declared: 'Since priests are supposed to be God's temples, vessels of the Lord and sanctuaries of the Holy Spirit ... it offends their dignity to lie in the conjugal bed and live in impurity.'[4]

After the Reformation all the Churches sprung from it adopted marriage for the clergy, since the prohibition was not to be found in Scripture. Unfortunately the theological bitterness of that period was such that its adoption by Protestants drove the Catholics more firmly in the other direction, as was the case with the vernacular liturgy.

However the Second Vatican Council radically changed the situation by what it stated theologically and by the climate of open debate which it inaugurated. All aspects of ecclesiastical organization were scrutinized critically to see if they promoted or impeded the Church's mission. It became clear that the exclusion of married men from the clergy did not enhance that mission. The Council's crucial theological pronouncement about priestly celibacy is as follows:

> With respect to the priestly life, the Church has always held in especially high regard perfect and perpetual continence on behalf of the Kingdom of Heaven ... It is not indeed demanded by the very nature of the priesthood, as is evident from the practice of the primitive Church, and the tradition of the Eastern Churches. In these Churches in addition to all bishops and those others who by a gift of grace choose to observe celibacy, there also exist married priests of outstanding merit. While this most sacred Synod recommends ecclesiastical celibacy, it in no way intends to change that different discipline which lawfully prevails in the Eastern Churches.[5]

That statement effectively demolished the theological basis of the law of obligatory celibacy, as has been shown by subsequent belated attempts to shore up the requirement in the Western Church.

By a special intervention in the Council's business in October 1965, Pope Paul VI prevented the bishops from debating the matter in any more detail or deliberating any practical changes to the law.[6]

In June 1967 the same pope published the encyclical *Sacerdotalis Coelibatus* (Priestly Celibacy) in which he commended the retention of compulsory celibacy, but he was unable to provide convincing reasons for it. In section 13 of the encyclical he praised the holiness and dedication of countless celibate priests and religious in past and present times. And without further justification he opened the next section with the words: 'Hence we consider that the present law of celibacy should today continue to be linked to the ecclesiastical ministry'. No coherent theological reasons were offered there or elsewhere in the encyclical. To his credit Pope Paul VI did face up to the different discipline for married priests in the Catholic Eastern rites. However he expressed the rationale for the different systems in words which must be among the most extraordinary that have ever featured in an official document of the Church:

> If the legislation of the Eastern Churches is different in the matter of discipline with regard to clerical celibacy, as was finally established by the Council of Trullo held in the year 692, and which has been clearly recognised by the Second Vatican Council, this is due to the different historical background of that most noble part of the Church, a situation which the Holy Spirit has providentially and supernaturally influenced. (section 38)[7]

Is this the ultimate theological suicide? Apparently we are expected to believe that the Holy Spirit has inspired two contradictory commands in the different disciplines of the Western and Eastern Churches.

It goes without saying that the advocates of married priests are unanimous in their respect for the gift of celibacy, when indeed it is a special grace from God and not merely a prohibition of ecclesiastical rules. Admittedly it is a rare gift, but when it is seen in the lives of those who have received it, it is wonderful to behold. It gives those individuals an inner freedom and generosity so that they can bestow unselfish love to all around them. I can think of a secular priest who used to have ex-Borstal boys living in his presbytery to help them to rebuild their lives. I can recall too an Orthodox archbishop whose talks on contemplative prayer were more inspiring than any other preacher whom I have heard. Such people are transparently inspired by a contagious love of God. But that grace is very rare.

The rarity of this gift ought to have caused the legislators to pause before attempting to bring this gift and the sacrament of orders into an inseparable relationship. There are two ways in which it could have been done. Either the legislators could have set out to discern the presence of the gift of celibacy in seminarians and then restricted ordination only to those who were judged to have received that particular grace from God. Alternatively they could set out to discern the signs of a vocation to the priesthood and then impose upon such aspirants the legal obligation to remain single. The former course would exclude from the clergy many men who had a vocation to the priesthood, and the latter course would deny the right to marriage to a whole class to whom God had not given the special grace of celibacy. Both alternatives are flawed because there is no intrinsic connection between priesthood and celibacy, as Vatican II stated clearly.

Ecclesiastical practice has been consistent ever since the twelfth century. Those who are deemed to have a vocation to the priesthood are deprived of the right to marry. Canon law simply forbids it. In the period prior to Vatican II it was unceremoniously referred to as part of the package deal. If a man wished to become a priest he had to put up with remaining single. What is really shocking is that the Code of 1983 (canon 277, section 1) repeated the old prohibition in spite of the clearly enunciated theological statement of Vatican II.

Needless to say events have not stood still, nor has the debate. It has been estimated that in the decades following Vatican II approximately 10 000 priests resigned from the ranks of the clergy, mostly in order to marry. The Vatican simply does not know how to cope with this problem. During the pontificate of Paul VI practically all those who applied for laicization were granted it, and also given the dispensation for a Church marriage. In the pontificate of John Paul II virtually none have been granted. This indicates that the policy is arbitrary. What is more disturbing is the fact that since about 1988 applications for laicization have simply remained unanswered without even an acknowledgement that the letter had been received at Rome. This is what psychologists call denial, that is the refusal to face up to a problem that is too difficult to cope with at the conscious level, so the individual acts as if it did not exist. At the collective and institutional level, that is exactly what is happening at the Vatican.

Public opinion within the Church has moved decisively in favour of ordaining married men. The number of candidates for the secular clergy has shrunk to a trickle and it is clear that the principal deterrent is the law of celibacy, which is now not supported by any pretence of theological coherence.

Vast areas of the Church are now effectively deprived of priests. This is the real tragedy. In rural parts of Africa and Latin America many Catholics do not see a priest for months on end or even years. The cynicism of the Vatican authorities is almost beyond belief. Traditionally it was always held that for Catholics the mass was of supreme importance, but it seems clear that for the administrators in the Vatican the retention of the law of celibacy takes precedence over the availability of mass and the sacraments. Apart from the implicit denial of the right to the sacraments enshrined in Canon 213, the absence of eucharistic communities has created a vacuum which others have not been slow to fill. The rapid progress of Pentecostal sects in Africa and South America is partly due to the absence of priests, and for this the Vatican has only itself to blame. Europe too is experiencing similar shortages, but having started with a greater number of clergy, concentrated more densely, the shortage has not yet caused the same problems as in Africa. But it is only a matter of time. For example just before the end of the millennium, it was reported by Bishop Georges Gilson (chairman of the French commission on ordained ministries) that the Tonerre region, 90 miles south-east of Paris, was now served by only four priests, two of whom were foreigners. One hundred years previously every one of the 73 villages had its own priest.[8]

Most surprising of all was the revelation that in 1998 Ireland, of all places, was suffering from an acute shortage of candidates for the seminaries. In September of that year it was announced that St Peter's diocesan seminary at Wexford was closing down because the number of students had sunk to 12, whereas there were 40 in that seminary a decade earlier. In 1998 there were only 220 seminarians in training in Ireland, whereas 20 years previously there had been 600 students in the regional seminary of Maynooth alone. The archdiocese of Dublin accounts for one-third of the population of Ireland, yet in 1997 not one candidate came forward in that diocese to start training in a seminary. Another large diocese, Cork, did not ordain a single priest in 1997 or 1998.[9] This was the country which until recently had so great a surplus of priests that many were trained for work in other English-speaking countries such as Britain and the USA. Paradoxically it was the 'export seminary' which provided one of the most significant pieces of evidence of the current trends. For more than two hundred years, All Hallows College in Dublin trained priests who would leave Ireland to work in practically all the English-speaking countries. In the 1950s it was not uncommon for the student body to number more than 200, yet in the autumn of 1998 it did not have a single clerical student. Instead it housed 550 laypeople studying theology.[10] If the crisis has hit Ireland, then there is no future at all for the centuries-old celibate form of priesthood.

England too has its problems. Admittedly they are not as urgent as in some other countries but the shortage of priests is already doing serious damage to the Church's mission. For example, in one small diocese in the south of England between mid-1996 to mid-1998 six priests resigned. In 1997 two priests died, but only one was ordained. In 1998 there were no new candidates to enter the seminary. This pattern is fairly typical of the whole of England. Since Vatican II deaths among the clergy almost always outnumber ordinations. There have been years when large dioceses like Liverpool did not ordain a single priest. The future looks bleak for several English dioceses. At the start of the academic year in 1998 51 men entered seminary or pre-seminary training, compared with 107 in 1988, which is a decline of more than 50 per cent in a decade. Several dioceses did not have even one candidate, namely Birmingham, Hexham and Newcastle, Middlesborough and Shrewsbury. The situation in Wales was even worse. The three Catholic dioceses which compromise the whole of Wales – Cardiff, Menevia, and Wrexham – did not have one candidate between them.[11] Furthermore, the overall decline in the number of priests is constantly aggravated by the steady stream of resignations from the clergy.

In the 1990s events moved with ever-increasing swiftness. Whereas all participants in the debate respect the special grace of celibacy spoken of in the New Testament, which must be accepted freely, the theological arguments against compulsory celibacy have become unanswerable. The German theologian, Dr Heinz-Jürgen Vogels, has disputed the intrinsic legitimacy of the law, that is to say, he has challenged its moral basis. His starting point is a principle, accepted by all moral theologians and affirmed by Pope John Paul II in his encyclical *Evangelium Vitae*, namely that no merely human law can invalidate a divine law. He then cites various popes, including Leo XIII and Pius XI, who declared that marriage was a fundamental human right of divine natural law which could not be abrogated by any human law.[12] The inalienable right to marry and raise a family was also stated by the Second Vatican Council. Its words on the subject are so clear that they deserve to be quoted verbatim: 'For in view of the inalienable human right to marry *(inalienabile hominis ius ad matrimonium)* and beget children, the question of how many children should be borne belongs to the honest judgement of the parents.'[13] Admittedly the context is that of family planning, which I will deal with in Chapter Ten, but the underlying principle is perfectly clear, and its implications are unanswerable.

As far as England is concerned, all theoretical debate was overtaken by events in 1983. In the spring of that year the Bishops' Conference agreed to seek permission from Rome to ordain convert married priests coming from the Church of England. The request was approved by Pope John Paul II, and since then there has been a significant number of married former Anglicans working as priests in English parishes.

In 1994 the Vatican's Congregation for the Clergy published a belated attempt to justify the retention of the law of mandatory celibacy for priests. It is to be found in the *Directory on the Ministry and Life of Priests* (sections 57–59).[14] The statement from Vatican II that there is no intrinsic connection between priesthood and celibacy is never mentioned in the document. The alleged reasons for the retention of obligatory celibacy are to be found at the end of section 59, in the words: 'The Church from apostolic times has wished to conserve the gift of perpetual continence of the clergy, and choose the candidates for Holy Orders from among the celibate faithful (cf. II Thes. 2:15, I Cor. 7:5, 9:5, I Tim. 3:2-12, Tit. 1:6-8).' This sentence is seriously misleading as can be seen by anyone who cares to refer to the Scripture citations and who has access to a library where the attendant footnote can be checked.

In the first place, a cursory reading of the New Testament passages in question will indicate that they have nothing to do with clerical celibacy, nor are there any other passages in the New Testament which enjoin it on priests. The lengthy footnote which accompanies those references to the Epistles cites various Fathers and several provincial councils and one general council. These witnesses are all from the fourth century or later. For the first three centuries the surviving documents are silent. There is no evidence from that period and the statement that celibacy was required from apostolic times is simply false.

I will reserve the detailed examination of the patristic and conciliar texts for the First Excursus at the end of this chapter, lest the details should confuse the overall argument of this chapter. By way of anticipating the conclusion, I can indicate here that cultic purity was at stake. It was assumed that the clergy were married, but after ordination they were required to abstain from sexual relations with their wives. This concept of ritual purity is an ancient pagan principle that occurs in many religions, and it implies that certain things, such as disease, contact with dead bodies, and sex, are incompatible with the sacred. It is to be seen in the Old Testament, though its origin is clearly part of the ancient culture which was established before Abraham. It is totally absent from the teaching of the New Testament.

It entered Christian thinking in the fourth century when other concepts related to the priesthood were borrowed uncritically from the Old Testament. At that time they did not realize that it was incompatible with Christianity. Vatican II has made it clear that the sexual relationship between husband and wife is intrinsically good, and that statement invalidated any appeal to cultic purity as a basis for excluding married men from the priesthood. Even in the fourth century the practical enforcement of such a prohibition must have been unrealistic. This is borne out by the sporadic and repetitive pattern of the legislation. Over the centuries it seems to have been widely ignored, which is not surprising in view of its being so much at variance with the spirit and teaching of the New Testament.

In effect the Church has lacked a satisfactory rational basis for the law of celibacy since Vatican II, and this is one reason for the massive exodus from the ranks of the clergy. The future holds out no prospect of any improvement. We can be confident that resignations will continue, recruitment is unlikely to increase, and the morale of the secular clergy will decline as they realize that they are being required to live within a prohibition that cannot be justified theologically. One simple example will illustrate the point. In 1997 the bishop of a certain English diocese telephoned one of the deans and asked him if there was a parish in his deanery whose presbytery was large enough to accommodate the family of a married ex-Anglican priest who had by then been ordained as a Catholic. The dean supplied the required information and a few days later sent in his own letter of resignation. The incident had brought home to him how little value now attached to his life of sacrifice. In simple practical terms it was clear that his ministry could be conducted from a smaller house than that of a married priest.

One fears that the next development will be an increase in the number of priests who have mistresses. This is a predictable consequence for priests who feel trapped in a system which their superiors cannot justify satisfactorily. Worse still is the fact that Pope John Paul II has forbidden bishops to discuss the matter publicly.[15] In spite of that prohibition a number of bishops have voiced their support for married priests including Cardinal König, the retired archbishop of Vienna, Bishop Iby of Eisenstadt in Austria, and Bishop Strecher of Innsbruck, back in 1995 as well as in his famous open letter (criticizing many aspects of Vatican policy) which he published the day before he retired in 1998.[16]

Case Study: The Priests of the Underground Church of Slovenia[17]

After the collapse of communist power in Eastern Europe the Church in Czechoslovakia had to come to terms with a large number of priests and bishops who had been ordained in secret and whose apostolate became public knowledge in 1990.

The main controversy centres upon Bishop Felix Davidek who was consecrated bishop by Jan Blaha in 1967. Despite the absence of records Blaha has insisted upon the validity of his consecration of Davidek, and the fact that he did so with the pope's authority. Blaha had himself been consecrated in Augsburg earlier that year by a Jesuit bishop Peter Dubovsky, whose own consecration was valid and lawful.[18] Subsequently Davidek consecrated bishops and ordained priests in numbers that were larger than had been envisaged and which were not recorded in Church archives on account of the persecution by the communist government. Estimates vary about the numbers. The total may be as high as 40 bishops and 200 priests.[19] Davidek himself spent a considerable time in prison, as did several of the clergy he had ordained.[20] Many of the priests and some of the bishops were married. Davidek had made a deliberate decision about that detail, estimating that the secret police would be less likely to suspect that married men were priests. Added to which it gave them a psychological advantage if they were imprisoned. Fridolin Zahradnik (a married bishop with three children) stated 'A celibate priest was alone in jail with God. I was there with God and with my family's love.'[21]

The Vatican's reaction to this situation has been totally lacking in generosity, in view of what those men suffered in order to keep the faith alive in time of persecution. The validity of their ordinations has been questioned because there are no records. They have been offered the opportunity to work as permanent deacons in the Latin rite or to have conditional re-ordination in the Greek Catholic rite which accepts married priests.[22] Some have accepted the conditional re-ordination, but others regarded such a step as simply insulting and strictly an injustice that the validity of their ordinations has not been accepted. The Vatican's attitude also shows a lack of trust, a virtue whose absence from much of the Church's administration was discussed in the chapter on Hope.

The absence of written records or their ordinations should not be a matter of surprise. Anyone who has done research into English Catholic history in penal times will have been aware of the lack of baptismal records. To have set down the matter in writing would have rendered the recipient liable to penalties. This cautious practice continued long after the Catholic Emancipation Act of 1829.

Clearly the hidden agenda is that those priests and bishops were married, and it is for that reason that the Vatican is unwilling that they should function among Latin-rite Catholics. The mean manner in which the Vatican has reacted to their underground mission and the dangers which they faced is another sad example of misdirected moral effort. The bureaucrats simply cannot come to terms with the heroes who have endured prison for the Church's mission but transgressed a man-made rule for the well-being of that mission. Small mindedness of this kind is damaging to the Church's credibility.

Personal Rights within the Church

The treatment of the heroic priests of the underground Church in Czecho-slovakia leads one logically to consider what safeguards exist in Church law to protect the rights of the Church's members against possible abuse from the system within which they work. The treatment of those priests gives rise to the serious question as to whether they were protected by any acknowl-edged rights in Canon Law. In view of what modern popes have pronounced on workers' rights, living wages, and political freedom, one would have hoped that within the community of the Church an adequate system of rights would be recognized. This expectation has been strengthened consid-erably by the decisions of Vatican II and its explicit recognition of the concept of human rights (which was discussed in Chapter Five).

The publication of the new Code of Canon Law in 1983 provided the ideal opportunity to codify the principles that had been stated by modern popes and the Second Vatican Council. Yet one searches in vain for an explicit acknowledgement of the concept of human rights deriving from natural law or Christian revelation. If this should seem to be a harsh judge-ment I will present in the next few pages the essence of what the 1983 Code has to offer by way of rights for members of the Catholic Church. Personal rights are dealt with in four sections of the new Code, according as they apply to four categories of people, namely Christians in general, laity, clergy, and fourthly members of religious orders.

Canons 208 to 228 deal with the obligations and rights of all *christifideles.* This is the technical term used in the Code for Christians who are members of the Roman Catholic Church, as is clear from Canon 204. A variety of rather indeterminate rights is indicated, such as the right of Catholics to express their opinions on Church matters to their pastors, and to communi-cate such ideas to other members of the Church (Canon 212, section 3). They have the right to receive preaching and the sacraments (Canon 213). Others are less specific, such as the right to worship in a particular rite, the Greek Catholic rite for example, the right to participate in the Church's mission (Canon 216), and the right to a Christian education (Canon 217).

Academic freedom is cautiously conceded with the words: 'Those who are involved in sacred studies enjoy a just liberty of research and of pru-dently disclosing their thoughts … observing due obedience to the Church's magisterium' (Canon 218).

If anyone should fall foul of Church law, the right to a fair trial exists, but it is described in somewhat ominous terms. Canon 221, section 1 states that the members of the Church are 'competent to vindicate the rights which they enjoy in the Church in the competent ecclesiastical court, according to the rule of law'. Section 2 of the same Canon states that they also have the right, if summoned before competent authority, to be judged by the precepts of law, applied with equity. Finally section 3 declares, with unconscious irony, that Church members have the right not to be penalized by canonical punishments unless they are applied according to the norm of the law. Presumably this is to safeguard people from arbitrary penalization through administrative decisions. But why should such a safeguard be needed in the Church of God? Is this not the ultimate cynicism?

Although that section of the Code does mention rights, they are not very far reaching. They are the kind of freedoms which are simply taken for granted in modern democratic nations. There is no indication of their origin. Thus far there is no acknowledgement that as human beings members of the Church have natural rights. The implication is that the rights are conferred on them by the ecclesiastical legislators; in which case they could be removed by the same authorities.

The second section of the Code which covers rights is that which is devoted to the obligations and rights specifically of laypeople, in Canons 224 to 231. It is stated that laypeople have the right to take part in the apostolate and in the promotion of the Church's mission (Canon 225, section 1). Parents are declared to have the obligation and right to educate their children (Canon 226, section 2). This would seem to have been an obvious place to state that it was a natural human right, but nothing here or elsewhere indicates the source of that right which is simply stated with no reference to its origin. In view of the disputes in the nineteenth century, one is tempted to surmise that it was included in the Code to safeguard Catholic parents against the incursions of the state, which might claim a prior responsibility. Canon 227 speaks of secular politics in language which bristles with latent problems. In that Canon laypeople are said to have freedom in 'the affairs of the earthly city' in the same way as other citizens. Well, why not? And is it implied that the ecclesiastical legislators have given them permission to do so?

Canon 229, section 1 states that suitable laypeople may be admitted to those ecclesiastical offices and functions that they are capable of discharging according to the prescriptions of law. It is rather vague and cautious, and one is left wondering how well they would be welcomed into the clerical preserve, and what safeguards they might enjoy. One instance that comes to mind was the appointment in the 1980s of a married woman (with five children) to teach ecclesiastical history in a seminary in England. She performed the task competently for a number of years but was then dismissed summarily by an administrative decision and was given no explanation as to why she had been replaced by a nun. Canon Law gave her no right of redress. There is nothing in the code similar to the right in English law for an employee to sue the employer for unfair dismissal. Out of a sense of loyalty to the Church, the woman in question did not take the bishop to the civil court, but the whole episode emphasizes the absence of humane safeguards in Church law.

Canon 229 also states the right of laypeople to acquire theological education and to gain diplomas and degrees therein. It is a sad reflection on the mindset of the lawgivers that this should be legislated for, rather than being taken for granted. One is reminded of the exclusion of women from British universities until the end of the nineteenth century. It is a serious reproach to the Church's ethos and organization that until comparatively recently laypeople were unable to study theology at university level. For example it was only in the 1960s that the University of Fribourg first conferred the doctorate in theology on a woman.

The obligations and rights of clergy are dealt with briefly in Canons 272 to 279. The only right which is stated is that of Canon 278, section 1, which acknowledges the right of association, whereby clerics may join together for purposes in keeping with the clerical state. The obvious question about priests' salaries is stated in terms which are frankly unsatisfactory. Canon 281, section 1 declares: 'Clerics, since they dedicate themselves to the Church's ministry, merit remuneration that is suitable to their condition.' In other words, they have no strict right to a living wage. Nothing more is said about the rights of the clergy.

The obligations and rights of members of religious orders are dealt with in Canons 662 to 672. A careful reading of this section indicates that they are accorded no specific rights by the Code of Canon Law over and above what they enjoy as *christifideles*.

In view of the insistence on workers' rights in papal encyclicals for more than a century, and the positive statements about human rights in Vatican II, it is disappointing to say the least that members of the Church are accorded so few rights in the Code. Its orientation represents a regression from the positive vision of Vatican II and suggests a reassertion of the spirit of authoritarianism. It is deeply disturbing to realize how swiftly the ethos of the Council was set aside. One looks in vain in the pages of the Code for an explicit assertion of the principle of human rights similar to that embraced by Vatican II or in the United Nations Declaration of Human Rights.

Other measures which modern governments have adopted for safeguarding justice are similarly absent from the legislation of the Catholic Church, such as the independence of the judiciary. Not only is this principle absent from Canon Law but just the reverse is proclaimed. Canon 391 states that the bishop in his own diocese enjoys the three powers of being legislator, judge, and administrator. The same principle applies to the Bishop of Rome, but to a more enhanced degree since Vatican I had declared his jurisdiction over the whole Church. In 1983 the pope alone promulgated the new Code of Canon Law on his sole authority as legislator, as had his predecessor with the Code of 1918.

Shortly after the publication of the current Code of Canon Law, an American ecclesiastical lawyer wrote: 'as with any bill of rights, it will take time to see what practical significance they will have in the life of the Church. They will probably be the means whereby the new Code will ultimately bring about a change in mentality in many areas of Church life.'[23] By the end of the century that optimism sounded hollow and the epithet 'bill of rights' is sadly inappropriate.

Conceivably it could be argued that the Code of Canon Law is not the place in which one ought to seek the vindication of human rights. Is not the Church the one area in human activity in which goodwill, generosity, and high-minded motivation can be taken for granted? It would be nice to think so. Experience tells a different story. In the absence of legal safeguards for human rights, the Church's own authorities not infrequently deal with their own subjects in a manner which falls far below the standards of justice, equity, and openness which are taken for granted in modern democratic societies. This has been particularly evident in the treatment of scholars who are suspected of doctrinal deviationism, and against whom anonymous denunciation has all too often been employed, as will be seen in the next section.

Case Study: The Treatment of Suspect Theologians

I will confine my attention to the events of the twentieth century. Although the anti-Modernist measures of Pope Pius X now seem rather far away, their effects were felt in the Church long after his death. The bishops and theologians who fashioned the documents of Vatican II had all pursued their theological studies in the shadow of those reprehensible measures.

In the aftermath of the French Revolution, strenuous efforts were undertaken to rebuild the normal functioning of the Church, not least in the field of scholarship. It was a period of immense potential. Archaeological discoveries in the Near East had opened up a whole new vista for the understanding of the Bible. Similarly the application of the methods of critical history to the origins of the Church held out hopes for a totally new appreciation of how the early Church and its doctrine developed. After years of stagnation it is not surprising that Catholic scholars were not the first in the field, and the authorities in Rome took up an attitude of antecedent suspicion, since the initiative in these fields had come from Protestants or non-believers.

Catholic scholars have always taken for granted the fact that they work within the community of a teaching Church which is endowed with the guidance of the Holy Spirit and the charism of infallibility. In times of crisis irreformable doctrinal pronouncements are made, as for example by General Councils. However such decisions are exceptional, and the normal progress of theology has always been by means of intellectual investigation. The most brilliant achievements have occurred at times when the magisterium is least intrusive, as can be seen, for example, in the work of Augustine and Aquinas. It is noteworthy that the Second Vatican Council made no irreformable declarations, and offered the world admirable statements in a spirit which was both supremely confident and humble.

Unfortunately that was not the spirit which prevailed in the time of Pope Pius X. He had inherited from the previous century the practice whereby suspect theologians were secretly reported to Rome in circumstances in which they had little chance of establishing their innocence. Not only were good men penalized unjustly but sensitive intelligent thinkers were inhibited by the climate of distrust. Cardinal Newman's career is a tragic example. In his 45 years as a Catholic, he published far less than in the 20 years of his adult life as an Anglican. Metaphorically speaking his creativity froze in such a hostile atmosphere.

As the Modernist problem unfolded in the early years of the twentieth century the climate of suspicion and denunciation intensified. No one was exempt from the poisonous atmosphere. For example, the archbishop of Milan became the victim of an unsubstantiated slander.[24] Archbishop Andrea Ferrati had held the post since 1894 and during his tenure of office he had shown himself to be a learned, pious, and sensitive pastor of what was then the largest diocese in the Catholic world. In the spring of 1911 a Catholic newspaper in Venice stated that the senior seminary in Milan was rife with Modernist tendencies. The archbishop (who was by then a cardinal) retorted bitterly in the press that the charge was groundless and irresponsible. He made a speech to the same effect to the students of the seminary in question, and one of the seminarians recorded it in shorthand and sent it to Rome. The Pope reacted by despatching a letter of reprimand to the archbishop and the seminary was taken out of his control and placed under the direction of an apostolic visitor sent from Rome. Throughout the whole unedifying episode, the archbishop of Milan had no opportunity to vindicate his innocence nor did he have any legal basis on which to do so.

In 1907 the situation became worse with the advent of Monsignor Benigni. He was employed in the Secretariat of State and had a flair for journalism. In the Vatican he put together a sort of press agency that supplied anti-Modernist propaganda to Catholic newspapers throughout the world, and also received information about alleged Modernists from sympathetic journalists all over Europe. In about 1909 Benigni founded an organization know as the Sodality of Saint Pius V, which was a secret society pledged to exposing crypto-Modernists and denouncing them to the Roman authorities. It grew out of the network of journalists and other informants whom Benigni had gathered throughout Europe. It provided the structure through which anyone could be reported secretly to Rome. Evidence did not have to be substantiated and there was no due process to evaluate the accusations. No one was safe in that climate of anonymous denunciations. The cardinal archbishop of Vienna was accused of sadly loose morals and doctrinal transgressions. The archbishop of Paris was delated for being soft on Modernism, as was Cardinal Mercier the primate of Belgium. The files of the society literally bulged with the names of alleged deviants.[25] (Those files began their passage into the public domain when they were discovered by German soldiers during the occupation of Belgium in 1915.) Unfortunately the Sodality had the full support of Pope Pius X.

During those terrible years some of the Church's greatest and most loyal scholars were penalized. The famous biblical scholar M.J. Lagrange was removed from the École Biblique which he had founded in Jerusalem. Pierre Battifol was dismissed from the post of director of the Institut Catholique in Toulouse. L. Duchesne's monumental and justly famous *Early History of the Church* was put on the Index of Prohibited Books. Those three intellectual giants survived with their scholarship and moral integrity intact, but one wonders how many less robust personalities were literally crushed by the programme of repression.

After the death of Pope Pius X the notorious Sodality was suppressed by his successor in 1921. Concerning its activities and the atmosphere of those times, Archbishop Mignot of Albi (who was thoroughly conversant with the whole problem), stated: 'The most innocent words and deeds, odiously parodied, have been presented as though they were acts of treason to the faith or to the hierarchy. The victim can do nothing but yield, because it is impossible to establish his innocence against a secret and anonymous calumniator.'[26]

After the suppression of the Sodality of Saint Pius V in 1921 the situation for scholars improved for a few years. However, after the Second World War the attitude of suspicion and censure reasserted itself. In the 1950s some of the Church's leading theologians were penalized for no good reason. Chenu, de Lubac, and Congar were all summarily dismissed from their teaching posts and ordered to depart from the towns where they had been teaching. Congar was exiled to England and forbidden to write. That latter prohibition is perhaps the most unjust of all since it amounts to a penalty for crimes which have not yet been committed but which the legislator presumes will be committed by the suspect. It is a tragic reversal of the principle that a person must be presumed innocent until proved guilty. Viewed from another standpoint, it is indicative of the vindictiveness of the authorities and of their immature attitude also.

After Vatican II various measures were enacted to give some kind of protection to scholars whose orthodoxy had been questioned, so that complaints against them could be dealt with by due process, rather than by administrative decisions which could become arbitrary, if not worse. However the most recent set of guidelines represent a return to repressive measures. They have been studied by a canon lawyer who finds them quite simply unsatisfactory.[27] In summary one can say that the process can take place without the suspect's knowing that his writings are being investigated, and in the process the same person is both accuser and judge. The procedures are at variance with the principles of natural justice, and as such they undermine the credibility of the Church. It is another sad example of the way in which the Church's administrative policies work against the authentic tradition of enlightened moral idealism.

Notes

1 Duffy, E. *Saints and Sinners: A History of the Popes.* New Haven, CT 1996, 89. Kuhner, H. *Lexikon der Papste.* Frankfurt 1960, 76.
2 ACOD 191, 198.
3 Ranke-Heinemann, U. *Eunuchs for the Kingdom of Heaven.* (English translation by Peter Heinigg) London 1990, 107.
4 Ranke-Heinemann, 110.
5 Vatican II, *Presbyterorum Ordinis*, section 16, DVII 565.
6 Wills, G. *Papal Sin: Structures of Deceit.* London 2000, 122.
7 *Sacerdotalis Coelibatus*, sections 13 and 38. English translation in *The Papal Encyclicals 1958–1981*, ed. Carlen, C. New York 1981, 206, 209.
8 *The Tablet*, 15 November 1997.
9 *The Guardian*, 2 and 15 September 1998.
10 *The Tablet*, 21 November 1998.
11 *The Tablet*, 6 February 1999.
12 Vogels, H.-J, *Priester dürfen Hieraten*, Bonn 1992. English translation *Celibacy: Gift or Law*, by G.A. Kon, Tunbridge Wells 1992, 98.
13 Vatican II, *Gaudium et Spes*, section 87, DVII, 302.
14 Published in English by the Catholic Truth Society, London 1994.
15 Sipe, A.W.R. *Sex, Priests and Power.* London 1995, 45.
16 *The Catholic Herald*, 11 August 1995, *The Tablet*, 3 February 1996, *Kirche Intern*, October 1998.
17 For this section I am principally dependent on an article in the journal *Religion, State and Society* 21 (ii) 1993, Corley, F. 'The Secret Clergy in Communist Czechoslovakia'. Also *The Tablet*, 11 July 1998.
18 Corley, 175.
19 *The Guardian*, 2 November 1966.
20 *Kirche Intern*, May 1996.
21 Corley, 185.
22 *The Tablet*, 16 May 1992.
23 Morrissey, F. 'Is the New Code an Improvement for the Law of the Catholic Church?' in *Concilium*, June 1986, 36.
24 O'Connell, M. *Critics on Trial: An Introduction to the Catholic Modernist Crisis.* Washington, 1994, 360.
25 O'Connell, M. 363.
26 O'Connell, M.365.
27 The academic lawyer is Ladislas Orsy SJ, whose detailed arguments are to be found in the Second Excursus at the end of this chapter.

The Vatican's Reasons for Retaining Compulsory Clerical Celibacy*

The reasons for obligatory celibacy presented in the *Directory on the Ministry and Life of Priests* (1994) are so misleading that they need to be quoted verbatim, so that readers who do not understand Latin and who do not have access to a comprehensive theological library can evaluate the evidence for themselves. The true underlying thought, namely cultic purity, soon becomes unambiguously clear.

The first council to be invoked is that of Nicaea in 325. Canon 3 states the following:

> The great synod totally forbids that a bishop or priest or anyone else in the clergy should be allowed to have a woman introduced into the house (*suneisakton* in Greek, translated as *subintroductam* in Latin), unless perhaps it be his mother, sister, aunt or those persons who are above suspicion.[1]

The unusual Latin word, *subintroductam* (and its Greek original) became a technical term in Christian usage. It meant a woman living in the same house as a man in a relationship of spiritual marriage. The potential abuses are obvious. It was opposed by various writers and councils, the prohibition in Canon 3 of Nicaea being the most important. The Canon says nothing about the wife of the bishop or priest, yet it is known from other sources that it was normal at that time for them to be married so her presence would not arouse comment.

To have quoted only Canon 3 of Nicaea is misleading. The Church historian Socrates records that the bishops of Nicaea deliberated about imposing perpetual continence on all those in major orders who had married before ordination. He records that Bishop Paphnutius from Egypt opposed the suggestion on the grounds that marriage is honourable and that not all men could practice continence. Admittedly there has been some dispute about the reliability of the report about Paphnutius. Bellarmine and Baronius (both being well-known champions of Catholicism) considered that it was a forgery, but one cannot avoid the suspicion that being so close to the reformation they might have felt uncomfortable with a witness who supported

---

* I published the substance of the following pages in an article in the journal *Priests and People* in November 1996. It is reproduced here in substantially the same form by kind permission of the editor.

Luther's view. Circumstantial evidence would seem to favour the authenticity of the Paphnutius episode. It is clear that the matter of clerical celibacy was discussed at the council. It is equally clear that the rigorous view, adopted by some local councils in the next century, did not prevail. Paphnutius was respected because he had been imprisoned in the persecution of Diocletian and had been punished by the gouging out of one eye. His advice was heeded and the measure was not proceeded with.[2]

The Directory next invoked a local council in Spain, that of Elvira shortly after 300 AD. Canon 27 states:

> A bishop or any other cleric may have with him only a sister or a daughter who is a virgin dedicated to God; it is our decision that he should never have a stranger (*extraneam*).[3]

The reference to the bishop's daughter needs no comment. His wife is not mentioned, probably because her presence was taken for granted.

Canon 33 of the same council, also cited in the *Directory*, presents something of a difficulty, because its plain sense is ambiguous:

> It pleased the synod completely to prohibit bishops, priests, deacons and all clergy serving in the ministry to abstain themselves from their wives and not to beget children: whoever should do this shall be removed from the ranks of the clergy.[4]

H.J. Vogels has made sense of this Canon, which is almost meaningless as it stands. He has shown that it was not one of the original 21 Canons of Elvira but comes from elsewhere. Its wording is identical with number 51 of a collection known as the Eastern Collection of Apostolic Canons, which forbade abstinence from meat, wine and sex. The background was the desire to protect the goodness of creation from an attitude of pessimism about the material world and expressed itself in a perverted abstention from life's intrinsically good pleasures. This gives a coherent meaning to the Canon but it undermines its usefulness in the case for clerical celibacy.[5] In fact, it is a sensible argument in favour of clerical marriage.

The next witness cited in the *Directory* is the letter *Ad Gallos Episcopos* (To the bishops of Gaul), from Pope Damasus, and issued in a synod in Rome in the year 374 or thereabouts. Chapter III is entitled 'Concerning the chastity and cleanness of priests'. The relevant passages are as follows:

> This is established in the first place concerning bishops, priests, and deacons, who of necessity must be present at the divine sacrifices, by whose hands the grace of baptism is conferred and the body of Christ is consecrated, they are compelled to be absolutely chaste, not only by our authority but also by the Holy Scripture, and the Fathers too command them to observe bodily continence ... those who offered the sacrifices in the Temple remained in the temple for a whole year, simply in virtue of their turn of duty, so that they should be clean, hardly knowing their homes ... If intercourse is a pollution, then indeed a priest

must stand ready for the heavenly duty since he is to intercede for the sins of others, lest he should be found unworthy ... and would the priest or deacon dare to contend, being subject to the *behaviour of animals (animalium more)*.[6]

It does not require much subtlety to understand what is the motive behind this statement: quite simply it is the primitive concept of ritual purity. Anthropologists have identified it as one of the most widespread concomitants of primitive religion. It was the attitude that established incompatibility between the sacred and the unclean. This concept applied to such things as disease, contact with dead bodies, and sex. The ancient Israelites held to these principles, derived no doubt from cultural influences in their prehistory prior to the patriarchal epoch. They were incorporated into the Pentateuch, like so much of their cultural heritage, and became a way of expressing obedience to the one true God. The establishment of the New Covenant abolished all such taboos (like the category of prohibited foods). It is puzzling to reflect why the Latin Christians from the fourth century should have revived this element of Pentateuchal law.

The same morbid attitude to sex and cultic purity can be seen in the next witness invoked by the *Directory*, namely the letter of Pope Siricius to the Bishop Himerius of Tarragona in the year 385. Section 9 of the letter, referring to the priests of the Old Testament, says as follows:

'Be holy, because I the Lord your God am holy.' (Levit. 20:7). Why were the priests commanded to dwell in the temple, far from their homes in the year of their tour of duty? Clearly it was for this reason, that they should not have carnal intercourse with their wives so that with conscience gleaming with integrity, they could offer an acceptable gift to God.

Priests and deacons are constrained by a binding law of continence ... all priests and Levites, we are bound by an indissoluble law, that from the day of our ordination we are constrained by sobriety and modesty of heart and body, so that we may please God in all things in the sacrifices which we offer daily. (Section 10)[7]

In addition to supplying further evidence for the understanding of cultic purity, which underpinned those regulations, the letter also affords evidence of how early the Roman community had adopted the daily celebration of the Eucharist. It has been suggested convincingly by R. Gryson that this was the decisive factor which brought about different disciplines in the Greek- and Latin-speaking parts of the Church.[8] The Greeks held to the older tradition of celebrating the Eucharist on Sundays only, and presumably the priests abstained from sex on Saturday evenings. The impurity incurred by sexual intercourse was deemed to wear off in the course of the day! Leviticus 15:18 explains the supposed problem: 'If a man lies with a woman and has an emission of semen, both of them shall bathe themselves in water, and shall be unclean until the evening.'

Pope Siricius had occasion to return to the matter again in 386 in a council attended by 80 bishops, whose decisions were recorded in a letter dated 6 January of that year. In chapter 9 we read:

> We consider that priests and Levites should not have intercourse with their wives because, in the ministry, the ministers are occupied with obligations which occur every day.

The document concludes with a list of Canons, the fourth of which declares:

> Bishops priests and deacons should abstain from their wives.[9]

Towards the end of the fourth century a number of councils in North Africa give evidence of the same prohibitions. The council of Carthage of AD 390 stated quite briefly in its second canon that 'Bishops priests and Levites must abstain from (conjugal relations) with their wives'.[10]

In the same city, the council of 401 stated the same principle but with more elaboration. Canon 4 declared:

> Bishops, priests and deacons shall not live with their wives; if they do so they must withdraw from their functions. The other clerics will not be held to continence.[11]

The distinction between the two classes of clergy is clearly because the former actually touched with their hands the consecrated elements of the Eucharist.

The Council of Telepte cannot be dated with exactitude, but it was about 418. Its ninth Canon stated:

> We wish to recommend that which is worthy, modest, and honest, namely that priests and Levites should not have intercourse with their wives because they are occupied by the daily demands of the service in the ministry.[12]

The next witness cited in the *Directory* is Innocent I, who was pope from 402–17. He dealt with clerical continence in his letter number 6, in which he gave replies to a number of enquiries about pastoral matters:

> You have asked what is to be observed, in the case of those who do not or did not observe continence, and produced children, although they were ranked in the ministry of deacons or priests. Concerning these the rule from the divine law is clear, and equally well known are the commands of bishop Siricius, of blessed memory. Namely that those who are placed in such orders who are incontinent, shall be deprived of all ecclesiastical rank, nor shall they be allowed to approach the service which continence alone should fulfil. For there is originally the sacred authority of the Old Law, which was a rule from the beginning, namely that the priests were commanded to inhabit the Temple for the year of their

service [Luke I] … Priests whose ordinary occupation is to pray and to offer sacrifice, must always abstain from this kind of intimacy. If he should be contaminated by carnal concupiscence how would he presume to take up the duty of sacrifice?[13]

As with other evidence cited by the *Directory* the motive is plainly that sex between husband and wife was regarded as morally unclean, so as to render a married priest ritually impure and debarred, at least temporarily, from the sacrifice of the Mass.

Leo the Great (pope from 440 to 461) is the next authority invoked by the *Directory*. He wrote about the matter in his letter 167, which is a series of answers to questions put to him about practical matters of Church discipline. The third enquiry was: 'Concerning those who minister at the altar, and who have wives, whether they may lawfully have intercourse with them?' Pope Leo replied:

The law of continence is the same for ministers of the altar, be they bishops or priests. When they were laymen or lectors it was lawful for them to contract marriage, and they were able to beget children. But when they were promoted to the aforementioned ranks, that which had been licit was no longer licit. Whence, in order that the carnal marriage may become a spiritual one, they ought not to dismiss their wives, but retain them as if they did not have them, by which means both connubial charity is safeguarded, and the activities of marriage cease.[14]

Clearly the underlying rationale is that those who actually handle the Eucharist must be ritually pure.

The Eastern part of the Church seems to have been far less worried about the whole matter. As with the Latins, there is no evidence prior to the fourth century, other than the fact that a married clergy is seen to be the universal practice when the documentation of the fourth and later centuries illuminates the scene.

The Council of Neocaesarea, which can be dated no more precisely than between 314 and 325, enacted in its first Canon that:

If a priest married, he will be excluded from the ranks of the clergy: if he should be guilty of adultery or fornication he will be excommunicated and must submit to penance.[15]

It is interesting to note that the same council's eleventh Canon prescribed that the minimum age for ordination should be 30. In a sense, this clarifies most of the practical matters. Those who wished to marry would have done so perhaps a decade earlier, and would probably have produced as many children as they wished for. Having derived that much fulfilment from their marriages, possibly the requirement of future continence was not regarded as an excessive burden.

Later in that century Eusebius, writing in his *Demonstratio Evangelica*, dealt with the matter obliquely. Commenting on the First Letter to Timothy 3:2, where St. Paul had stated that a bishop should be a man of one wife, he stated:

> Those who have been consecrated and who are occupied with the divine service are recommended (*prosekei*) to refrain from intercourse with their wives.[16]

In the latter part of the fourth century Epiphanius furnished two pieces of evidence which are referred to by the *Directory*. In his major work *Against All Heresies*, he touched on the matter in the section against the Montanists (Book II, vol. I chapter 9), in which he stated that a second marriage was forbidden to priests.[17] That is all. In the same work in the section against the Cathars he declared (chapter 4) that remarriage after the death of a wife was permissible because of human frailty, but not for the priest 'who would have refrained from intercourse with one wife'.[18]

Epiphanius returned to the theme in his *Expositio Fidei* (Book 3, vol. 2, chapter 21), once again in the context of forbidding a second marriage to a priest: 'It is customary to elevate to the priesthood those who refrain from their wives, or who are living as widowers after one marriage.'[19]

All things considered it is a meagre amount of evidence from the Eastern Church, which was clearly less anxious about supposed sexual deviation than the Latins. The classical statement for the Greek-speaking Christians, which set the tone for the whole future pattern, was the Council in Trullo of 692.

- Canon 3 forbade a second marriage to anyone in the clergy.
- Canon 6 decreed that only those in minor orders were entitled to enter upon a marriage (as opposed to the ordination of a man who was already married).
- Canon 12 stated that bishops should not live with their wives after their consecration.
- Canon 13 deals with priestly continence and I will quote it in full:

> In the Roman church, those who wish to receive the diaconate or priesthood promise to have no further intercourse with their wives. As for us who keep the Apostolic Canons, we permit the continuation of the conjugal life. Whoever wishes to dissolve such unions will be deposed, and the cleric who under pretext of religion abandons his wife, will be excommunicated. The subdeacons, deacons and priests must always abstain from sexual intercourse with their wives during the time when they exercise their sacred functions, for the council of Carthage has ordained that whoever serves in the sanctuary must be pure.[20]

The last sentence of that canon indicates that the Greeks at that period shared the same attitude as the Latins to the concept of cultic purity. However, as Gryson pointed out (see above) the retention of the older practice of mass on Sundays only ensured that their practice and law would remain different from that of the Latins, whose priests celebrated mass daily from at least the fourth century.

That is the sum total of evidence, presented by the *Directory*, and it is frankly inconceivable that it should have been published in the twentieth century. It has nothing to do with the grace of celibacy by which a man will choose to remain single for spiritual reasons and thereby leave himself available for ordination, according to the present discipline of the Western Church. The only evidence advanced by the *Directory* is that of concern about cultic purity. Frankly, the *Directory* is misleading, to put the matter mildly. Cultic purity is a primitive pagan concept which entered the Church's discipline in the fourth century via the Old Testament, together with the quaint notion that impurity wore off in the course of the day (Lev. 15:16)! With the wisdom of hindsight we can see now that they were badly mistaken. Such an attitude is incompatible with what Vatican II stated explicitly about the intrinsic goodness of sex between husband and wife.[21]

If the Roman Curia wishes to base the law of mandatory priestly celibacy on arguments such as those, then presumably they have their own reasons for doing so. However on the basis of the evidence presented in the *Directory* they can hardly expect to command confidence among the generality of the Church.

The only thorough treatment of the matter from the conservative point of view, since Vatican II, is that of Christian Cochini who invoked the argument from cultic purity a few years before it was adopted by the *Directory*. Although he cites mostly the same ancient authorities as the Vatican's document, he does not seem to realize that it was a pagan concept which has nothing to do with the letter or spirit of the New Testament. He invokes a somewhat vague notion of the separateness of the tribe of Levi, which symbolized their sacred functions. It is almost superfluous to point out the inconsistencies of such symbolism, since the Levites continued to reproduce in a healthy fashion.[22]

The Vatican's *Directory* represents a very serious misdirection of moral guidance, because it is based upon such faulty reasoning. Least of all can they expect intelligent young men to commit themselves to a lifelong privation on the basis of pagan cultic purity.

Notes

1   ACOD 7. For *suneisakton*, see *A Patristic Greek Lexicon*, ed. G. Lampe, Oxford, 1961, 1317,1318.
2   Socrates, *Ecclesiastical History*, I.11 London 1874.
3   DS 118.
4   DS 119.
5   Vogels, H.-J. *Celibacy: Gift or Law*, London, 1992, 29.
6   MPL, vol. 13, 1181-94. [Italics, mine.]

7   DS 185.
8   Gryson, R. *Les Origines du Célibat Ecclesiastique*, Gembloux, 1970, *passim*.
9   Bruns, H. (1839), *Canones Apostolorum et Conciliorum Saec. IV–VII*, Berlin. Reprinted Turin, 1959, vol. 2 (i), 154–5.
10 Hefele, K. and Leclercq, J. (1908–49) *Histoire des Conciles*, Paris, Vol. II (i) 77.
11 Hefele and Leclercq, vol. II (i) 127.
12 Hefele and Leclercq, vol. II (i) 71.
13 MPL, vol. 20, 496,497.
14 MPL, vol. 54, 1204.
15 Hefele and Leclercq, vol. I (i) 327.
16 MPG, vol. 22, 781.
17 MPG, vol. 41, 868.
18 MPG, vol. 41, 1024.
19 MPG. vol. 42, 824.
20 Hefele and Leclercq, vol. III (i), 560–78.
21 Vatican II, *Gaudium et Spes*, section 49, DVII, 253.
22 Cochini, C. *Apostolic Origins of Priestly Celibacy*, English translation, San Francisco, 1992, 418, 429, 430.

Excursus 2

Procedures Against Suspect Theologians*

On 29 June 1997, the Congregation for the Doctrine of the Faith promulgated new procedural rules entitled *Regulations for the Examination of Doctrines*. They have superseded the norms published in 1971.

The explanatory note issued by the Holy See said that after 25 years of experience it had been decided 'to prepare new regulations that might respond even better to the demands of the present day'.

By referring to 'demands of the present day' – demands of justice, obviously – the document itself invites us to consider whether it meets them.

Part I: The Regulations

Let us look first at the provisions for an 'examination in ordinary form' where the aim is to decide whether there are erroneous and/or dangerous propositions in the writings.

The process consists of two sequences: the first is internal and takes place in complete secrecy. The congress (that is the senior administrators of the permanent staff of the Congregation for the Doctrine of the Faith) commissions a council of consultors to examine the writings in question and to ascertain if the author's doctrine does, or does not, conform to the Church's teaching.

To help these experts, the congress appoints a 'relator for the author'. His task is to represent and uphold the author's interest, ensure that the author's opinions are correctly understood, and see that the examiners are informed of the 'positive aspects' of the author's writings.

The consultors conclude their investigation with a formal session. Taking into account the earlier study prepared by the office, they discuss the case. The relator for the author must be present and has a voice; the Ordinary (that is the bishop of the diocese where the author lives) of the author may also be invited to participate in the debate (if so, he is bound to secrecy). Once the formal discussion is over, the consultors alone decide if the author's writings contain erroneous propositions and/or dangerous opinions.

The criteria for the identification of an offence are much broader than the denial of an article of faith. They include not only the Nicene Creed, subse-

---

* The substance of this section was originally published by Ladislas Orsy in *The Tablet*, 16 January 1999, and is reproduced here by kind permission of the author and editor.

quent solemn definitions, and determinations by the ordinary magisterium or teaching office but also 'definitive teachings' given by the popes and the episcopal college and official pronouncements even if not intended to be definitive.

We have to recall that the formula of the profession of faith introduced in 1983 by the Congregation for the Doctrine of the Faith contains a novelty: it includes acceptance of doctrine definitively declared by the magisterium and submission to non-definitively intended official pronouncements. It would be hard to find a precedent in Christian history, Eastern or Western, for such a presentation of a profession of faith.

The council's judgement with all the acts and minutes is then brought before the ordinary session of the Congregation. The members may decide either not to pursue the case any further or to continue it by confronting the author with his erroneous propositions and/or dangerous opinions. The Congregation's decision must in any case be submitted to the pope.

If the pope agrees to the confrontation, the case moves on. For all practical purposes the author under investigation is charged with spreading erroneous or dangerous opinions. His Ordinary, all other Ordinaries who may have interest in the case, and the competent departments of the Holy See are informed.

There follows a second sequence with limited publicity. The focus of the proceedings now turns from an examination of the writings to a trial of the person. The author is informed of the findings through his Ordinary and is given a list of the erroneous or dangerous propositions found in his writings with due explanations for the negative judgements. The regulations do not say who is competent to provide these explanations and the identity of the 'explainer' cannot be revealed.

With the consent of his Ordinary, the author is entitled to appoint an 'adviser' for himself. This adviser is not an advocate with the legal right of defending the author; he is closer to a private counsellor who has the right to be present at his side. The author has three months to respond to the Congregation concerning the propositions that are contested. His Ordinary is encouraged to express an opinion. The author has no right to appear before his judges, but the Congregation [presumably the Prefect] may grant him permission, with his adviser present, to hold a dialogue with the delegates of the Congregation. At the meeting minutes must be taken and signed by all.

If the author does respond in this way, the congress is competent to receive his answer. Should it contain new grounds for reconsideration, the congress may choose to remit the case again to the council of consultors. The response of the author with the result of the renewed consultations [if any] must finally be submitted to the ordinary session of the Congregation. If the author does not respond, the same ordinary session is competent to take 'an appropriate decision'.

So much for the examination in ordinary form; let us now consider the provisions for an 'examination in urgent form'. This is a shortened version of the ordinary process described so far, to be used in an emergency. A 'process in urgency' is authorized whenever it is clear and certain that the writings of an author contain errors that are either directly threatening the faith of the people or effectively causing damage among them.

The congress is competent to determine the existence of an emergency and the need for immediate action. Once this is done, it sends information to all Ordinaries who may have an interest in the case and to the competent departments of the Holy See. Then it appoints a commission to identify precisely the erroneous and dangerous opinions. The harmful propositions are submitted to the ordinary session of the Congregation which must give precedence to the case. If its judgement is condemnatory, the decision must go to the pope for his approval. If the pope ratifies the sentence, the author is notified and is given three months to correct his opinions. He may, however, request permission to offer a written explanation. The ordinary session is competent to receive it and to judge it.

Incidentally, there is an inconsistency, real or verbal, in this section of the regulations. First the text states that the emergency procedures should be used openly in the case of clear and certain 'errors'; then it speaks of its use in the case of 'erroneous and dangerous propositions'. They are not the same.

The Congregation then has to decide the punishment. If the author has not corrected his errors 'in a satisfactory way and with adequate publicity', and the ordinary session found him guilty of the 'offence of heresy, apostasy, or schism', the congregation proceeds to declare the *latae sententiae* – that is automatic – penalties incurred. The reference to a Canon of the Code of Canon Law makes clear that the penalty is excommunication. 'Against such a declaration no recourse is admitted.' If the author has been found guilty of a lesser offence, the Congregation is entitled to impose a lesser sanction according to the general norms of the law.

The two articles on sanctions have been specially approved by the pope; that is, they have the binding force of a pontifical law.

Part II: The Legal Wisdom of our Age

As I reflect on the legal wisdom of our age, I am really speaking of expectations because we do not have anywhere in the world a perfect judicial system. We have convergent expectations that express the best that can be distilled from the experience and prudence of many nations. The more a judicial process fulfils such expectations, the better the cause of justice is served.

On purpose I avoid speaking about 'due process' because the expression can generate misunderstandings in two ways. First, the literal meaning of 'due process' is a process 'according to the requirements of the law' – hence not arbitrary. By dry logic, it could be argued (and has been) that even judicial systems which are of poor standard are observant of 'due process' since they conform to the local laws. Secondly, since the expression is known as referring to the procedural rules of the common law of English origin, it can (as experience shows) provoke in persons unfamiliar with the common law fear and suspicion that to invoke due process is to introduce alien conceptions into canon law.

The expectations I speak of go beyond the boundaries of any one legal system; they exist the world over among citizens of many nations. They focus on a 'fair process' which includes also much of what is best in the 'due process' tradition.

Legal Principles and the Regulations

In each of the following paragraphs, I shall state first a general principle held in honour by modern jurisprudence and meant to protect human rights; then I shall see how the procedures set out in the regulations correspond to such an expectation.

Justice demands the precise definition of an offence.   The principle speaks for itself: the less precise the definition of a crime or offence is, the greater the danger of injustice in court proceedings because a great multitude of actions can be brought under the definition. A vague term opens the way to broad accusations and restricts the scope of the defence: that is why totalitarian states like to have definitions of crimes broadly drawn such as 'crimes against the state' or 'subversive speech'.

The regulations name two offences (without giving any precise definition) that warrant investigations: 'erroneous doctrine' and/or 'dangerous doctrine' found in published writings.

'Erroneous doctrine' can have different meanings here. Catholic theology has always carefully distinguished between revealed articles of faith, beliefs connected with revelation [in various degrees], opinions commonly held by theologians, and so forth. If a position is judged erroneous, to understand the gravity of the error one must know the authority of the truth that it seems to deny. The regulations do not take into account such a hierarchy of truths insisted on by the Second Vatican Council. They allow proceedings (and condemnation) against the author even when he fully assents to the doctrine of faith but dissents from an official 'definitive' or 'non-definitive' proclamation.

The expression 'dangerous doctrine' gives a broad scope to the examiners: with its help they can reach far and wide. The concept has no firm and objective limit. Dangers can be detected in many places; persons and communities can be seen as exposed to dangers in many ways. The perception of a danger can be subjective and deceptive: much depends on the mind of the observer. Many times at the Second Vatican council, before the doctrine of episcopal collegiality was finally approved, its opponents demanded that the doctrine should be discarded since it was dangerous. It would undermine the primacy they warned. Yet today we all hold that collegiality belongs to the core of Catholic beliefs. Down through Christian history, many more instances could be found when true insights emerged but many cried 'Danger'. Is this not what happened in the case of Gallileo? To make 'danger' (ill-defined or not defined) a juridical ground for condemnation is to endanger the operation of justice itself.

Justice is best served when, in the process, the respective roles of the judge, the prosecutor, and the defendant are kept apart. The aim of any judicial process is to help the judge (or jury) to arrive at an impartial and detached judgement. The accumulated experience of courts and tribunals (an experience originating in ancient civilizations) has shown that when the roles are fused, justice is imperilled. The dynamics of the investigation and of the trial carry the prosecutor (or the examiner) in one direction, the defendant in another. If either assumes the role of the judge as well, the objective outcome of the trial is put in jeopardy.

In the *Regulations for the Examination of Doctrines* this classical distinction is not honoured. The same organs of the Congregation for the Doctrine of the Faith initiate the investigation, establish the charges, and then pronounce judgement over both the writings and the writer. In practice, the same persons are investigators, prosecutors, and judges.

Equity [which is the perfection of justice] postulates that each of the opposing parties has a similar opportunity to plead their case before the judge. A trial is nothing else than a dialectical argumentation to bring the judge (and all others concerned) as close to the truth as possible. Justice postulates 'fair play', that is, a similar measure for both sides. If one of the parties is not heard as well and as fully as the other, that party is exposed to the risk of not being heard at all.

The regulations, however, grant different measures (far from any equal time) respectively to the accusers and the defender. During the first part of the ordinary process, where a crucial decision is taken about the meaning of the author's writings, he is absent; he does not even know that there is a process. A relator appointed by the investigators is called to defend him and to clarify the sense of his contested publications. (Is there not a conflict of interest?)

If the outcome of the investigation is negative and the Congregation finds the author's propositions erroneous or dangerous, his Ordinary and the competent offices of the Holy See are informed. In other words, the notice of the condemnation is spread and the author's reputation is affected without his ever having been notified of any problem, let alone having had the possibility to say a word in his own defence.

Many scholars, researchers and writers live and work in a culture and use a language different from those of the Roman examiners. The risk, therefore, of a serious misunderstanding is high. We have only to recall how theological misunderstandings between the Greeks and the Latins arose leading to mutual accusations and condemnations, and finally to the tragic separation of the Churches. Today we know that, in spite of seemingly conflicting expressions, the doctrine of faith has never been endangered.

The Church has nothing to lose and much to gain by taking all precautions against mistaken perceptions and letting a writer explain in person his position right at the moment when a serious problem first emerges.

The duty of the judge is to presume the accused innocent [and protect him] until the evidence proves beyond reasonable doubt that he is guilty. In a developed system of justice, the principle of the presumption of innocence is an inviolable part of criminal proceedings. To speak of the duty of the judge may be an unusual way of presenting this principle, but it is a good way of stating it. It names the person who is mainly responsible for upholding the principle.

The presumption is not mentioned in the regulations. The first part of the 'ordinary proceedings' is concerned with writings; in theory the person himself is not affected. So far, perhaps one can say that no presumption of guilt or innocence exists in the examiners one way or another.

If, however, their conclusion concerning the writings is negative, they must confront the author with the propositions that they have already judged erroneous and/or dangerous. How could they then presume the author to be innocent? There would be no problem if the examiners were merely accusers and an independent judge (or judges) watched over the confrontation. But that is not the case: the examiners (who are now accusers) will have a part in the final decision.

Incidentally, there is no reason why even within the Congregation a system could not be set up where the judges remain distinct in every way from the accusers. After all, the Code of Canon Law prescribes that in every ecclesiastical tribunal there should be judges and a 'promoter of justice' (whose task is analogous to that of the examiners). It is unthinkable that the same person should assume both tasks; if it ever happened, the sentence would be irreparably null and void.

All that affects a public sentence ought to be done openly. [Not only ought justice to be done; it ought also to be seen to be done]. The virtue of justice (as integrated with faith, hope and love among Christians) is a powerful factor in forging unity in the community. For this reason the whole judicial system of the Church should be a visible witness to evangelical justice for all who care to look. This is not to deny that prudence and discretion may require some confidentiality; it is to affirm that all that affects the public sentence should be done openly. A trial is never about one single individual: the accused is a member of a community of believers. Whether he is guilty or not, the community nurtured him and suffers with him. It should be informed. Such openness should not become unbridled publicity; there are many ways of communicating with responsible people.

Overall, the regulations fall short of the standards of an open trial: in particular, the first part of the ordinary proceedings is shrouded in complete secrecy.

The opportunity for appeal is an integral part of any good judicial system. To leave room for appeal is to acknowledge our human condition: we are fallible human beings – judges not excepted. A process with no possibility of appeal is a scary system for any lawyer to contemplate: it leaves no room for the correction of mistakes.

The regulations state that once the Congregation has declared that the author has incurred automatic excommunication, 'against such a declaration no recourse is admitted'. In the explanatory notes the reason is given: throughout the process, the pope himself is involved so there cannot be any room for appeal. It is hardly conceivable, however, that the pope would invoke his full apostolic authority to pronounce an infallible judgement in an ordinary process. Further his infallibility cannot be delegated to the Congregation. It would, therefore, be rash to exclude the possibility of a miscarriage of justice.

We are touching on a substantial structural weakness in the regulations: a trial is directed immediately to the highest level involving the pope himself. Sound jurisprudence would postulate a court or tribunal of first instance at a lower level from which there would be an appeal to a higher court. In marriage cases the Roman Rota admits an appeal even against its own decisions: how much more prudent it would be to admit an appeal in doctrinal cases! As things are now, the pope must be involved in every single 'doctrinal examination'. Should ever a miscarriage of justice occur, it would immediately reflect on the papal office. Not a good prospect to contemplate.

The penalty of automatic excommunication. Excommunication is an extreme penalty in a Christian community: it is a wrenching of a member from the body of the believers. As with all extreme penalties, it punishes both the individual and the community. The individual is spiritually incapacitated: he cannot receive the sacraments. The community suffers the trauma of an amputation: it loses the support of an organ. Automatic excommunication is an anachronism that hurts modern sensitivities: it operates in secrecy without control. The offender is mandated to be his own accuser and judge. He must cut himself off from the body.

It would be difficult to decide whether excommunications have done more good than harm to the Church throughout history. What we know for certain is that some excommunications have done enormous harm. We can recall the hasty and tragic gesture of Humbert, the papal legate in Constantinople, who in 1054 excommunicated the Patriarch and thus contributed to the enduring severance of the two sister Churches, East and West. Or we may ponder the impact of the excommunication in 1570 of Elizabeth I by Pius V; it was a harsh sentence that effectively destroyed any hope of reconciliation between the English monarchy and the see of Rome.

The regulations warn that if an accused does not correct his position within the time allotted to him, the Congregation can proceed to the declaration of excommunication. This may happen even if the author has never had the opportunity to explain his mind to his judges.

The regulations ignore a crucial problem: the crime of heresy is an 'obstinate denial' of an article of faith (Canon 751); it is a surrender to falsehood while one sees the light. Such an act of self-destruction is certainly possible, no less than suicide is possible, but it is not an ordinary event. Even if it has been established that the writings of a person contain heretical propositions, it does not follow necessarily that he is guided by a perverse intention. To rush into the imposition of an extreme sentence (perhaps without ever having listened to the author) can hardly be the sign and symbol of justice – let alone Christian mercy. Most of the time, for the good of the community, it should be enough to state with authority what our Catholic doctrine is, and what our tradition is not – and then let time, fraternal correction, and divine grace have their gentle impact on the author.

Many thoughtful theologians and canonists suggested before the last revision of the Code of Canon Law that automatic excommunications (their name was Legion) should be abolished altogether. The revision cancelled out many but retained a few. To delete them all from canon law would be no loss to the faithful – or to the reputation of the Church.

One story that is unfolding now should give us pause: there is an increasing consensus among theologians and historians that, on several counts, the Council of Trent misunderstood the teachings of the Reformers and consequently several anathemas were misplaced. Ecumenical scholars are putting immense effort into the disentangling of such mistakes; and as truth reveals itself the expressions of regrets are becoming more numerous. If such misunderstandings could occur at an Ecumenical Council, they could surely occur within the Church's ordinary administration.

Conclusion: Creating a Climate of Trust

An immediate conclusion emerges in stark simplicity: for anyone educated in the sensitivities of modern jurisprudence, the regulations do not in fact respond 'to the demands of the present day'. Overall, they are not signs or symbols of justice. They have their roots in past ages which did not have the same vision of the dignity of human persons and the same respect for honest conscience that is demanded the world over today.

On reflection, the conclusion expands: the regulations do not really fulfil the mandate of the Congregation for the Doctrine of the Faith, as this mandate is stated in its own documents. The integral mission of the Congregation goes well beyond investigating, prosecuting, and punishing offences against the faith. It embraces the 'promoting and safeguarding' of the 'doctrine of faith and morals throughout the Catholic world'. In the Catholic world, the best way of promoting and safeguarding the doctrine of faith is to create a climate of trust where the process described by St Anselm of Canterbury as 'faith seeking understanding' (*fides quaerens intellectum*) can flourish. Such a search for understanding is carried out mostly (not exclusively) by professional theologians. To attract young and talented persons to choose theological research and reflection as their vocation, to strengthen those who are already dedicated to that work, and to lift the spirit of those who are struggling with the hard issues of our days, an environment of freedom and confidence is absolutely necessary. Such an environment cannot exist if investigations, accusations, and even condemnations are allowed to take place in secrecy.

Creative thinkers who scrutinize the divine mysteries and give us a language to speak about them must be constantly aware that the Church trusts them and protects them. If norms are needed to prevent deviations, norms are even more needed to secure legitimate freedom for creative thinking.

In truth, creative thinkers are one of the greatest assets of the Church today – and ever. The recent encyclical of Pope John Paul II on faith and reason, *Fides et Ratio*, is, every page of it, a solemn proclamation of this truth. As our world evolves, new questions are continually addressed to the Church about how to understand revelation, about the role of religion in political society, justice in the distribution of the resources of the earth, issues of morality and so forth. Learned persons who are capable of reaching new insights into our old tradition can be of valuable (even indispensable) assistance to the hierarchy who have the final judgement in doctrinal matters and to all the faithful who are seeking insight into the mysteries with a sincere heart. This was the ministry of St Thomas Aquinas or of Cardinal John Henry Newman.

The judicial procedures of the regulations are entirely of human composition. They are not rooted in any venerable tradition: they are the product of post-Tridentine defensive policies. To work for their reform is not to harm any divine institution, quite the contrary. It is to accept, honour and obey the forceful admonition of the Second Vatican Council. 'Christ summons the Church, as she goes her pilgrim way, to that continual reformation of which she always has need, insofar as she is a human institution here on earth,' said the Council in its decree on ecumenism.

Ultimately we should trust the internal strength of the word of God. Cardinal Newman's insight in his *Essay on the Development of Christian Doctrine*, chapter 5, remains as valid today as ever: 'The stronger and more living is an idea, that is, the more powerful hold it exercises on the minds of men, the more able is it to dispense with safeguards, and trust to itself against the danger of corruption.'

There is no stronger 'idea' given to the human family than the 'idea' of Christianity. It is born of God and the source of its 'internal vigour' (Newman's words) is the ever-living Spirit. Its power over the minds of human beings is immense. It follows that the prime purpose of our norms, regulations, and procedures should not be to protect the idea (since it can trust to itself against the danger of corruption), but to secure an environment of freedom where it can spread, take roots in minds and hearts, and bring forth fruit a hundredfold.

Chapter 7

Obedience or Subservience

Obedience – this virtue is a paradox. Its importance has been stressed by many moralists[1] yet, as I will show in the course of this chapter, it is arguable that as much harm has been done in the name of obedience as has been done by disobedience. On the one hand it has facilitated the activities of politicians like Hitler when he wanted docile people to do his bidding, and in the same way it has inhibited Christians from taking an independent line when nonconformism was required.

Aquinas classified it with justice. To use his own technical terminology it is a potential part of justice.[2] In spite of the quaint language, it has the advantage of preparing the agenda so that we can evaluate its harmful excesses as easily as its harmful shortcomings, that is being too obedient or insufficiently obedient. At this stage it is useful to reflect that obedience as such is morally neutral. That is to say, to submit one's actions to the decision of another has no intrinsic goodness. It is arguable that for an adult it is in principle wrong to relinquish one's moral autonomy by handing over responsibility for one's practical decisions to another. In many situations people have no choice in practice, granted the necessity of earning one's living and thus submitting to the dictates of one's employer.

The moral quality of obedient behaviour arises mainly from the purposes linked to the total process of the one who commands and the collaboration of his subordinates. For example, it may be invoked to curtail conflicting ambitions or to coordinate the work of a group like the interaction of teachers and pupils in a school. In such a case it is reasonable and therefore morally acceptable to abide by the orders of the head teacher.

Whereas an individual might offend against obedience, quantitatively so to speak, by giving too much submission to superiors (like Hitler) or too little (like teenage rebels), the Church as a community has offended qualitatively by imitating a style of authority derived from secular models. Authoritarianism and autocratic behaviour are unnecessary and repulsive even among politicians, generals, and captains of industry. When this style of leadership is adopted by Church leaders it constitutes an affront to the gospel. Jesus stated clearly that secular models of authority had no place among his followers: 'You know that the rulers of the gentiles lord it over them, and their great men exercise authority over them. It shall not be so among you but whoever would be great among your must be your servant' (Matt. 20:25). The Second Vatican Council took up that theme and applied it explicitly to the manner in which authority should be exercised in the

Church. In the section devoted to the hierarchical structure of the Church we read the following:

> For the nurturing and constant growth of the People of God, Christ the Lord instituted in His Church a variety of ministries, which work for the good of the whole body. For those ministers who are endowed with sacred power are servants of their brethren, so that all who are of the People of God, and therefore enjoy a true Christian dignity, can work toward a common goal freely and in an orderly way, and arrive at salvation.[3]

The same message was repeated in the context of the bishops' responsibility for the Church's worldwide mission. 'Now, that duty which the Lord committed to the shepherds of his people, is a true service, and in sacred literature is significantly called "diakonia" or ministry.'[4] The ramifications of that understanding of the nature of authority as service were studied extensively in the period of the Council.[5] The practical realization soon showed itself in small but significant details such as the abandonment of the old custom of genuflecting to a bishop to kiss his ring on meeting him. From then onwards lay people and priests started to shake hands with bishops as they would with other members of the human race.

The worst departures from the gospel ideal of authority were to be seen in the high Middle Ages when the Papal States were functioning in the same way as the other sovereign states in Europe. At that period the popes acted in the same way as their secular counterparts. Other members of the ecclesiastical hierarchy in countries other than the Papal States tended to adopt the same style of exercising authority in purely ecclesiastical affairs. Moreover there was a further source of confusion between spiritual and political activity in the careers of men like Cardinal Wolsey who were entrusted with high office in both Church and State. Unfortunately the loss of the Papal States in the nineteenth century did not see the end of that style of authority and the corresponding manner in which obedience was required.

In spite of such abuses, the balanced exercise of obedience does have value. One example, chosen more or less at random, can illustrate its usefulness. At the start of the Second World War a group of conscientious objectors decided to work a smallholding together and live under the same roof. They were all recent graduates from university, and extremely high-minded. Very soon tensions developed within the group. These became more intense and after a few months the group was riven with the most bitter dissensions. At that point one of them made a journey to a nearby monastery, took instruction, and became both a Catholic and a lay oblate of the monastery.

His turning to a monastery is instructive since it seems that a group of zealots, living together, can easily turn to fanaticism unless their enthusiasm is carefully regulated. St Benedict seems to have perceived this in the writing of his Rule which has undoubtedly stood the test of time. It is worth noting that voluntary bodies like Amnesty International and the War on

Want have also experienced destructive tensions among their workers. It is probably the success of the Benedictine rule that has earned a high reputation for the virtue of obedience.

One caution is necessary at the beginning of an analysis of obedience. St Benedict's model was the Roman extended family, and the abbot occupies the place of the paterfamilias. Without being carping or mean, it is worth noting that this is not a model that is offered by the New Testament. Indeed the gospels and epistles say very little about obedience. When St. Paul uses the word, it is usually a synonym for faith. Occasionally the concept occurs in the injunctions for children to obey their parents, wives to obey their husbands, slaves to obey their masters, and all to obey the emperor and magistrates (cf. Eph. 5:23–6:9, Col. 3:18–25. I Peter 2:13–3:6). (It is interesting to note that the New Testament makes no distinction between obedience to secular or religious superiors.) Since these injunctions are so much at variance with St Paul's constant teaching on freedom from law, their interpretation has occasioned some difficulty. It has been suggested that they are interpolations into the original text. But this is difficult to sustain, since it would have entailed tampering with two Pauline letters and one of St Peter, all of which were circulating independently prior to the establishment of the New Testament corpus.

Schillebeeckx has suggested that they represent the desire of the infant Church not to disturb the existing social order lest they should incur more hostility from the pagans than was inevitable; instead, they should accept the social order as it stood and live out their Christian convictions within it.[6] Clearly the infant Church had enough problems in defining its self-identity and independence of Judaism, and establishing itself as a unique international community in which all races, cultures, and nationalities were equal, without wanting to add to their problems by openly provoking hostility by battles over what were regarded as non-essentials. Loyalty to their essential beliefs was earning them quite enough persecution!

The concept of obedience presents considerable difficulties for the modern mind since we have grown up in societies where democratic freedoms are taken for granted. A glance at the past is instructive. After Gutenberg had invented printing in the fifteenth century, the governments of the day perceived its potential for fomenting political unrest. The licensing of printers as well as the censorship of books and plays became normal. This can be seen in such disparate examples as the invigilating over the printing presses in Tudor England, and the theatre of Molière and Voltaire in France. In Italy the practice survived well into the nineteenth century, and in the north, under Austrian hegemony, the composer Verdi had constant problems with the censors in the production of his operas. At the same time, in Russia the serfs were still making their annual token of loyalty to the landowners by prostrating before them on the latters' birthdays. In such a climate of opinion, Pope Pius IX's desire to hold on to every scrap of authority is understandable. His condemnation of the proposition that the abrogation of his temporal power would be conducive to the well-being of the Church is not so outlandish.[7] In the twentieth century it looks like an unwarrantable thirst for power.

In a world that experienced so much political repression and control, the Church's insistence on obedience did not seem out of place. The twentieth century changed all of that. We are now accustomed to giving our loyalty to governments which we criticize openly in the columns of a free press and which we can vote out of office. In the Westminster parliament the Leader of the Opposition is an official position with its own salary attached. These are marks of a mature society, and this pattern of activity should be regarded as one of the authentic achievements of human progress. Uncritical obedience to superiors has an ever-diminishing role in such a society.

Paradoxically it is alive (but not well) in the Church, and therein lies our problem. It is my contention in this chapter that immense moral harm has been done by the Catholic Church's overemphasis on obedience, and the concomitants which attend it, namely the absence of free speech, consultation, and criticism. As I pointed out in a previous chapter, at the homely level of the parish, the laity have no say in the choice of their parish priest nor the duration of his stay among them. His relationship to them is governed by law and custom, in which obedience is the central ingredient. It is not compensated for in any realistic way. Church law enables him to conduct parish business virtually in secret, and he is answerable only to the bishop, to whom he owes obedience!

The pervasive influence of the concept of obedience can be traced, in part, to education. Up to the end of the nineteenth century practically the whole field of Catholic education was under the control of religious orders. Nuns, priests, brothers, and monks did the actual teaching in most of the classrooms of Catholic schools. At that period laypeople were beginning to enter the field as a wage-earning profession, but their formation as teachers would have taken place in colleges which were owned and directed by religious orders. Since obedience occupied so large a place in the lives of priests and nuns, it is not surprising that its practice, and the concomitant attitudes, were unconsciously transmitted to their pupils. Nowhere was this influence as powerful as in the inculcation of religious and moral values.

The nineteenth century saw an enhancement of the role of obedience in the Church. All over Europe the upholders of legitimate government had been terrified by the events of the French Revolution. When the Napoleonic wars were over, and Europe was restructuring itself at the Congress of Vienna, many members of the ruling classes looked favourably on the Catholic Church. It represented a reliable survivor of the revolutionary epoch, whose age-old authority was intact and which could command obedience to legitimate government. It was a reassuring presence in a situation that had witnessed too much undermining, and indeed destruction, of the rulers' control over their subjects. It did not augur well for the Church's coming to terms with the inevitable progress of democracy.

Free speech in the church emerged with difficulty in the 1950s in the latter part of Pius XII' pontificate. It was ratified by Vatican II.[8] So far, it is the only example of normal democratic freedoms yet to be found within the Church's internal activities.

Anti-Semitism in Germany

Of all the abuses of obedience, none has been more damaging to the concept than its use in the Nazis' persecution of the Jews. If and when the perpetrators, like Eichmann, have been brought to justice, their defence has always been that they acted in obedience to their lawful superiors.

Constant research, since the end of the Second World War, has gradually uncovered the extent of the operation to exterminate the Jews in German occupied territories, and the number of people who were commanded to take part in it.

In addition to the straightforward obedience to military orders when soldiers were commanded to transport Jews to concentration camps and bring about their deaths, there was the all-pervasive climate of acquiescence to the policy. The appropriate moral antidote to both attitudes would have been a thoroughgoing independence of mind and action that could have withstood both the climate of opinion and the specific commands. Unfortunately, Catholicism had not taught its members in the German nation, or elsewhere, the habit of independent moral decision-making and opposition to unreasonable demands of authorities, be they of Church or State.

D.J. Goldhagen has studied the climate of German anti-Semitism during the Nazi period and beforehand.[9] His general contention is that anti-Semitism in Germany was so strong and widespread that it provided the enabling cause for Hitler's policy of obtaining racial purity by exterminating non-Aryans. Or to use his own words: 'The average German wanted to eliminate the Jews in general.'[10] Hitler's Minister of Propaganda, Dr Goebbels, held basically the same estimate of the situation. Before the large-scale executions had begun, he considered that the Churches – Catholic and Protestant – would not hinder the process.[11] Goldhagen also revealed that the Churches, while not specifically cooperating, facilitated the genocide by acquiescence. There was no coherent opposition, either from Church leaders acting as public spokesmen of the nation's conscience nor by their guidance of individuals in their Churches.

Whereas anti-Semitism was widespread in all Christian societies, German anti-Semitism had particularly virulent elements in it that ultimately led to the Holocaust.

It was in the nineteenth century that German anti-Semitism assumed its particularly aggressive form, but one should bear in mind that other European nations were only marginally less bad. In Austria, for example, after the *Anschluss*, the Nazis received almost total cooperation in their work of arresting and deporting the Jews.

German anti-Semitism, which had been inherited since the Middle Ages (which I discussed in Chapter Three), went through a complicated evolution in the nineteenth century. In the wake of Napoleon's invasion and the acceptance of principles of the Enlightenment, the legal restrictions against Jews were repealed. However, irrational prejudices remained and there were many petitions to the authorities to rescind the liberties.[12] With Bismarck's unification of the nation came the question of what constituted the essence of being German. The Jews were deemed to be outside the concept. At that period they constituted no more than one per cent of the population. In practice, they were excluded from the officer corps and the civil service. The universities too became hostile to them. Most sinister of all was the literary campaign. Between 1861 and 1895 many writers discussed what was then called the 'Jewish Problem'. Among them 28 authors proposed practical solutions, and among them fully two-thirds advocated extermination.[13] The Catholic leaders could not possibly have been ignorant of the threat.

In the twentieth century the hostility hardened. Jews were accused of not contributing to the war effort, particularly by not serving in the forces (although they were denied entry to the officer corps!). Hitler made his hostility quite clear when he published *Mein Kampf*. When the Nazi party was formed, article 4 of its programme declared that Jews would not be regarded as members of the nation. The boycott of Jewish businesses occurred on 1 April 1933.

When the Party came to power these prejudices were enshrined in the Nuremburg Laws in 1935. Under that legislation Aryan Germans were forbidden to marry Jews. Ironically the Catholic Church's law also forbade such marriages, not specifically to Jews but to all non-Christians. Whereas the code of Canon Law enshrined a long standing attitude of hostility to marriages with non-Catholics, the context of the Nuremburg Laws made it plain that they were deliberate acts of anti-Semitism. In his notorious book *Mein Kampf* Hitler had likened such a marriage as being like a union with an ape.[14]

Most dramatic of all were the events of Kristallnacht, 9–10 November 1938, so named because of the smashing of the windows of all known Jewish shops, and the burning of most of the synagogues. At the end of November a report from Heydrich to Goering indicated that 7500 Jewish shops and businesses had been destroyed or plundered and 250 synagogues had been burnt or demolished.[15] In the violence, about 100 Jews were killed and 30 000 were subsequently deported to concentration camps. The event was celebrated on the following day by a large-scale rally at Nuremburg. On 1 September 1941, Jews in Germany and conquered territories were ordered to wear a yellow star on their clothing. Clearly this was an unambiguous sign of prejudicial public discrimination, which was unworthy, to say the least, of any civilized society.

Any one of the half-dozen events noted above could have provided the Church authorities with the psychological opportunity to initiate a protest, but none was made. In fact anti-Semitic pastoral letters continued to be published throughout the period, notably by Cardinal Faulhaber of Munich and by Archbishop Grober.[16] There was no protest in 1936 when detention without trial of large numbers of people began. Representations were made to the government about the availability of mass and the sacraments to the detainees. One bishop, Berning of Osnabruck, actually visited a number of camps, reminded the prisoners of their duty of obedience to the state, and praised the conduct of the SS guards.[17]

The silence of the Catholic leaders over anti-Semitic measures is all the more significant in view of the successful protests that were made against other elements in the Nazis' programme. In 1936 the German bishops published a joint statement condemning the policy of sterilizing those whom the state considered unfit to produce children. In 1941 they published a joint pastoral letter protesting against the measures to forbid prayers or display crucifixes in schools. In 1942 there was another joint pastoral letter against the government's policy of euthanasia.[18] Towards the end of the war when the extermination of the Jews was being pursued with maximum intensity, the bishops produced nothing but an anodyne statement reiterating well-known general principles in relation to killing. The joint pastoral letter of 19 August 1943 mentioned such matters as the inviolability of non-combatants, and unarmed prisoners as well as members of different races or origins.[19] The precise word Jew was not mentioned, and that omission is simply astounding in view of the fact that by then millions of innocent Jews had been gassed in the camps and yet more millions were destined to follow them. For the rest of the war the German bishops did not hold another plenary meeting. No further joint statements were issued, and Archbishop Bertram refused to make any more pronouncements on the ground that they would be useless and harmful.

A modern writer has summarized the attitude of the Church in the following words: 'The papacy and members of the German hierarchy in the pre-war years had at times denounced the cult of racism, of blood, and soil. But there were no clarion protests against the anti-Semitic policy of Nazi rulers then or during the war years.'[20] In other words, nothing which could add up to an authentic act of witness to the truth, in spite of some discreet statements of principle.

The mass killings of Jews began in 1941, initially in Russia and Poland, and were widely known throughout the nation thanks to the information supplied by soldiers on home leave. Still the Church leaders made no protest. In 1946 when the full extent of the Holocaust became known to all, Martin Niemöller (an erstwhile anti-Semite), declared that Christians bore more responsibility than the Gestapo.[21]

It has been necessary to devote some space to this survey of German anti-Semitism and its causes, but what is of more relevance to this study is the attitude of Christians and particularly Catholics in the face of the active persecution. In general they acquiesced to the prevailing climate of virulent anti-Semitism, and in particular they obeyed all the government's measures against the Jews, even to the point of collaborating with the actual deportations and killings. Their Catholic moral formation had not taught them the virtues of independence of mind, and the moral value of active disobedience. When one reflects upon the massive scale of the operations and the individual atrocities that it entailed, the whole episode constitutes an inexcusable lapse in the moral programme of the Catholic Church. As I have observed in previous parts of this book, it should not surprise us if serious-minded people, particularly young idealists, turn elsewhere for their moral inspiration

Battalion 101

One particular aspect of the Holocaust, namely the attitude of the police, has been studied by C.R. Browning in his book entitled *Ordinary Men: Police Reserve Battalion 101 and the Final Solution in Poland.*[22] The author shows how totally average men took part in the Holocaust under the command of their superior officers or under pressure from their peer group. Christianity had not taught them to refuse obedience nor to take a radically independent line against crowd pressure.

In 1939 roughly two-thirds of the German population were Protestants and one-third was Catholic. My principal concern is with the latter. At that period they were well organized and well educated in their faith. The parishes were adequately staffed by well-educated priests, religious houses were flourishing, as were the faculties of Catholic theology in about half a dozen state universities. It is difficult to think of any other nation where conventional institutional Catholicism was functioning so well. Yet when the testing time came, the moral programme of the Church was seen to be ineffectual in the real moral crises of the period.

The so-called Reserve Police Battalions had been created in Germany in the 1930s to combat any recurrence of the revolutionary outbreaks and general breakdown of law and order such as those which occurred after the end of World War I. They were armed and trained like soldiers but were recruited and deployed locally. Their status was a legal fiction to evade the limitation on the numbers of the regular army which had been imposed upon Germany by the Treaty of Versailles. In 1933 they numbered 56 000 men, but by the outbreak of World War II the total had risen to 131 000. It was an attractive alternative to regular conscription, since the men normally lived at home and were exempt from front-line service.

In the case study, Battalion 101 was recruited and based in Hamburg. In the light of subsequent atrocities it is paradoxical to reflect upon the social mix of the unit. Browning describes it as follows:

> Of the rank and file, the vast majority were from the Hamburg area. About 63 per cent were of working-class background, but few were skilled labourers. The

majority of them held typical Hamburg working-class jobs: dock workers and truck drivers were most numerous, but there were also many warehouse and construction workers, machine operators, seamen, and waiters. About 35 per cent were lower-middle-class, virtually all of them white-collar workers. Three quarters were in sales of some sort; the other one-quarter performed various office jobs, in both the government, and private sector. The number of independent artisans and small business men was very small. Only a handful, (2 per cent) were middle class professionals, and very modest ones at that, such as druggists. The average age of the men was 39 ... about 25 per cent were Nazi Party members.[23]

On 20 June 1942 Battalion 101 received orders for special action in Poland, and was moved to the Lublin district. They were destined to take part in the rounding up of all Polish Jews for forced labour or for extermination if they were too old, too young, or too weak to work.

Action began on 12 July when the battalion was transported to the village of Jozefow. Their commander assembled them in the village square and explained exactly what was to be done. All the Jewish people in the village were to be rounded up and taken to the marketplace. Able-bodied men were to be kept there for transportation to labour camps, women, children, and the elderly were to be taken to the nearby woods to be shot. Any people who were too ill to walk to the marketplace were to be shot on the spot. This order applied to children as well. Those who attempted to escape were likewise to be shot. The commander offered the men the choice of dropping out if they felt that the task was too repulsive. About a dozen did so, out of approximately 500. One of them later described how he was vilified by his colleagues, who shouted at him expletives like 'shit-head' and 'weakling'. The commander did not go to the woods because he could not bear the sight. He was seen to be in tears, and muttering 'orders are orders'.[24]

The actual killing was done in cold blood. Browning's description is as follows:

> When the first truck load of 35 to 40 Jews arrived, an equal number of policemen came forward and, face to face, were paired off with their victims. Led by Sergeant Kammer, the policemen and Jews marched down the forest path. They turned off into the woods at a point indicated by Captain Wohlauf, who busied himself throughout the day selecting the execution sites. Kammer then ordered the Jews to lie down in a row. The policemen then stepped up behind them, placed their bayonets on the backbone above the shoulder blades as earlier instructed, and on Kammer's order fired in unison.[25]

The atrocious business went on without interruption from dawn till nightfall, by which time 1800 people had been deported or shot. When the battalion returned to barracks the men were depressed, angered, embittered, and shaken. They ate little, but drank heavily. Generous quantities of alcohol were provided and many of the policemen became completely drunk.

The commanding officer made the rounds, trying to console and reassure them, and again placing the responsibility on higher authorities. Within the battalion the matter was never spoken of again, until the official investigations some time after the war from which reports Browning obtained his information.[26]

Operations of the kind described above continued throughout the summer and by the end of September 1942 Battalion 101 had participated in the shooting of approximately 4 600 Jews and 78 non-Jewish Poles. They had also helped to deport approximately 15 000 Jews to the extermination camp at Treblinka. The savagery was not confined to the official policy of eliminating the Jews. On 25 September a German sergeant was killed by the Polish resistance. The regional commander at Lublin ordered that 200 Poles had to be executed in the village where the German sergeant had been ambushed. This hideous act of revenge was carried out by the men of Battalion 101.[27]

The next task for the battalion was the deportation of the Jews from the town of Miedzyrzec. It occupied units of Battalion 101 from the end of August until 7 November, in which time they had rounded up and deported at least 25 000 Jews for the extermination camp at Treblinka. The most horrific detail of these actions is that children were among those who were individually shot.[28]

Browning devoted considerable space to analysing the motives and psychology that prompted such brutal killings.[29] Unlike other war situations, they were not in the position of having to kill their enemies or be killed themselves. Obedience to authority was one factor but not the overriding one. It seems that peer group pressure was the determining factor.[30] This factor works in various situations where solidarity is required by the group. In warfare it is connected with the survival instinct, by which the natural propensity for self-defence is gradually extrapolated on to a larger canvas. A man is put under social pressure to defend his family from assailants, then the village or clan (in primitive times). Any man failing in his perceived duty in that situation was under immense social pressure in those small communities, with the insinuation of cowardice which, in the village, was more daunting than the fear of death at the hands of the enemy. For centuries men have been conditioned by these pressures, and they become ever more powerful when men are bound into a strongly structured community like the army, with uniforms and other factors of social control. In short, it takes great independence of mind and considerable moral courage to take an individual stand against the prevailing ethos and pattern of action. The moral programme of the Catholic Church had not prepared those men for that sort of independent decision-making and it must stand as one of the most serious failings of the Church's pastoral strategy.

Was the Church Ignorant?

At this point it is worth noting that the Catholic Church was fully aware of what was going on. As I have already noted, knowledge of the atrocities could not be kept a total secret since so many soldiers and police were involved in it. At the highest level there was the important achievement of Rudolf Vbra, the only man known to have escaped from Auschwitz. He alerted the Papal Nuncio in Prague, who in turn forwarded the information to the Vatican.[31] He escaped from Auschwitz on 10 April 1944 and after a couple of weeks managed to reach the safety of Zilina in Czechoslovakia. There he met with Dr Oscar Neumann who was the spokesman for all the Jews of Slovakia. This man was instrumental in putting Vbra in contact with the Papal Nuncio. A meeting between the two was arranged at a monastery near Svaty Jur in the vicinity of Bratislava. After careful discussion the Nuncio was convinced that he was genuine and promised to take his report to the International Red Cross headquarters at Geneva. Thence it went to Pope Pius XII, Churchill, and Roosevelt. Within a month the Papal Nuncio to Hungary made use of the information to warn President Horty (who was a Catholic married to a Jewess) that deportation and execution was being planned for the Jews of Hungary.[32]

With the passage of time, the Catholic Church has tried to make amends. In the pontificate of John XXIII the liturgy of Good Friday was altered to remove the offensive word 'perfidious' from the prayer for the Jews. The Second Vatican Council spoke warmly of the spiritual patrimony of Judaism,[33] and in 1986 Pope John Paul II paid an official visit to the synagogue in the former ghetto of Rome. On that occasion the pope recited psalm 113, and the congregation replied with psalm 150. Commenting on the event, Barnet Litvinoff observed: 'This gesture of reconciliation, unprecedented in the history of the pontificate, may well have drawn a line under the centuries of conflict and mutual recrimination. History cannot be re-written, however, much has been achieved that may prevent its repetition.'[34] Without wishing to appear cynical and ungenerous, I cannot help feeling that something much deeper and more far-reaching is needed if the Catholic Church is to make adequate reparation for the centuries of cruelty which has been inspired by our cultivation of anti-Semitism.

In all fairness to the Catholics in Hitler's Germany, one must remember that they were not the only group that failed to make the appropriate acts of protest and disobedience. As I will show later on British and Americans proved to be no better in comparable situations of indiscriminate violence and cruelty.

One further remark is relevant before resuming the main argument of this chapter. The amount of time and energy devoted to instilling correct attitudes to the papal teaching on birth control is seen to be seriously misplaced in comparison to the silent acquiescence of the Church authorities to the cruelties which have been described above. It is a perfect example of the parable of Jesus about straining at the gnat and swallowing the camel.

Silent Acquiescence

The human propensity to conformism and obedience has been tested experimentally in a now famous laboratory exercise devised by the American sociologist Stanley Milgram.[35] He advertised in a local newspaper for subjects to take part in an experiment at Yale. In spite of being offered only $4, hundreds of people (postmen, professors, salesmen, housewives, and students) responded. On arriving at the laboratory they were told that they were to take part in a study investigating the effects of punishment on learning. In fact, they were the subjects of a very different experiment. Each subject was introduced to a stooge and told that one of them would be asked to teach the other a simple task. They pulled lots from a box containing two slips of paper. 'Teacher' was written on both slips so that the volunteer wrongly believed that he had been randomly assigned the teaching role. The experiment was, apparently, to test whether the 'pupil' – who was in fact, a carefully trained actor – could learn to associate one word with another. The teacher had to administer electric shocks when the pupil failed to perform the task correctly (which of course, he regularly did). A supervisor – the figure of recognized authority (with white coat and clip-board) – stood by and instructed the teacher.

The pupil-actor, watched by the teacher, was strapped into a chair in order to prevent him from moving when shocks were administered. The teacher could give shocks ranging from mild (15 volts) to the most severe (labelled as 450, intense and dangerous). The teacher-subject was instructed to give a shock every time the pupil made a mistake and to increase the shock level by level, moving up to the possibly fatal 450 volts. If he demurred, the supervisor had a set number of phrases to utter in order to persuade him: 'Continue please', 'The experiment requires that you go on' and so on. If the teacher still refused, the experiment would be halted. Of course, no shocks were actually delivered; it was all a surrealist charade, a grim theatrical *tour de force*.

But the results were astonishing and horrifying. The pupil-actor protested verbally at the low level of volts, cried out in pain as the shock was increased, whimpered and howled as it moved to the 150 level; desperately appealed to be let out of the chair; shrieked with unendurable pain and, at 330 volts, slumped in the chair and did not respond further. During the first series of experiments, there were 40 volunteers, all male. None of them refused to administer shock treatment. A horrifying 26 went all the way, sending intense and possibly fatal shocks into the apparently comatose body of the pupil. The rest also went to high levels, apparently causing severe pain and distress.

The experiment was repeated with variations by Milgram, and then tried in other universities in other countries and the results were always about the same. When women volunteers were used instead of men, it made little or no difference. Social class, age and culture made no difference either. Most people did what they were told to do.[36] As C.P. Snow has remarked, 'More hideous crimes have been committed in the name of obedience than have ever been committed in the name of rebellion.'[37]

Obedience Damages the Church

Earlier in this chapter I pointed out that the Church's failure to inculcate independence of mind had harmed humanity. That is to say in situations like the Holocaust, or the Death Squads of Latin America, the silence of the Catholics amounted to acquiescence which allowed the villains to perpetrate mass crimes unchecked even by protest. The time has now come to examine how much damage is done within the community of the Church by over-reliance on obedience. The proper moral development of a human being requires that the will should be educated to use its freedom with deliberation and if necessary with courage. All too often the Church leaders have invoked obedience to their authority in what would seem to be the policy of quick results. In situations where people really need to be convinced, the processes of education and persuasion would have taken much more time and trouble. This regrettable situation was also compounded by a systematic instilling of fear, particularly the threat of mortal sin for non-compliance, whose punishment was eternal damnation of the soul.

Among the various areas of human behaviour where unquestioning obedience has damaged the lives of Catholics, it would appear that the way in which the Sunday mass obligation has been presented has been arguably the most harmful. After a complicated history, attendance at Sunday mass came to be perceived as the supreme moral obligation of Catholics and its omission was the mortal sin *par excellence*. In terms of badness, it was equated with murder or adultery in the popular mind and was judged to merit eternal punishment. The orchestration of its badness seems to have been the creation of the theologians rather than the popes. In this respect it is a perfect commentary on Professor Mahoney's criticism of the voluntaristic tendency in moral theology, which made obedience the supreme virtue and which gave too much influence to theologians. The voluntaristic stance in moral theology stresses the will of the legislator as opposed to the intrinsic reasons for any obligation. To quote the author's own words:

> the third defect of this particular moral system or mental attitude – that at heart it implies that the most important moral stance and the only moral virtue which really counts for salvation, is obedience to, and compliance with, the will of another, and ultimately with the will of God, conceived quite separately from the mind of God who is ultimate reason.[38]

The quest to discern the will of God the legislator led to the development of probable opinions by theologian, on points where Scripture and Tradition

were silent, and of these opinions, the same author declared that they were
destined to carry so much weight that they 'ominously placed the authority
of theologians before the intrinsic force of arguments'.[39]

Lest that contention should seem to be an exaggeration, I will illustrate it
briefly from the history of the Sunday mass obligation. Over the centuries
the popes and Councils have urged it upon the faithful by persuasion, but the
theologians commanded it with threats, and it was the fear induced by the
latter which came to predominate ultimately in popular perception.

In antiquity the Church's sense of community was strong, and gradually
the practice of attendance at Sunday mass acquired the force of customary
law. Occasionally it was bolstered by legislation in local councils, such as
that of Elvira in 305 AD, which threatened temporary excommunication for
those who were culpably absent on three successive Sundays.[40] Not surprisingly the obligation featured in Gratian's mediaeval collection of Canon
Law, where it is stated that the people must be present, and if they were to
leave before the end of mass they were to be reprimanded publicly by the
bishop.[41] The Council of Trent adopted the same attitude, commanding the
clergy that they should urge their people to attend the parish churches on
Sundays and Festivals.[42]

Popes in the post-Tridentine period upheld the same message. In 1566
Pope Pius V directed bishops, magistrates and governors of the Papal States
to enforce mass attendance, and he authorized them to inflict fines (25
ducats for example) for certain kinds of irreverent behaviour in church.[43] It
is important to take note that the threatened penalties belong to this life and
not to the other side of the grave. In 1642 Pope Urban VIII reduced the
number of Festivals on which mass attendance was obligatory. He spoke of
the importance of the obligation, but made no mention of sin for non-
attendance.[44]

During the pontificate of Innocent XI there was one decision which is
inconsistent with the general trend. In 1679 the Holy Office condemned 65
propositions from the writings of Michael du Bay, one of which (item 52)
had declared that the precept of observing the Festivals was not binding
under pain of mortal sin.[45]

In the middle of the eighteenth century, Pope Benedict XIV spoke about
Sunday mass on about half a dozen occasions,[46] but in the sixteen volumes
of his decrees and decisions there is not one mention of sin as the deterrent
for non-attendance at mass.

Pope Pius IX perpetuated the same attitude in his encyclical letter
Amantissimus Redemptoris of 1858. The laity are to be commanded to
attend mass on Festivals and Sundays, but there is no mention of penalties
in this world or the next for non-compliance.[47]

Whereas the popes had used exhortation, reprimands, and occasionally
civil penalties to urge people to attend Sunday mass, the theologians were
much more severe in their approach. To cite all of them would be too
lengthy so I will start with St Alphonsus Liguori, since his influence domi-

nated the whole field of moral theology after the eighteenth century. In his famous and influential *Theologia Moralis*, which was published in 1753, he stated unambiguously, concerning the Sunday obligation: 'He who does not hear the whole Mass is in sin; venially if he should omit a small part, mortally if he should omit a notable part such as a half or a third.'[48] He adduces no intrinsic reason for this sweeping condemnation. However he cites in his favour other theologians of previous centuries such as the Salmanticenses, de Soto, Suarez and others. Liguori was followed uncritically by the generality of moral theologians.

To cite but a few examples from the twentieth century, the threat of mortal sin was upheld by Noldin,[49] H. Davis,[50] and by Dom P.C. Augustine commenting on Canon 1247 of the Code of Canon Law (of 1918).[51] Via the theologians and canonists the gravity of the obligation found its way into the Penny Catechism (question 232), and influenced the outlook of generations of uncritical laypeople who imbibed its message in childhood. Even in the adult years, the fear of hell haunted them should they miss mass on a Sunday. It overshadowed all other moral precepts and in their minds it was equivalent to murder or armed robbery.

I do not wish to minimize the value of assisting at Sunday mass but the manner in which the obligation was presented and maintained represents a serious example of moral infantilism. It is one of the worst examples of the misuse of obedience, and is part and parcel of a misdirection of moral effort in the Catholic Church, in which really serious issues were ignored. One consequence has been massive moral infantilism matched by apathetic compliance or quiet emigration from the visible community of the Church.

Of the vast number of examples that I could quote, one incident remains clearly in my memory. It was Sunday mass in a Manchester church in the 1980s. The building was large, with seating for about 500. Its style could not be described precisely as ugly but it was devoid of beauty and suggested an atmosphere of joylessness which was certainly reflected by the attitude of the congregation. About half the seats were occupied, and the people spaced themselves out so as to achieve the maximum dilution, subconsciously (or deliberately?) distancing themselves as far as possible from any other person. The liturgy was totally lacking in animation. Every action of the people, whether they stood, or knelt, whether they spoke or remained silent, indicated apathy. Joining in the prayers was desultory, many remained silent, and as for taking part in the singing, it was tantamount to inviting passive resistance. Very few people under the age of 40 were present, except for children who were obviously bored and had been brought along by parental command.

The whole sad performance was the complete expression of Mass by compulsion. Those who were present complied with the rules out of fear of mortal sin but without enthusiasm or conviction. In the course of their Catholic formation since infancy, no one had taken the trouble to convince them that Sunday mass was intrinsically worthwhile, that it was integral to the life of an authentic community. Nor had the clergy felt the need to ensure practically that it was enjoyable.

It is difficult to exaggerate the damage done to prayer and worship by reliance upon rules enforced under the threat of mortal sin. Admittedly there have been serious attempts since Vatican II to make the liturgy meaningful. The vernacular makes it inescapable but many priests are unable to rise to the demands of a truly participated community experience. Old habits die hard and the compulsion pattern of the old Latin mass still influences the attitudes of many priests and laity.

Until the mass was celebrated in English it was almost impossible to make it an interesting experience. Not only was the Latin unintelligible to the vast majority of the congregation, but the restriction of the responses to the altar servers only meant that for the congregation it was a totally silent experience. (Sung masses were always in a minority and even then, the music was so unfamiliar that it had to be left to the choir for the most part.) Bilingual missals for the use of the laity had long ago been forbidden by the Vatican. John Gother published the first English–Latin missal in 1718, and Dom Cabrol produced a better one at the beginning of the twentieth century. Strictly speaking, both men were breaking the law. Sadly, the use of such books was too difficult for most people. Those whose reading habits were limited to tabloid newspapers could not cope either with the language or the cross-referencing between the ordinary and the proper of the mass. (The educational failing may be the fault of the nation's schooling system, as much as the Church.)

The pews and kneelers in the old churches were always uncomfortable, and central heating was introduced only after the First World War. It all added up to a penitential exercise that had a pseudo inner logic. If the church was cold, ugly, and uncomfortable, and if the liturgy was silent, incomprehensible, and unparticipated, then it all constituted one grand penitential suffering for which there would be an eternal reward. And in case this did not motivate the faithful, there was the reminder that they would be in mortal sin if they were absent. All this was underpinned by obedience to authority.

If this should seem to the reader to be an exaggeration, I would like to draw attention to those exercises of public worship which are not commanded under pain of sin. What has happened to Benediction? Even before evening mass had threatened its place in the Sunday timetable, the priest often had difficulty in ensuring the presence of 12 people which was the minimum number below which the exposition of the Blessed Sacrament was not allowed. Since the 1970s Benediction has for all practical purposes vanished from the public prayer life of the Church and it has not been replaced by anything else. The former habits of compulsion have conditioned the majority of Catholics to attend Church only when compelled to do so as an act of obedience. It is difficult to comprehend the extent of the spiritual harm done by this atrophy of true conviction in the public prayer life of the Church.

At this point it is appropriate to consider damage of a more serious kind, which has been inflicted on countless Catholics by basing their moral behaviour on obedience and its sanctions. Not only has it distorted the perception of duties like mass attendance, but it has also infantilized the basic moral formation of vast numbers of Catholics.

It is obvious that very young children must be guided by commands that require obedience, in order to protect them from dangers which they are too young to appreciate intellectually. At the most trivial level they must be forbidden to put their fingers into electric sockets, to turn on the gas taps, or to run across a busy road. This system of command by their parents covers the whole area of their life and behaviour at the early stages of life.

Psychologists in the field of child development have come to a broad agreement about the moral formation of infants. In general terms it is now accepted that they must make a transition from obedience to external rules to the acceptance of moral norms which they understand, accept, and which are internalized. This state of mind, in a child who has grown beyond the age of infancy, is known as autonomy, and has been described succinctly by Piaget, one of the founders of modern child psychology:

> With advances in social cooperation and the corresponding operatory progress, the child arrives at new moral relationships based on mutual respect which leads to a certain autonomy. Two facts should be noted … First, in games with rules, children before the age of seven, who receive the rules ready made from their elders … regard the rules as sacred, untouchable, and of transcendent origin [parent, the government, God, and so on]. Older children, on the contrary, regard rules as the result of agreement among contemporaries, and accept the idea that rules can be changed by means of a democratically arrived at consensus. Second … as early as seven or eight and increasingly thereafter, justice prevails over obedience itself and becomes a central norm.[52]

As children develop towards adulthood, a properly integrated moral development entails outgrowing the commands of parents and teachers to the point of taking personal responsibility for their own moral choices. This is not a regression to anarchy but the proper achievement of responsibility for their own actions and his life. R.S. Peters has expressed it thus:

> Our moral expectation of a person is that he is a chooser – that he can be deterred by the thoughts of the consequences of his actions … but such a person might be a time-serving, congenial conformist, or an easy going, weak willed opportunist. To this must be added the characteristic of autonomy. There must be some feature of a course of conduct, which the individual regards as important, which constitutes a non-artificial reason for pursuing it as distinct from extrinsic reasons, provided by praise or blame, reward and punishment, and so on, which are artificially created by the demands of others.[53]

The popular evaluation of obedience has been influenced to no little extent by the discipline of the armed forces, which is presented as necessary and virtuous. This area of human conduct is something of an anomaly that has acquired disproportionate influence. Although the time spent in actual fighting is short compared with the length of time that a man might spend in the army it is for that short-lived activity that the whole enterprise is organized. In action there is no time for debate and discussion, and the success of battle depends to no small extent on the prompt and unquestioning compliance with commands. It is also a way of ensuring that the men will overcome the emotions of fear and the instinctive loathing for the act of killing one of their own species, a fellow human being. Courageous soldiers who have carried out orders at great personal risk have always been held up as heroes. In subtle ways the concept of blind obedience has acquired status in our society. It is also a method of getting quick results with the minimum of trouble, as for example in school or at work. The conformist personality is appreciated in many areas of life because he does not cause trouble, but as a moral ideal his pattern of behaviour falls below the proper integration of freedom, responsibility, and awareness of the needs of others.

Douglas Graham has expressed it succinctly:

> The submissive person is one who will not initiate action: He relies on authority, and may have a reputation as a responsible person, based on conscientious performance of what he is required and expected to do.
> He tends to have strong moral standards and a well developed sense of duty ...
> But he has formed his standards as a result of accepting standards imposed by authority, and is little capable of thinking or acting independently.[54]

Sadly, much of this applies to the moral training given by the institutions of the Catholic Church. Obedience is put at a premium and personal responsibility for moral decisions has been discouraged. In the pre-conciliar period the parochial clergy acted mostly in a paternalistic fashion and expected docility from their parishioners. The conformism of German Catholics in Hitler's time is a sad commentary on the limitations of that kind of moral behaviour. Catholics of other nationalities showed themselves equally compliant in carrying out immoral orders during the war, as I will show in subsequent chapters.

After the Council much of this ethos was questioned critically, leaving something of a vacuum in its wake. After the publication of *Humanae Vitae* in 1968 a mood of defiance set in, since the ban on contraception was presented to the laity as a matter of obedience and without any attempt to justify it by sound theology or coherent reasoning. One bishop in Wales commended the encyclical to his diocese with the injunction that 'the Vicar of Christ has spoken'.

Quite simply, the Church authorities' reliance on obedience by the laity and clergy has undermined authentic moral development. Its limitations are now widely recognized, but until an entirely new approach is developed in moral theology and its pastoral applications Catholics are living in something of a vacuum.

Another aspect of this misdirected virtue is the damage done to the lives of the clergy, particularly the secular priests. The 1980s produced something of a paradox. During that decade, half a dozen Catholic priests occupied professorial chairs in British universities in theology or related subjects, and one was the Master of one of Oxford's most ancient colleges. All of them had resigned from the clergy before occupying those posts and most of them had married. Could it be that obedience to the ecclesiastical system that they had left behind had constrained their brains as well as their hearts? Regrettably this is the case, and actually it is worse than that.

The distinguished scholars mentioned in the previous paragraph were merely the tip of the iceberg. Others were pursuing similar careers at less spectacular levels. Clearly their intellectual abilities had been curtailed while they remained in the ranks of the clergy. This poses a problem similar to the repression of their emotional lives by the law of celibacy.

The lives of the secular clergy, in particular, are blighted by the twin forces of obedience and celibacy, neither of which has been thought out with the care and safeguards with which they are accompanied in religious orders. There is a subconscious process which muddles along somewhat on these lines: Celibacy is a privation, but it is said to be good for the soul. Obedience counteracts the harmful effects of self-seeking in a clerical career. Asceticism is painful by definition. So, if something hurts it must be good spiritually. Even if the priest is unhappy, the sacraments that he administers are still valid; and so it goes on. Curates were never consulted about which parishes they were appointed to, nor did they know how long they would work there. Without warning a letter from the bishop would arrive one day telling them where to go next, sometimes at a week's notice. Allegedly it inculcated the virtue of detachment. That is questionable, but undoubtedly it indicated to them that their work was unimportant since it could be curtailed so abruptly.

Clearly this system has not produced spiritual dynamos. In old age, many priests are just dispirited, if not worse. That contention can be proved by countless examples drawn from experience. Limitations of space prevent an exhaustive listing of them. One poignant case will have to suffice. It was the fate of the late Canon D.J.B. Hawkins with whom I worked as a curate up to the time of his death in the early 1960s. Since all his close relatives and friends are now dead, I can speak freely about his wasted talents.

The frustrations began in Rome where he was studying in the 1920s. He derived little from the lectures at the Gregorian University, but he was obliged under obedience to attend them. So as to use the time profitably he sat at the back of the large lecture halls, withdrew his attention from the lecturers, and read the whole corpus of Plato and Aristotle in the original Greek. After ordination he was appointed as a curate in South London, and his intellectual abilities were never utilized by the Church. When he became a parish priest he wrote half a dozen brilliant but brief books on philosophy. Unexpectedly at about the age of fifty, he was invited to be the first occupant of a chair of scholastic philosophy at the University of Belfast, but the plan misfired and he was left as the rector of a small country parish.

Shortly afterwards I joined him as his curate and it soon became apparent to me that he had lost interest in life. Probably the opportunity at Belfast, which had not materialized, had brought home to him that he would never be allowed to use his immense talents in the service of the Church, or the world of scholarship. Living under the same roof was intellectually stimulating. Each mealtime was like a tutorial (he had no small talk), and I learnt as much in those mealtimes as I did at any of the universities at which I have studied. He died at the age of 58 from what I discerned to have been psychological causes. Subsequently when I found myself at Cambridge as a post-graduate student, I came to realize that Hawkins had been possessed of a better intellect than any of the six professors then in divinity school of that university. More than 30 years have passed since his death but I have never ceased to grieve over the waste not only of his talents but his whole life. He was the archetypical victim of obedience.

What is equally sad is that it need not be so. The Anglicans have worked it out quite well for their clergy. A candidate for ordination is allowed to study at the college or university of his own choosing. (Catholics have no choice about the seminary to which they are sent.) Once ordained the Anglican priest will normally serve his first curacy in the diocese that sponsored him. After that he is free to apply for vacant posts in any Anglican diocese with as much freedom as people in any other walk of life. If he wishes to specialize as a university chaplain, for example, he can take the initiative to find such work. If he wants to pursue further theological study, it is not only permitted, but facilitated. The result is a generally contented workforce with many able scholars in the ranks of the clergy and, more to the point, several first-class theologians in the ranks of their episcopate.

The last example, which I will discuss in this chapter, of damage which obedience inflicts on the Church is that of the selection of bishops. Very occasionally priests receive secret enquiries from the papal nuncio asking their opinion, in confidence, of the suitability of Father X, or Y, or Z to be made a bishop. The document contains a series of questions as to his education and practical experience. However the crucial question is about his unswerving loyalty and obedience to the pronouncements of the popes. (One cannot help feeling that the Vatican has *Humanae Vitae* in mind.)

As a result of this kind of selection, the Church has for many years been blessed with a set of utterly obedient bishops. Without being cynical in one's observations, it is perfectly legitimate to ask whether there might be other qualities in a bishop's personality which might serve the Church even better than his being predominantly obedient. There is a grave danger that the present system produces dull, unimaginative, conformist bishops. Without being too specific about the personalities in question, the English and

Welsh hierarchy since 1918 (when the popes took over the sole nomination of bishops) has not been notable for outstanding qualities of leadership. Not one diocesan bishop since that time has been a renowned scholar who has written an authoritative book on theology or held a university teaching post. Many of them have had little pastoral experience either. A disturbingly large proportion spent the majority of their priestly lives as bureaucrats working in the diocesan curias.

The one exception was the Benedictine, former abbot of Downside, B. C. Butler, who was a renowned scholar. As president of the English Benedictine Congregation he attended the Second Vatican Council and made a significant contribution to its deliberations. The sad irony was that after the Council he was made an auxiliary bishop in Westminster and not archbishop. Had he been archbishop, and hence leader of the Catholic community of this country in the immediate aftermath of the Council, the adoption of the Council's vision would have been a much happier affair. He was passed over in favour of a man who could not be described as intellectually brilliant.

The Importance of Protest

Although too much obedience has damaged the Church and its mission, I am not advocating disobedience or anarchy as the remedies. The authentic response to excessive authoritarianism is protest, which in the Christian context is closely allied to witnessing to the truth, whose highest expression is martyrdom.

Of the various Christian Churches whose particular gifts have enriched the religious scene, it is the Quakers who have most strongly demonstrated this quality. For centuries they have taught their followers to adopt an independent way of life, standing apart from fads and fashions and if necessary refusing obedience to authorities and laws which they perceive as being at variance with the values of the New Testament. From the occasion in the seventeenth century, when George Fox refused the offer of a captaincy in the Parliamentarians' army (as the price of release from prison), they have been the leaders in working for peace rather than war. Elizabeth Fry showed similar independence of mind when she pioneered prison reform at a time when public opinion required her to be at home with her children. In commerce too the Quakers have consistently treated their employees well, against the prevailing current of keeping down wages to remain 'competitive'.

The Catholic Church still has a lot to learn from the Quakers in the difficult task of diagnosing real moral evil and making the appropriate kind of protest. Our own record is not reassuring, as a couple of examples will illustrate. When slavery was still legal in the United States prior to the Civil War, the Catholic bishops did nothing to work for its abolition. An American historian has given this assessment of their inaction: 'Concerning the issue of slavery in the 1850s, not a single bishop spoke in favour of abolition preceding the war. Rather than stir their congregations on this controversy, most bishops merely assented to their Church's cautious acceptance of slavery, and advised their people, in the words of Bishop Kenwick, that "Nothing should be attempted against the law." '[55]

A century later an even worse example was to be seen in Brazil. In 1964 Cardinal Angelo Rossi became archbishop of São Paolo and president of the Brazilian bishops' conference. In the same year the military dictatorship came to power in Brazil and commenced their regime of repression of political opposition. Rossi was quite incapable of facing up to the military dictatorship. In spite of censorship, the evidence of torture, persecution, and the disappearance of political opponents became well known. Rossi always seemed to be on good terms with the dictators. When Bishop Helder Camara of Recife in the north of Brazil appealed to the world to denounce the torture being practised in Brazil, Rossi thought that Camara's action showed lack of patriotism. In October 1970 Pope Paul VI transferred him from São Paolo to become prefect of the congregation for the Evangelization of Peoples in Rome.[56]

Case Study: One Successful Protest against the Nazis

Among the many examples of excessive obedience doing damage to the Church's moral standing, in modern times none was worse than the failure to protest against the Nazis. Pius XII has been blamed for his silence but the German moral theologian Bernard Häring, in one of his last press conferences before his death, pointed out that the Church in Germany was far too obedient, and that the German bishops should have raised their voices against Hitler.[57]

In the context of the Nazi regime in Germany, it is both instructive and humbling to recall that a totally successful protest against the deportation of a certain category of Jews did take place in Berlin in 1943. It was the demonstration of women in the Rosenstrasse. In February of that year the authorities started to arrest the Jews who were still at liberty in Berlin, including the Jewish spouses of non-Jewish partners. In fact most of this group were men and they were separated from the other prisoners and confined in a Jewish social centre in the Rosenstrasse.

As soon as the location of their confinement became known, a group of about 150 women, mostly their wives, gathered outside the building to protest and ask for the release of their husbands. For the next three days and nights an ever-increasing crowd of women maintained their vigil in the street shouting in unison 'We want our husbands back'. On the night of Monday 1 March there was a heavy air raid on the city. The SS guards retired to shelters but the women stayed where they were in the street. On Tuesday 2 March the police and SS were unable to disperse the women in spite of threats. The crowd of women increased steadily as news of the protest spread by word of mouth. Eventually the SS aimed their rifles and threatened to shoot the women. At this they sought refuge in side streets, but soon returned to the Rosenstrasse. Eventually on 6 March Goebbels ordered the release of the Jewish prisoners who were married to non-Jews. Seventeen hundred were set at liberty. His deputy, Leopold Gutterer admitted that the government feared that the protest might spread further. In the aftermath of Stalingrad the authorities were sensitive about civilian morale.[58]

That incident speaks for itself. The women of Berlin, motivated by love of their husbands, had made the perfect moral response to the government's act of cruelty. Surely the Christians (and my concern is mainly with the Catholics) could have done something similar, motivated by the love of God. The Church's failure at that juncture is a sobering reminder of the damage that can be done to morality by excessive obedience.

How did Obedience get Out of Hand?

The exercise of authority in the Church and the demand for obedience has become frankly unchristian in its manner of dealing with people; it has become autocratic in the extreme. This is partly due to the fact that so often, Church institutions and their functions have been fashioned in imitation of secular models taken from the political sphere. I alluded to this tendency in Chapter Five in the context of justice. It is necessary to return to it again because of the way in which ecclesiastical obedience has been exacted under the influence of secular models of government.

This tendency started when Constantine made Christianity the religion of state, and it became more pronounced in the Middle Ages when the popes themselves had become the political rulers of an independent state. Eventually the Papal States comprised a large part of central Italy, whose governing required an administrative system, the levying of taxes, armies, law courts and all the apparatus of political life. The style of government, which went with administering the Papal States, spilled over into the sphere of conducting the purely ecclesiastical affairs of the Church. In the high Middle Ages, when the popes and emperors were locked in titanic struggles over the independence of the Church, the papacy had become a world power competing with the Holy Roman Empire on the latter's secular terms.

It was in this period that the concept of jurisdiction became firmly entrenched in the governmental and spiritual activities of the Church. Jurisdiction (*ius dicere*) is the competence to enact laws and judge of their observance. It belongs to the nation-state and not to the voluntary societies within it. Smaller communities within the nation will have their own rules for functioning and also for disciplining troublesome members. These activities may be as homely as the rules of a golf club, or as important as the licensing of doctors by the British Medical Association or the conferring of degrees by universities. However the obligations which they impose are hypothetical, depending upon the desire of individuals to seek membership, to avail of their benefits and abide by their conditions. It is a sort of implied contract. The nation-state does not admit of that degree of choice. I cannot refuse to pay taxes on the plea that I wish to opt out. The government will say, if you live and work here you are not free to opt out of our laws. Citizens are automatically members of the nation and thus come within its jurisdiction.

In antiquity the Church had been content to live as a voluntary organization within the state, operating its own rules for the conduct of its members in religious matters. That degree of authority was sufficient to assure the faithful transmission of the teaching of Jesus and the conferring of valid sacraments. It was still basically an exercise of service, or *diakonia* to use the technical term employed by Vatican II. There was as yet no notion of the exercise of jurisdiction in the strict sense of the term. With the passage of time and the vast increase in the number of Christians, a qualitative change occurred. Eventually all the citizens of Europe embraced Christianity, but it is clear that for many of them it was not a decision of faith. All too often in the early days of evangelization kings were baptized and the entire nation followed them into the Church. It lies outside the scope of this study to evaluate that particular aspect of the increase in the number of Christians. By the time that Church and state has become coterminous, the Church had adopted the notion of jurisdiction in the rules (thenceforward called laws) which it enacted for its members. Clearly this qualitative change in the control of the Church's members had nothing to do with its supernatural mission: it was the result of historical accidents.

The same processes were at work in the imitation of secular models for the rulers of the Church. In short they copied the behaviour of the kings, and as time wore on the popes came to resemble the absolute monarchs of the eighteenth century. Those were the rulers who governed without elected parliaments and whose activities were not limited by any practical system of checks and balances. There was no division of powers such as the independence of the judiciary. Equally damaging to the reputation of Church authority is the fact that most modern refinements in the art of government, such as accountability and evaluation, have likewise been ignored. The pope is answerable to no one for his decisions, and practical policies are never subjected to realistic evaluation. For example, what is the role of hospitals conducted by religious orders in a nation which has a national health service? Do they provide poor people with care which would otherwise be unobtainable for them? Do they effect religious conversion among rich people who pay for their services? In short, what is their contribution to the Church's mission? Their work could be examined by scientific evaluation, but it is not. The reason is that all the Church's activities are influenced, indirectly at least, by the pattern of absolute monarchs and the ways in which they commanded their subordinates. Evaluation would have been tantamount to criticism, and a plea for accountability would have suggested rebellion.

In the nineteenth century the popes overtook their secular counterparts, most of whom had been eliminated by revolution or had to share power with elected parliaments. In 1870 the First Vatican Council declared that the pope's power over the Church was universal, supreme jurisdiction. It is pertinent to observe that when that Council defined papal infallibility it surrounded the power with carefully thought-out limitations, but the pronouncement of universal jurisdiction received no similar restrictions. The absence of such constraints showed itself for instance in 1918. The newly codified Canon Law gave the pope competence to nominate all bishops throughout the whole Church. This was the most spectacular augmentation of papal power that the Church had ever witnessed in its long history. As I pointed out in Chapter Two, at the end of the eighteenth century the popes nominated bishops for merely 24 dioceses throughout the world. Other episcopal appointments were made through election by cathedral chapters, or nominations by royal houses and other secular rulers. As a result of the Code of 1918 the popes at the end of the twentieth century were nominating the bishops of more than 3000 dioceses.[59] The pope also nominates all the cardinals (who elect his successor), all the Papal Nuncios, and all the senior administrators in the Roman Curia. The amplitude of his unconstrained power over the Church is frankly terrifying. With the exception of dictators like Hitler and Stalin, no political leader in the modern world has such complete control over the organization that he rules.

The same Code of Canon Law declared that in his own diocese each bishop was legislator, judge, and administrator. The model of the absolute monarch had been consolidated totally. Consequently it is not surprising that obedience, which is the concomitant attitude in the subordinate, should be exercising a disproportionately influential role in the life of the Church.

Lutheranism also had an unexpected influence on the manner in which Church authority was exercised. After he had made his shattering protest which took millions from the Catholic Church obedience was seen as a quick remedy for his challenge to authority. To be precise, Luther denied the teaching authority of the bishops, the pope, and General Councils. In its place he declared that the Christian should be guided by the Bible and by the individual's own interpretation of it. The Catholic Church repudiated this and, to make the position even more secure, they tended to curtail private decision-making in the individuals' moral choices. This was not a conscious policy decision but it arose out of the general orientation away from private judgement and in favour of obedience to authority.

From that time onwards the study of moral theology became more and more dominated by rules. By contrast, in the Middle Ages the classical moral theology of Aquinas had been a systematic exploration of the three theological and four cardinal moral virtues. From the sixteenth century too, we see an increasing volume of decisions emanating from popes or departments of the Roman curia, giving practical decisions on matters where neither scripture nor rational ethics could supply a clear answer. Frequently these decisions were presented in a way that did not supply reasons for their injunctions, and it was implied that they would be obeyed simply on the authority of the pope. This represented a great change in moral theology and the basis upon which Catholics were expected to make their moral choices. One example will illustrate the process. In Cardinal Manning's time English Catholics were forbidden to attend the universities of Oxford and Cambridge. The decision came from the Roman curia because it was assumed that attendance at those universities would constitute a danger to their retaining allegiance to the Catholic faith. A few years later the ban was lifted, but the situation at the universities had not really undergone a significant change.

As far as laypeople were concerned a whole series of rules were elaborated concerning marriage, sex, the education of children in Catholic schools, birth control, sterilization, cremation and many more. In most cases some sort of legitimation was offered from Scripture or reason, but in essence they were presented as matters on which the Church leaders must be obeyed. Quite apart from the intrinsic moral issues at stake, the act of obedience to authority was judged to be virtuous in itself. Rarely did the clergy or teachers advert to the underlying principles of whether it was right to hand over one's moral decision-making to another.

This collective attitude of mind lasted until 1968. With the publication of the encyclical letter, *Humanae Vitae* which repeated Pius XI's condemnation of contraception, people started to ask for the reasons which underpinned the decision. No satisfactory reasons were forthcoming, as will be shown in the chapter on temperance, and from that time the practice of unquestioning obedience came to an end. Catholics no longer accepted what the clergy told them to do. The results have been far-reaching, for example in the increasing number of parents who do not send their children to Catholic schools. 1968 marked a watershed, after which obedience has counted for less and less. Unfortunately the authorities in Rome have not faced up to the reality, no alternative system has been put forward, and in many matters the laity are now living in a moral vacuum.

Notes

1 The literature on the subject is vast. A few of the standard sources are these: Tillard, J.M. (1982), 'Obeissance' in *Dictionnaire de Spiritualité*, Vol.11, cols. 535–63, Paris; Theolbald, M. and others (1995), 'Gehorsam', in *Lexikon für Theologie und Kirche*, Vol. 4, cols 358–63, Freiburg; Truchlar, K.V. (1967), 'Obedience' in *New Catholic Encyclopedia*, vol. 10, 602–6, New York; Auer, A. (1977), 'Freedom to be Autonomous or Freedom to Obey', in *Concilium*, Dec. 1977.
2 *ST* II–II, q.104.
3 Constitution on the Church, *Lumen Gentium*, section 18, DV II, 37.

4   *Lumen Gentium*, section 24, DV II, 47.
5   Two accessible books on the matter in English are: *Problems of Authority* ed. J.M. Todd, London 1961, and *Power and Poverty in the Church* by M.J. Congar, London 1964.
6   Schillebeeckx, E. *Marriage: Secular Reality and Saving Mystery*. London 1965, vol.1, 271, 272.
7   *Syllabus of Errors*, number 76. DS 2976.
8   *Gaudium et Spes*, section 26, DV II, 269, 270.
9   Goldhagen, D.J. *Hitler's Willing Executioners*. London, 1996.
10 Goldhagen, 14.
11 Denzler, G. and Fabricius, V., *Die Kirchen im Dritten Reich*. Frankfurt 1984, 95.
12 Goldhagen, 62.
13 Goldhagen, 71.
14 *Mein Kampf*, Munich 1933, 444, quoted in Denzler and Fabricius, 135.
15 Hofer, W. in *Anti-Semitismus* edited by H.A. Strauss and N.Kampe, Frankfurt 1988, 182.
16 Goldhagen, 101, 109.
17 Denzler and Fabricius, 78.
18 Denzler and Fabricius, 114, 106, 130.
19 Denzler and Fabricius, 156.
20 Helmreich, E.C. *The German Churches under Hitler*. Detroit 1979, 361.
21 Goldhagen, 114.
22 Browning, C.R. *Ordinary Men: Police Reserve Battalion 101 and the Final Solution in Poland*. New York, 1993.
23 Browning, 47.
24 Browning, 57, 58, 66.
25 Browning, 61.
26 Browning, 69.
27 Browning, 101.
28 Browning, 109, 113.
29 Browning, 159–89.
30 Browning, 174, 175.
31 Vbra, R. and Bestic, A. *I Cannot Forgive*, London 1964, passim.
32 Vbra and Bestic, 257.
33 Vatican II, *Nostra Aetate*, section 4, DV II, 663–67.
34 Litvinoff, B. *The Burning Bush: Anti-Semitism and World History*. London 1988, 420.
35 Milgram, S. *Obedience To Authority*, New York 1969.
36 Comment by Nicci Gerard in *The Observer*, 12 October 1997.
37 Snow, C.P. in *The Observer*, 12 October 1997.
38 Mahoney, J. *The Making of Moral Theology*, Oxford 1987, 244.
39 Mahoney, 244.
40 Häring, B. *The Law of Christ*, Cork 1963, vol. 2, 309.
41 *Decretum Gratiani*, Pars III, Dist. I.C. LXIV, in the Leipzig edition of the *Corpus Iuris Canonici*, 1879, 737.
42 Council of Trent, Session 22, in 1562. *Decree on Reform*, Canon 1, ACOD 737.
43 Decree *Cum Primum* of 1 April 1566, sections 3 and 7, printed in *Bullarum Diplomatum et Privilegium S. Romanorum Pontificum*, ed. Aloisio Bilio, Turin 1868, vol.8, 434, 436.
44 Decree *Universa per Orbem*, of 13 September 1642, in Bilio, vol. 15, 206, 207.
45 DS 2152.
46 *Sanctissimi Domini Nostri Benedicti Papae XIV, Bullarium*. Malines 1826, edited by H.J. Hanicq. Decrees of: 30 March 1742, vol. 1, 277; 12 August 1742, vol. 1, 423; 24 August 1744, vol. 2, 231; 5 November 1745, vol. 3, 280 and 285; 14 November 1748, vol. 16, 276.

47   *Enchiridion delle Encicliche*, eds E. Lora and R. Simionati, Bologna 1996, vol.2, 406.
48   Liguori, A. *Theologia Moralis*, Rome, 1911 edn, vol.2 , 163.
49   Noldin, H. *Summa Theologia Moralis*, Innsbruck, 1951, vol. 2, 239.
50   Davis, H. *Moral and Pastoral Theology.* London 1949, vol. 2, 59.
51   Augustine, P.C, *Commentary on the Code of Canon Law.* St Louis 1923, vol.6, 173.
52   Piaget, J. and Inhalder, B. *The Psychology of the Child*, London 1969, 127.
53   Peters, R.S. *Moral Development and Moral Education.* London, 1981, 120, 121.
54   Graham, D. *Moral Learning and Development: Theory and Research.* London 1972, 173.
55   Byrnes, T.A. *Catholic Bishops and American Politics.* Princeton 1991, 16.
56   *The Guardian*, 31 May 1995.
57   *Kirche Intern*, November 1997.
58   N. Stolfuss, *Resistance of the Heart*, New York 1996, 210–48.
59   These remarkable statistics were researched originally by Canon Garret Sweeney and published in the book *Bishops and Writers*, ed. A. Hastings, Hertford, 1977, 207.

Chapter 8

Truthfulness

This virtue is so central to Christianity that in the perspective of the fourth gospel it is the way in which Jesus defined his mission. When he was questioned by Pilate he stated his objective thus: 'I was born for this, I came into the world for this: to bear witness to the truth' (John 18:37). Correspondingly he promised to his disciples a similar central relationship with truth: 'If you make my word your home, you will indeed be my disciples, you will learn the truth, and the truth will make you free' (John 8:32).

In addition to the simple practice of truthfulness, which has been acknowledged in all ethical systems since the ancient Greeks, Christianity has a specific contribution to this virtue. It is the injunction to bear witness to the truth. This is something more positive and creative than merely avoiding falsehood in the field of communication. It entails publishing the truth with increasing emphasis in areas where questions of morality are at stake. The discussion on slavery presented a perfect example. A variety of authors and popes can be cited, as having condemned slavery in their textbooks or decrees. As long as those laudable sentiments remained merely within the pages of the documents, their authors could not claim to have fulfilled the Christian injunction to bear witness to the truth. Nor, at the other extreme, is a Christian obliged to walk round the streets carrying placards about sin or the end of the world. Something more subtle yet realistic is required, like the action of Bartolomé de las Casas in refusing the sacraments to landowners who had not granted liberty to their indentured labourers in the hacienda system. The most heroic examples of witnessing to the truth were the sufferings and cruel deaths of the martyrs.

Mere internal agreement with the truths of the gospel is not sufficient. Faith has to be acted upon in the manifold vicissitudes of life and even in the face of persecution and death. The possible ways in which this practical expression of witnessing to the truth could be realized are too numerous to describe exhaustively. In spite of this practical complexity, the principle of witnessing to the truth is integral to the practice of this virtue by Christians, although the need to do so may not be felt by even well-intentioned atheists.

For the body politic the importance of truth cannot be overestimated. Governments are prone to concealing anything that might reflect badly on their efficiency or wisdom. This is particularly to be seen in totalitarian regimes where criticism can be stifled by censorship, secret police, and other agencies of control. Solzhenitsyn described it in his novel *The First Circle*, where well-educated prisoners in a labour camp were researching for the secret police into the possibility of voice detection to identify speakers on bugged telephones. The prisoners had deceived the prison authorities about the progress of their research. The prison authorities had deceived their superiors about their prisoners' progress in the matter. In short, everyone was deceiving everyone else.

Outside the realms of enlightened fiction, the habit of deception seems to have penetrated every level of Soviet life. A homely example may serve to illustrate the point. In the 1980s I was travelling to Cuba via Shannon airport where I had to change on to the Russian Aeroflot plane for the final part of the journey. The take-off was delayed, and the passengers were told to return to the departure lounge while the plane had one of its wheels changed. Two hours later we returned to the plane. None of its wheels had been changed, but the cause of the delay became apparent. A Soviet trade delegation came aboard, having been with the Soviet ambassador to Ireland in the VIP lounge for the past two hours. Clearly they had been drinking heavily and were shrieking with laughter. Why this had to be concealed from the passengers by the story about the wheel is intelligible only when one reflects that deceit had become endemic in that society.

If the Church is to give moral guidance and inspiration to the human race, this area of public truthfulness in the activities of governments and corporations is extremely important. It is imperative that the Church's own conduct at this level is above reproach. Unfortunately, as will appear in the course of this chapter, such is not always the case, to put it mildly!

At the level of individual conduct the moral position is simple. Telling lies is reprehensible, and on that point all are agreed. The Church's teaching on the matter has been uncomplicated and clear.

However, at the level of community behaviour the matter is not so clear. Its relevance to morality can be seen in relation to a simple paradigm which accounts for most of humanity's collective wickedness. Namely, human conduct tends frequently to selfishness, which, if frustrated, quickly leads to violence and then to concealment (when the violence is tacitly recognized as unjustifiable, even by its perpetrators). Of the many examples that could be cited, the conduct of the tobacco companies comes to mind. Many years ago scientists realized that there was a connection with lung cancer and that the habit of smoking was addictive. In the 1990s it became apparent just what efforts had been made to conceal those facts and how strenuous were the legal battles to ward off compensation claims. Much the same could be said for the asbestos industry. Asbestos continued to be used widely for heating insulation, long after its dangers were known, and kept from public knowledge. At the level of government, the 1980s and 1990s provided all too many examples of the concealment of discreditable activities, such as gigantic armaments contracts with undesirable regimes, which were concealed from the public and from parliament as long as possible.

A simple human remedy for that kind of activity has long been known and practised, namely openness in business and government. In the Greek city states, when they had thrown off the political power of dictators, public business was conducted openly in the assemblies in which all male adult free citizens participated in the decision-making. Somewhat later in history Anglo-Saxon England applied it to law courts as well. Thence was born the famous adage that justice must be done and must be seen to be done. From then onwards the activities of law courts were transacted in public, as was the business of government, from parliament down to the humblest parish council.

Unfortunately the complexities of the modern world have proved difficult to control in this respect, as concealment has proved to be quite easy for large corporations, and departments of government. For example, in the 1990s the United States Navy Academy at Annapolis was shaken by serious criminal activity and by the attempts to conceal it. The first scandal occurred in December 1992 when more than 100 midshipmen were found to have cheated in a final exam. It emerged that some students had stolen the entire exam paper and that others lied to cover up the crime. In 1996 a student was charged with sexually assaulting four women, five more were indicted for running a car-theft ring, and on the same day another was convicted of selling LSD, the first of 24 suspects charged with drug offences.[1]

The large-scale corruption was exposed by one of the professors at the academy, whose only course of action was to write an article in the *Washington Post* in order to get a hearing. The professor claimed that the trouble was systematic and that the academy fostered an atmosphere of arrogance and cynicism. He claimed that midshipmen learned that success came to those who bent the rules, who covered for their friends, and who never spoke out. 'Wonderful young people become immersed in an ethically corrupting system', he wrote. In the article's most devastating passage, the professor described how the navy's once pristine values had become warped. 'Particularly frustrating is the ascendance of loyalty over truth, as in the adage Never bilge (report) on a classmate. In one class I asked: What is the difference between you and the Mafia who are also loyal to a fault? We wear uniforms, was the reply.'[2]

As is so often the case in such instances, the professor was immediately suspended from teaching duties. Fortunately he was later reinstated. It illustrated the final moral badness in the paradigm: selfishness, violence, lies, and then the vindictive treatment of anyone who exposes the untruths.

The somewhat undignified name 'whistleblowers' has been coined for those who expose massive corporate dishonesty. In reality they deserve to be honoured as witnesses to the truth, and since they all incur considerable danger, their actions deserve to be classified as a form of martyrdom. The evil is present in practically every walk of life. The Bank of Credit and Commerce International was investigated in 1995 for malpractices that resulted in losses of more than two billion pounds worldwide. Judge Bingham concluded that the bank had fostered an autocratic environment in which no one dared to speak out against a fraud of nearly twenty years' duration. The only employee known to have reported alleged financial malpractices was an internal auditor who was subsequently made redundant.[3]

It will be obvious to the reader that dishonesty and concealment on the scale which I am describing here dwarfs into insignificance individual failings like white lies and giving short change in shops. One has to ask what kind of guidance and example has been given by the Catholic Church over such large-scale acts of dishonesty? I will revert to that later in the chapter; for the moment it is necessary to give a few more indications of the scale of the problem.

In addition to the artificially cultivated loyalty systems of the armed forces and commerce, the public administration itself is equally prone to these pressures. In the 1960s, a scientist, Dr Clair Patterson pioneered research into the contaminating effects of lead in the air, and particularly its effects on children. His concern sprang initially from a report produced by the United States Surgeon General's Department in 1962 stating that urban lead levels in America were not greatly above historical 'background' levels. Patterson knew this to be untrue, and by 1970 his research showed that lead levels in American cities were about 1000 times higher than those of the pre-industrial era. He also showed that the major source of contamination was petrol, which earned him the wrath of powerful commercial lobbies who spent three decades maliciously attacking the integrity of his work. To its great credit, the California Institute of Technology where he worked resisted powerful commercial pressures to have him dismissed.[4]

Unfortunately for its moral credibility, the Catholic Church also dismisses researchers and scholars whose views are threatening to the establishment. But of that, more later.

Parliamentary business in the 1980s and 1990s was not without its attempts to deceive the public but the most notorious case concerned the sinking of the Argentinian cruiser the *General Belgrano* during the Falklands War. The British government had declared a 200-mile exclusion zone round the Falkland Islands, within which any hostile ship would be attacked. The *General Belgrano* was well outside the zone and had been sailing back to its home port for more than 11 hours at the time of its sinking. It is arguable that this incident took place to ensure that the Peruvian peace plan would be wrecked and that the Royal Navy would have the opportunity to prove its worth. When the incident was explained to parliament certain facts were falsified, including the date, to make it appear that the sinking had taken place before the Peruvian peace plan had been communicated to the British government. A massive operation was undertaken by the government to deceive parliament and the public.

The details are irrelevant to this book but the moral issues are important. A civil servant, Clive Ponting, was caught up in the deception, and he described his growing sense of moral revulsion as the actions of the politicians became ever more devious:

Ministers had decided to continue to mislead Parliament. The cover-up now looked as though it was bound to continue. Consistency not truth was to be the order of the day. I found myself wondering whether the Civil Service was really going to be party to the deliberate deception of Parliament, simply to try and preserve the illusion that Ministers had told the truth, and thus protect their political reputation.[5]

Ponting blew the whistle, was prosecuted under the Official Secrets Act, but was exonerated by the jury.

Until recently public life, including politics, the law courts, police, and commerce had been protected from deception and financial dishonesty by what has been termed The Non-conformist Conscience. Its establishment at the heart of public life was a magnificent achievement of the Methodists and other nonconformist Churches, largely during the nineteenth century. The whole nation has reason to be grateful to those Churches. Even as late as the 1960s it was taken for granted that the police and law courts were above corruption, that truth would be respected in the universities, and that promotion in the armed forces would be on the basis of merit. The idea that any MP would lie to parliament was unthinkable and in the 1960s Profumo paid the price for doing so and had to resign his ministerial post in the government.

In the context of the nonconformist conscience, one is led to reflect upon the combination of truth and justice that produces one of the most positive of moral attitudes, namely integrity. Its roots stretch back to the Old Testament and it is frequently to be found in the Psalms as a component of Israelite morality. The Hebrew root *TAMIM* means basically completeness or wholeness and is best rendered in English by 'integrity'. It resembles closely that poetic insight of Shakespeare when he put into the mouth of Polonius these unforgettable words:

> This above all: to thine own self be true,
> And it must follow, as the night the day,
> Thou cans't not then be false to any man.[6]

Humorous anecdotes abound which illustrate the hold that it had upon the popular imagination. The poet Robert Graves described how he evaded paying for a train fare when he was a schoolboy. At the end of the school holidays he went to Waterloo Station to board the special train taking boys to Charterhouse School at Godalming. The crowd of schoolboys was so numerous that the ticket collector at the barrier did not notice that the young Graves had slipped past without a ticket. The same thing happened at Godalming Station so the boy had a free ride and deceived the ticket collectors.

In his first letter home, he mentioned this minor triumph to his parents. His father was reading the letter as he ate his breakfast. When he came to the paragraph describing the deceitful action he put down his knife and fork, left the bacon and eggs uneaten, left the house immediately, and took a cab to Waterloo Station. There he purchased a single half-fare from London to Godalming. As soon as the ticket was in his hands he tore it up and threw away the pieces. Only then could he return home and finish his, now cold, breakfast. The narrative of this episode is touching and faintly comic but the smooth running of society depended upon thousands of such delicate consciences.

The few examples which I have cited in the preceding pages indicate how diversified are the offences against truth and how serious is their impact upon the well-being of society. What is of immediate concern to this book is the way in which the Church responds to this evil. Has the Catholic educational system equipped every one of its past pupils to act like Clive Ponting? Clearly it has not. Does the Church's own bureaucracy act as a shining example of transparency, honesty and integrity? Unfortunately no, as I will show in subsequent pages.

Admittedly there have been some circumstances in the Church's long and complex history when secrecy was required. Papal elections are a clear example. In the dark ages the elections of the bishops of Rome were controlled by local politicians within the city or by international magnates like the German Emperor. The well-being of the Church was not their major concern! The first step in securing satisfactory elections was to protect the electors and the confidentiality of their business. This was the origin of the elaborate ritual of sealing the cardinals in the Sistine Chapel by literally bricking up the door, and burning the ballot papers, so that there would be no evidence as to which way any one of them had voted. In the modern period it has become a charming, and immensely popular ritual as the crowds in St Peter's Square anxiously watch for the emergence of white or black smoke from the chimney, signifying an inconclusive or a decisive vote.

In some circumstances secrecy may be necessary to protect individuals and the whole community. However it is a dangerous practice and, if abused, concealment can be as damaging to truth as is straightforward lying.

Unfortunately the habit of secrecy has been extended much too far in the Church's administrative life into fields which do not warrant it. In this matter the Church is much less open than enlightened secular organizations. For example, in the army, the annual reports on officers' work are shown to them before being sent off to the Ministry of Defence. If they think that the assessment of their year's work is unfair the officers are entitled to dispute the report. In the secular clergy the bishops have files on priests which the latter are never allowed to see.

To clarify this point I will cite a number of examples, taken from very recent history, of the Church's habit of concealment or deception. I have chosen examples from the trivial to the tragic to illustrate just how wide is the extent of this abuse in the practicalities of the Church's everyday life.

At the homely level of the parish it is almost impossible for the laity to know just how much money the community possesses. Canon Law makes the parish priest the sole administrator of the money and he is not obliged to disclose any details to parishioners. Conscientious parish priests publish voluntarily an annual statement of accounts, usually of income and expenditure, but it is very difficult to find out about savings or investments. In short, few people know how much money any given parish possesses.

Diocesan accounts are even more impenetrable. Once again the bishop is not obliged in law to publish them. If high-minded bishops do so, it is usually on the basis of income and expenditure. For example in England and Wales, no one has ever published figures to show just how much money the Catholic Church possesses. This kind of secrecy inevitably gives rise to wild speculations. The visit to England and Wales of Pope John Paul II in 1982 cost a large sum of money. When the bills had been paid for the hire of football stadiums, police overtime pay and so on, it was announced that there was a debt of £8 million still outstanding.

This figure prompts two thoughts. First of all, at that time mass attendance was approximately two million each Sunday, so the debt could have been cleared by a donation of merely four pounds by each practising Catholic. Their reluctance to do so should have been noted by the authorities as a sign of how little real impact had been made by the papal visit. The second thought is that the £8 million deficit was not heard of again. Evidently it had been taken up effortlessly in the general financial ebb and flow of ecclesiastical money. So just how rich is the Catholic Church in England? If £8 million could be written off so easily, the organization must be considerably wealthier than one is led to believe.

Recent legislation in parliament has required registered charities to lodge their annual accounts with the Charity Commission and there they are open to public inspection. Since all the Catholic dioceses and most religious orders have registered themselves as charities to benefit from taxation concessions, their accounts are now available for examination by anyone who cares to visit the London office of the Charity Commission. It is an admirable example of open government in the political arena but it is a sad anomaly that the secrecy of the Catholic institutions has been penetrated in this fashion, rather than by their own transparency.

A different kind of offence against truth was the practice, quite widespread until recently, of forbidding troublesome theologians to write any further books. I have dealt with this matter already in the context of justice since it offends against that virtue. It is pertinent to the subject matter of this chapter to allude to it once again because it is also at variance with the practice of truthfulness.

Probably the best known victim of this kind of action was the famous Dominican theologian Father Yves Congar. After the publication in 1953 of his famous book *Vrai et Fausse Réforme dans l'Église*,[7] he came under suspicion at the Vatican. As a punishment he was exiled from France, sent to the Dominican house in Cambridge, and forbidden to write anything further. A number of other eminent theologians like de Lubac and Chenu received similar treatment at that time.

The nature of those penalties gives cause for serious reflection on the Church's disciplinary procedures. First of all the measures were infantile and spiteful. It is difficult to understand what the authorities hoped to achieve by such actions. As an offence against justice the prohibition can be regarded as a punishment in advance for a crime which might never be committed, if indeed Congar's as yet unwritten books were to be regarded as crimes. Worst of all is the offence against truth. To forbid a theologian to write again in the future is a blatant offence against truth.

Fortunately Pope John XXIII summoned a General Council, revoked the penalties and invited the victimized theologians to become expert advisors for the Council. Later still Congar and de Lubac were made cardinals by way of making amends, but the initial measures against them must be regarded as serious offences against truth.

Another instance of the Church's offences against truth was the hushing up of child abuse scandals that came to light in the 1990s. It seems clear to me that the official policy of almost automatic and routine secrecy exacerbated the problems entailed in the child abuse cases. The suffering that the children endured was bad enough in itself but the reputation of the Church suffered equally by the cover-up.

As early as the 1960s unsubstantiated rumours about child abuse by Catholic clergy were circulating in England. The reaction of the bishops in those days was to move the priest in question to another parish or diocese, presumably to enable him to make a fresh start morally. Everything was done to ensure silence so as to preserve the reputation of the institution. It should have been clear to the authorities even then that this class of deviant seems always to have the propensity to reoffend. It would have been better to laicize them and provide them with psychotherapy and counselling. The opportunity for a fresh start was indeed taken up, but with the same offences. Even after serious lapses some priests were simply moved on and on. The bishops failed to face up to the problem realistically and compounded the harm to both perpetrators and victims by secrecy. There comes a point in such cases when the only honest course of action is to call in the police and treat the matter as a criminal offence, regardless of the adverse publicity.

Concealment broke down in the 1990s. What seems to have sparked off the open allegations of abuse were the highly publicized misdemeanours of two bishops, one in Ireland and the other in Scotland. The media revealed that they had fathered children years beforehand and that they had concealed the affairs totally. The exposure of the two bishops seems to have broken down a powerful inhibiting taboo of treating the clergy with deference. After that a volume of complaints began appearing in the public domain against priests, nuns, and brothers who had abused children in their care. Allegations of sexual abuse and appalling cruelty were made mainly against the nuns and brothers who had run orphanages in Canada, Australia, Ireland, Scotland, and England.

I do not intend to dwell at length on the details as the events have been widely aired in the press but a few salient facts must be noted. Early in 1998 the Glasgow solicitors Ross Harper were dealing with 260 claims against various Catholic institutions in Scotland for systematic abuse in childhood which took place between 1935 and the late 1950s.[8] The children were either orphans or those in care mainly because their parents could not provide for them for one reason or another. One of the claimants, Allister McNulty, remembered the punishment that he received at the age of eight in a childrens' home, Bellevue, run by the Sisters of Charity at Rutherglen. 'I was dragged naked up stone stairs by these two sisters and I was held down while I was beaten with a thick leather strap. Then I was put in the coal cellar and they wouldn't let me out because they said I was evil and they were God's children. I can't remember what I had done.' In September 2000 a nun, who had worked in the Sisters of Nazareth childrens' homes in Aberdeen and Midlothian, was found guilty on four charges of cruelty in the Aberdeen Sheriff's Court.[9]

Allegations of sexual abuse of children by priests were made in distressingly large numbers during the latter part of the 1990s. One priest was jailed for seven years in April 1998 by Warwick Crown Court for sixteen charges of indecent assault on boys in an orphanage and two charges of buggery.[10] Hitherto those activities had been concealed since the 1950s when they had taken place. If the boys complained about his treatment of them, they were beaten by the nuns who were in charge of the orphanage. It is almost impossible to imagine the extent of human misery that is indicated by those facts. His victims, some as young as six, were so haunted by the memory of the abuse that many later withdrew into reclusive lives or turned to alcohol for comfort. At least two of them were so guilt-ridden that they committed suicide, according to the police who carried out he investigation.

One is literally bewildered in trying to comprehend how such wickedness could come about. The children were the most vulnerable in society. The organizations that cared for them enjoyed complete public confidence, and they abused it. The personnel were supposedly trained for years in the love of God and neighbour. Any rumour of ill-treatment was concealed. Perhaps it is the dishonesty of the concealment that is the most disturbing.

Another aspect of institutionalized child abuse which involved Catholic institutions was the deportation of orphans and other children in care from Great Britain to Canada and Australia in the years immediately after the Second World War. Years of allegations of cruelty and abuse were confirmed by the publication in August 1998 of a report by the House of Commons Health Committee.[11]

As far as Canada was concerned, the migrants' welfare organization Home Children Canada alleges that 67 per cent of the children sent there were abused in some way. Australia received an estimated 7000 to 10 000 children between 1947 and 1967. Only a minority were orphans, and the parents of the others were neither consulted nor informed that their children were being deported. In many cases birth records have been destroyed making it difficult, if not impossible, for the survivors to trace their families in Great Britain. Child welfare organizations other than those of the Catholic Church were also involved in these deportations, but to quote the report: 'The worst cases of criminal abuse in Australia appear to have occurred in the institutions run by agencies of the Catholic Church, in particular the Christian Brothers and the Sisters of Mercy.'[12]

Regarding the abuse of boys by the Christian Brothers, the report states: 'It is hard to convey the sheer weight of the testimony we have received. It is impossible to resist the conclusion that some of what was done was of a quite exceptional depravity, so that terms like "Sexual abuse" are too weak to convey it.' One man said that as a boy, he had been repeatedly raped by the Christian Brothers at Tardun, one of the Brothers' orphanages in Australia. He had been in terrible pain, bleeding, and bewildered, trying to beat his own eyes so that they would cease to be blue and the Brothers like blue eyes, or being forced to masturbate animals, or being held upside down over a well and threatened in case he ever told.

Sadly, pages and pages could be written on this subject, since so much information was published in the public domain the 1990s. Amassing more evidence lies outside the scope of this book, but the incidents cited above are sufficient to demand serious reflection by those who are concerned with the theory and practice of the Church's moral programme. Admittedly it is difficult for novitiates, seminaries and similar organizations to filter out potential child abusers from among their trainees. In spite of this, there must be something radically wrong with organizations dedicated to child welfare which produce such abuses.

The Christian Brothers' series of tragedies in Australia were made worse by concealment and secrecy. Former victims of abuse brought claims against the Order in New South Wales Supreme Court in Sydney. The action was eventually dropped in the light of the Order's 3.5 million dollar voluntary settlement, but significant information was disclosed in open court. Most disturbing was the fact that offences were taking place before World War II and were known about at that time. In 1935 an Australian Brother wrote to the Superior General in Dublin saying: 'If we do not take a determined stand with regard to this matter, we are bound to have numerous scandals in the near future.' One wonders if the fear of publicity weighed more with him than the cruelty inflicted on the children in their care. Another senior member of the order wrote to the Superior General in the same vein: 'The weakness being a deplorable one, and scandalous in the extreme, the ever present possibility of publicity being given to the incident gives abundant cause for the most serious concern.' Fear of disclosure was also raised by Brother Conlon the superior of the Brothers' orphanage at Tardun, who wrote: 'As long as outsiders do not become aware of these things, we may hope for better times after the war.'[13]

In 1994 the Order's official historian for Australia, Brother Coldrey, drew up a report for the private consideration of the superiors. He admitted that there was a pattern of sexual abuse from the 1920s and possibly earlier. It was all hushed up in secrecy. Concerning one case of sexual abuse in the pre-war period, Coldrey wrote: 'The police were not called. The matter was handled within the Catholic community to avoid scandal.'

It would have been reasonable to suppose that the lessons of the past might have been learnt after the disclosure of such tragic events: but no. Although the order commissioned a book in1933, entitled *The Scheme*, to set right the record of the orphanages and child immigrants in Western Australia, its impact was undermined by another book. Entitled *A Secret Report*, this book goes much further in detailing the events in the orphanages. Its existence became known only after a copy came into the hands of the lawyers representing the former orphans and was used as evidence in the court hearings. The way in which this book came to light merely confirmed the public suspicions of a massive cover-up.

If the Church had practised openness instead of secrecy back in the 1930s a whole chapter of cruelty in the orphanages of Australia might have been avoided. But quite apart from such practical speculations, the offences against truth by systematic secrecy are indefensible, and have done great damage to the Church's credibility.

To illustrate how widespread is the disregard for truth in Church policy, I will take the next examples from other continents. The extent of the AIDS epidemic in the Third World needs no emphasis. The most satisfactory remedy so far devised is the use of condoms. The Vatican's opposition to their use will be dealt with in the chapter on temperance in the context of sex and birth control. In this chapter I wish to draw attention to a particular twist to an agonizing problem by the sheer dishonesty of the Church's message. In Indonesia the Catholic clergy are frightening the people by telling them that condoms are porous to the AIDS virus. In Africa a similar falsification is current. A Catholic doctor reported that she has seen a letter written on the headed notepaper of the Kenyan bishops telling the faithful that not only do many condoms have holes but that they may be laced with HIV.[14]

Disinformation of that kind can only arise in an organization that is habituated to relegating truthfulness to a subordinate position. Other considerations such as obedience and the public image of the Church have taken precedence over truth and this is indefensible.

The offences against truth which have been cited above pale into insignificance in comparison with the next two cases which I will discuss, namely the scandals of the Banco Ambrosiano and the disappearance, during the Second World War, of gold belonging to Jews.

If may come as a surprise to many Catholics to know that the Vatican has its own bank. It would seem to be alien to the Church's mission to own and run such an institution, and this perhaps explains its rather coy title. It is called the *Istituto per le Opere Religiose* (The Institute for Religious Works), IOR for short. In 1971 a certain Archbishop Marcinkus became its director. He was an American from Chicago, whose parents were immigrants from Lithuania. This gave him a direct affinity with Pope John Paul II, since his mother tongue enabled him to converse with reasonable facility with the Polish pope.

The IOR became internationally notorious in 1982 when the Banco Ambrosiano of Milan became bankrupt. It was Italy's largest private bank and the collapse involved the IOR. The main cause of the bank's collapse was the inability to honour a series of bad loans (amounting to $1.3 billion) to a string of ghost companies registered in the Bahamas, Luxembourg, and elsewhere. These loans had been guaranteed by the IOR, although as was subsequently disclosed, the IOR was directly or indirectly the owner of ten of them.[15] The chief executive of the Banco Ambrosiano, Roberto Calvi, was arrested in 1981 when the Italian government was investigating the affairs of the Banco Ambrosiano. When he was released on bail, he persuaded Marcinkus to issue letters of patronage affirming IOR's support for the ghost companies' debts. Marcinkus took the precaution of obtaining from Calvi a secret letter nullifying the letters of patronage. In June 1982 Calvi went to London allegedly to obtain documents which would force the IOR to rescue the Banco Ambrosiano. In the course of that journey he was murdered and his body was found hanging under Blackfriars Bridge. His secretary met her death in Milan, in mysterious circumstances, the day before.

On 17 June 1982 the Banco Ambrosiano collapsed because Marcinkus refused to honour the letters of patronage. He denied that the IOR owned any of the mysterious ghost companies. Under pressure from the Italian government's official investigation and enormous publicity from the world's press, the Vatican was forced to take action. On 3 July Cardinal Casaroli, the Vatican's Secretary of State (for Foreign Affairs), appointed a committee of three 'wise men' to investigate the links between IOR and the Banco Ambrosiano. On 22 July the *Financial Times* of London disclosed that the IOR owned seven of the ghost companies. This was denied by the Vatican.[16] On 29 July the Italian press announced that the three chief officers of the IOR were under investigation by the Italian government, namely Marcinkus, Luigi Mannini, and Pellegrino de Strobel. The Vatican took umbrage protesting that they were subjects of the Vatican in their work and exempt from the jurisdiction of the Italian Republic. After repeated denials and revisions of the story, the Vatican was forced to admit that the IOR did own ten of the ghost companies. It was stated that Marcinkus refused to pay their debts because the IOR did not own them all![17] The three wise men declared that in July 1981 the IOR did not know that it owned the ghost companies, that is after the money had been borrowed. Subsequent research showed this to be untrue.

The dramatic events and the exposure of denials fuelled immense speculation in the world's press about what was really happening. In the absence of complete transparency, rumours flourished. Speculation was rife about who killed Calvi, was it the Mafia or the Masonic Lodge P2? Who else was set to profit from his death and consequent silence? Who had received the money which was unaccounted for? Could it be Poland and the fledgling Solidarity trade union movement?[18]

Events moved slowly but in 1984 the Vatican agreed to a voluntary payment of $244 million to the creditors of the Banco Ambrosiano. This action still left many questions unanswered. In 1987 the Italian government issued a warrant for the arrest of Mennini, de Strobel, and most significantly for Marcinkus too. The Vatican claimed that this infringed the Lateran Treaty of 1929 which guaranteed the independence of the Vatican City State. The government insisted that it was acting within its rights, and Archbishop Marcinkus had to retreat (geographically) inside the Vatican's walls. There he remained, virtually a prisoner, liable to arrest should he leave that tiny enclave. It was rumoured that the pope was going to make him a Cardinal so that he would have complete and permanent immunity from arrest by the Italian authorities. However, that promotion was not given to him.

It is almost impossible to count up the amount of concealment and the number of lies told by the Church authorities in the course of that discreditable episode. Many questions are still unanswered and as long as silence reigns, the Church's reputation will suffer. In addition to the concealment of embarrassing facts two other aspects of the case are damaging to the Church's reputation, namely the alterations of official explanations when the secular press has shown that they were false, and the double standard in relation to the Vatican's immunity. That is to say, the Church authorities were prepared to invoke the Lateran Treaty to save Archbishop Marcinkus from arrest but they were perfectly content for the IOR's activities to cross the frontier and operate in the Italian financial markets.

The whole episode has done immense damage to the Church's reputation since it is clear to people of intelligence and integrity that truthfulness was betrayed on a massive scale.

The second major failing on the part of the Vatican has been the problem of Nazi gold. At the end of the Second World War it became clear that the Nazis, having stolen vast amounts of gold and other valuables from the Jews whom they subsequently killed, then used this wealth for commercial and other purposes via the Swiss banks and the Vatican. For years the Swiss banks resisted attempts by Jewish survivors' organizations to obtain information about such monies, pleading always the rule of confidentiality that is the hallmark of the Swiss system. The Vatican was equally silent, insisting on the hundred year rule for the opening of its archives.

After many years of campaigning, hope began to dawn for the survivors and the descendants of victims. In December 1997 in London, an international conference representing 40 nations agreed to increase the pressure on

Switzerland and the Vatican to disclose information. Several other countries including Britain have not been totally open about their involvement with Nazi gold during and at the end of the Second World War. The USA and Britain set up a fund to help the Holocaust victims, and by 1997 the UK had donated to it £1 million, the USA £2.3 million, and Austria £5.2 million. These sums are dwarfed by the amount of gold and other assets looted by the Nazis. A new study commissioned by the Swiss government estimates that it received about £2 billion in gold stolen by the Nazis.

The Vatican was represented at the conference by two observers, Monsignor Giovanni d'Aniello, and Father Marcel Chappin. They came under heavy pressure from the USA and other countries to open up the Vatican's archives, but they remained silent. The World Jewish Congress released a declassified letter from the US Treasury which showed that in 1946 the Americans were told that money and gold to the value of £80 million stolen from Jews and Serbs were sent to the Vatican. The funds stolen by the fascist Ustasha regime in wartime Croatia were sent through a Vatican 'pipeline' to Argentina and Spain, according to the letter. But the US Treasury said the reports may have been a 'smokescreen' and that the gold may still be in the Vatican. Elan Steinberg, a spokesman for the World Jewish Congress, said that the archives of the Vatican are desperately needed for the kind of information and transparency that we require.[19] Declassified documents also show that the Vatican Bank (IOR) was dealing with the Reichsbank and Swiss banks that had been blacklisted by the Allies.[20]

Eventually, after years of acrimonious debate, public pressure and diplomatic negotiations, the Swiss banks agreed to a settlement. On 13 August 1998 in New York, it was announced that the Swiss banks had agreed to pay $1.25 billion to the survivors and descendants of the Holocaust victims.[21]

In spite of the Vatican's refusal to cooperate by opening its archives to researchers, Jewish organizations have not abandoned the quest for the truth. In 1998 a group of Jews and others connected with the Holocaust Education Trust went to Rome in order to discuss the matter with the Vatican's Secretariat of State. The only information that they were given was a presentation set of the 12-volume edition of documents, namely *The Vatican and World Jewry during the Second World War*. The same group of people sponsored research in the British Public Records Office, the archives of the Bank of England, and a variety of published sources. As a result it became clear that the documents in the Vatican's 12 volumes had been carefully selected to stress only positive efforts by the Vatican to resist the Nazis or to save victims. Even so, the researchers were able to extract a number of key questions that they addressed to the Vatican authorities. They have received no answers.[22] Until the Vatican authorities allow independent researchers into the archives to examine the material at first hand it will be impossible to vindicate the truthfulness of the Holy See.

Another dimension of the Holocaust that has remained shrouded in secrecy is the extent to which the Vatican was aware of the Nazis' plans and activities in exterminating the Jews. Recently it has been alleged that as early as March 1942 Pope Pius XII knew of the policy. A member of the World Jewish Council, Gerhard Riegner then living in Geneva sent a telegram to the pope revealing the existence of the gas chambers and the plans to exterminate the Jews. This telegram is not mentioned in the Vatican's 12-volume authorized account of the war years. It is unlikely that Riegner's memory played him false. Almost the same conclusion was published in the narrative of Rudolf Vrba, who was the only man to escape from Auschwitz, and who made it his principal objective to convey the information about the camp to the papal nuncio in Prague,[23] as has been mentioned in the previous chapter.

In July 2001 events took a dramatic turn for the worse. The group of five Jewish and Catholic scholars who had been investigating the Holocaust and the Catholic Church's silence were denied access to the Vatican archives. They had been appointed in 1999 by the Vatican and various Jewish groups, but before publishing a final report they requested access to the Vatican archives covering the Nazi period. Access was denied to them, allegedly for technical reasons. That excuse is palpably untrue. Either something discreditable has to be hidden or the habit of concealment is so ingrained in the Vatican's staff that they cannot break out of it. The five scholars were left with no other course for men of integrity but to suspend their work and pull out of the investigation.[24]

In view of the allegations which have been made, the veracity of the Vatican and hence the Catholic Church in general will remain compromised until there has been a satisfactory open investigation into the archives. The refusal to initiate such an examination inevitably gives rise to the supposition that records of discreditable episodes have to be concealed.

The examples cited in this chapter show how great is the gap between the doctrine about truth and the activities of the Catholic Church in recent history. As with other matters discussed in this book, it is damaging to the Church's credibility and may well account for its diminishing appeal to high-minded people, especially among the young.

Notes

1 *The Guardian*, 2 May 1996.
2 *The Guardian*, 2 May 1996.
3 *The Tablet*, 8 July 1995.
4 *The Guardian*, 22 February 1996.
5 Ponting, C. *The Right to Know*. London 1985, 129, 139.
6 Hamlet, Act I, scene 3, lines 78–80.
7 Subsequently translated into English as *True and False Reform in the Church*. Published in Paris, by the Editions du Cerf.
8 *The Observer*, Colour Supplement, 3 May 1998.
9 *The Observer*, 3 May 1998; *The Guardian*, 20 September 2000.
10 *The Guardian*, 1 May 1998.

11   *The Tablet*, 8 August 1998.
12   *The Tablet*, 8 August 1998.
13   *The Tablet*, 8 August 1998.
14   *The Tablet*, 8 March 1996.
15   Gurwin, L. *The Calvi Affair*, London 1983, 170.
16   Gurwin, 169.
17   Gurwin, 170.
18   Gurwin, 176.
19   *The Guardian*, 5 December 1997.
20   *The Guardian*, 12 February 1998.
21   *The Guardian*, 14 August 1998.
22   *The Tablet*, 18 March 2000.
23   *The Guardian*, 10 October 1998; R.Vbra and A. Bestic, *I Cannot Forgive*, London
     1964, 257.
24   *The Guardian*, 25 July 2001.

Chapter 9

Is Bravery Virtuous?

Undeniably the greatest evil which one human being can inflict on another is killing, because of its finality. Every sin can be repented but this offence must always be without restitution. To face suffering and death for a noble cause has always been admired and the moral strength to do so has been called fortitude since the time of the ancient Greeks.

During the first three centuries of its history, the Church offered a model of still greater heroism in the courage displayed by the martyrs in their sufferings and the endurance of cruel deaths. The cult of the martyrs was the earliest form of honouring saints. They were held up as examples of virtue because of their constant witness to Christ, and because they displayed greater courage than military heroes, insofar as they offered no resistance to death. In other words their triumph over danger and fear was complete.

To kill another human being is so much at variance with our basic psychology and inbuilt taboos that it has always required some justification, however far-fetched. The legitimacy of self-defence has been extrapolated to the larger situations of defending the clan, tribe and nation. It becomes harder to sustain the logic when the notion is extended to cover wars of aggression and not simply defence. Yet in view of its intrinsic cruelty, men have always felt the need to try to justify the activity.

Powerful elites have often had so much to gain from compelling others to fight on their behalf that it should not surprise us if the basic immorality of the activity has been obscured by propaganda. What is really surprising and tragic is the extent to which the proponents of war and violence have succeeded in harnessing the poets, musicians, artists and publicists to their cause. One of the reasons why warfare has played such an unexpectedly large part in humanity's history is that its cruelties and injustices have been disguised and its heroism has been overstated and glamorized by the poets.

A few examples will indicate just how widespread has been the effect of the writers. At the very dawn of European literature, Homer immortalized the martial virtues in his masterpieces the *Iliad* and *Odyssey*. Virgil did the same for Latin literature with his *Aeneid*, starting with the unforgettable words 'Arma virumque cano' (which G.B. Shaw lampooned in the title of his play *Arms and the Man*). In the English language Shakespeare has been the most influential poet extolling the glories of heroism in war. Before the battle of Agincourt, King Henry V exhorts his soldiers with these well-known words:

This story shall the good man teach his son;
And Crispin Crispian shall ne'er go by,
From this day to the ending of the world,
But we in it shall be remembered;
We few, we happy few, we band of brothers;
For he today who sheds his blood with me
Shall be my brother; be he ne'er so vile
This day shall gentle his condition:
And gentlemen in England now a-bed
Shall think themselves accurs'd they were not here,
And hold their manhoods cheap whiles any speaks
That fought with us upon Saint Crispin's day.
                              (*Henry V*, Act IV, scene 3)

The rhetoric is powerful and influential even for those who are implacably opposed to war. In the same play we see another strand of publicity which has had an equally pernicious influence on the popularizing of war, namely that the benevolence of God has been hijacked in its propaganda. After the battle of Agincourt King Henry evaluates his victory in the following high-flown sentiments:

O God! thy arm was here;
And not to us, but to thy arm alone,
Ascribe we all. When, without stratagem
But in plain shock and even play of battle,
Was ever known so great and little loss
On one part and on the other? Take it, God,
For it is none but Thine!
                              (Henry V, Act IV, scene 8)

In all fairness to Shakespeare, it must be remembered than in another play he described the pathos of war more effectively perhaps than any other writer. In *Henry VI* Part III, he emphasizes the particular tragedy of civil war in an incident after the Battle of Towton. Two soldiers enter the stage, each bearing the dead body of the enemy whom each has killed in single combat. They search the bodies for money and other plunder. As they remove the helmets of their victims one man realizes that he has killed his father and the other sees the face of his son. The speeches that follow are among the most tragic in our language, and are a profound meditation on the iniquity of warfare (*Henry VI*, Part III, Act II, scene 5).

There is one group of writers who broke with the fashion. The First World War produced a remarkable group of English poets who wrote about the horrors and evils or war. Writers like Robert Graves, Siegfried Sassoon, Wilfrid Owen, Isaac Rosenberg and others, who had served in the front line, wrote about war as it really is and stripped of all glamour. In the overall perspective of the world's literature they represent merely a small counterculture. Their readership cannot rival the millions who have been inspired by the deeds of King Arthur and other heroes.

Sentiments of the realists are in a minority among the poetic and popular output. The praise of war and the assumption that our victory is God's will has far outweighed the down-to-earth understanding of its cruelty and injustice. It is difficult for us at the start of the twenty-first century to understand how Elgar could have set to music the sentiments in A.C. Benson's *Land of Hope and Glory*:

> Wider yet and wider,
> Shall thy bounds be set,
> God who made thee mighty,
> Make thee mightier yet.

Possibly the most blatant example of this tendency was the poem which Kipling composed for Queen Victoria's diamond jubilee. It was entitled *Recessional* and was published in *The Times* of 17 July 1897, in the same column as the Queen's Jubilee letter to the people:

> God of our father, known of old,
> Lord of our far-flung battle-line,
> Beneath whose awful hand we hold
> Dominion over palm and pine-
> Lord God of Hosts be with us yet,
> Lest we forget – lest we forget!
>
> The tumult and the shouting dies;
> The Captains and the Kings depart:
> Still stands Thine ancient sacrifice,
> An humbled and a contrite heart.
> Lord God of Hosts, be with us yet,
> Lest we forget – lest we forget!
>
> Far-called, our navies melt away;
> On dune and headland sinks the fire:
> Lo, all our pomp of yesterday
> Is one with Nineveh and Tyre!
> Judge of the nations, spare us yet,
> Lest we forget – lest we forget!
>
> If, drunk with sight of powers, we loose
> Wild tongues that have not Thee in awe,
> Such boastings as the Gentiles use,
> Or lesser breeds without the Law
> Lord God of Hosts, be with us yet,
> Lest we forget – lest we forget!

For heathen heart that puts her trust
In reeking tube and iron shard,
All valiant dust that builds on dust,
And guarding, calls not Thee to guard,
For frantic boast and foolish word –
Thy mercy on Thy People, Lord!

A century later it rings hollow but one cannot doubt how it echoed and reinforced the bombastic sentiments of the age. Possibly it has required the horrors of the two world wars in the twentieth century to convince thoughtful people that God was not necessarily on our side in the wars.

Classical musicians and poets were not alone in the idiom. They were emulated by the writers of music hall songs, such as:

There's something about a soldier,
There's something about a soldier,
That is fine, fine, fine.
Oh the banging of the drum,
And the shouts of Here they come,
There's something about a soldier
That is fine fine, fine.

Songs such as those were written by the dozen in the latter part of the nineteenth century when England was engaged on a seemingly endless series of (successful) colonial wars. Their sheer banality grates on the sensibilities of a more critical age. Considered as a means of disguising the real nature of war, they are a sobering reminder of how easily clear-headed reasoning and moral considerations can be brushed aside by shallow patriotic sentiment.

In addition it is worth remembering that generations of schoolboys have been influenced by narratives of heroism in the *Boys' Own Paper*, the Biggles books and many similar stories. Even nursery rhymes constituted part of the conspiracy of deception:

Every little girl would like to be,
A fairy on a Christmas tree.
Every little boy would like to fight.
With a trumpet and a gun.

The list could be extended indefinitely. For centuries the cruelties and injustices of war, in short its reality, have been disguised. This has been done by poetry that ranged from the sublime to the trivial as well as the use of gorgeous uniforms, military bands, and magnificent parades.

The massive culture of deception was necessary in order to persuade men to perpetrate the activity against which we have the strongest inbuilt inhibitions. All of this prompts two questions. First of all what has the Catholic

Church done to counteract this with a more influential moral programme? And secondly, how could human beings act in this manner? To begin with the second question, it is necessary to investigate just what motivates one man to kill a fellow human being in the course of wars in which the two individuals have virtually no personal stake.

A variety of explanations have been suggested. The simplest is that men are put into a situation where they must kill or be killed. This explanation was given to me by a thoughtful man, a conscript, who had been a tank commander. He was awarded the MC for dragging all the crew to safety when their tank was ablaze. He certainly knew what he was talking about.

Another explanation was advanced by Lord Trenchard who, in the inter-war years, organized the Royal Air Force in its present form. He considered that men would kill when influenced by a greater fear such as their reputation in the community. The insinuation of cowardice, particularly in something like a small village, is more daunting than the fear of being killed in battle.

An equally negative motive was described to me by a sailor who served all through World War Two. Early in the war, as a very junior officer, he was on the bridge of a battleship and he recalled the admiral saying, as he looked down on the seamen busy on the decks below, 'Do you think that these men will fight?' (He was aware that before they had been conscripted, many of them had been unemployed since the Depression and had little prospect of any personal advantage from a British victory.) Turning to his fellow officers he declared, 'They will fight if they are more afraid of their own side than of the enemy'. That was the constant verdict of old soldiers who were interviewed on television on the various anniversaries of the end of the First World War. When ordered to leave the trenches and go over the top to attack the enemy, they realized that the probability of death was high but equally they knew that refusing the command carried a higher probability of subsequently being executed by a firing squad.

A recent exhaustive investigation into the matter has revealed the disturbing fact that a minority of men enjoyed killing.[1] For the most part the evidence is anecdotal (quotations from letters and so on), and it is difficult to establish what proportion they constituted in the armed forces. Nevertheless, it is deeply disturbing to realize that some men (who are not professional criminals) actually gain pleasure from killing, as the following quotation shows:

> As a trench-mortar officer, I was given command over what is probably the most murderous instrument in modern warfare … One day … I secured a direct hit on an enemy encampment, saw bodies or parts of bodies go up in the air, and heard the desperate yelling of the wounded or the runaways. I had to confess to myself that it was one of the happiest moments of my life.[2]

The majority of men lack that kind of pleasurable aggression, and it has to be instilled by training. This became an acute problem for the British forces after 1916 when universal conscription of young men was introduced. The army then had to increase the emphasis in its training on stirring up the killer instinct. The men had to be taught how to become practical realists, conscious only of the necessity to kill or be killed.[3] During the First World War that objective was supposedly obtained by concentrating on bayonet drill. During World War Two a more sophisticated approach was tried, namely the employment of psychological measures to increase the hate factor. However during the course of the war it was found to be largely useless, as one commentator noted:

> In the course of most wars, individuals or small groups in training or back areas not infrequently become convinced that we must learn to hate the enemy and that blood lust is an important component of the combatant morale. Fascinating as this idea is, to the officers and men who are chafing over inactivity or struggling with boredom, experience shows that attempts to arouse primitive passion – even if they are successful in overcoming the British solder's sense of honour – have not been found useful as a method of increasing combatant efficiency.[4]

Once a unit was in action, it seems that group pressure on its members to conform was the most powerful motivator for a man's conduct. This applied to atrocities against civilians as well. In the Vietnam War the conscripted men had a real fear of ostracism or ridicule if they did not take part in massacres. Worse still, they might be killed by their own comrades if morale was at a particularly low ebb. It has been calculated, on the basis of data from the US Defence Department, that in the Vietnam War over 1000 officers and NCOs were killed by their own men.[5]

In spite of all the influences of military discipline and group pressure many soldiers found ways of contracting out quietly. For example unofficial truces were more common than the historians acknowledged. The most famous was that of Christmas 1914 when thousands of German and British soldiers came out of the trenches to celebrate Christmas in no man's land. In the middle of the Second World War an American official survey of 400 infantry companies found that no more than 15 per cent of men had actually fired their weapons, although at least 80 per cent had been in a position to do so.[6]

By contrast it seems that in particular circumstances all rational or moral restraint had been discarded in incidents like killing prisoners or large-scale massacres of civilians. The My Lai massacre in Vietnam in 1968 attracted worldwide publicity because in that village literally hundreds of innocent civilians were slaughtered.

The whole tragic business presents a moral and psychological vacuum in the field of human conduct. Most of those who are caught up in it try to make some sense of the activity by looking upon it as an unpleasant, but necessary duty.[7] In case that simple rationalization did not satisfy the leaders, there was always the apparatus of courts martial to ensure that the fear of their own side would outweigh the fear of the enemy.

This was certainly the presumption behind the courts martial which dealt with alleged cases of desertion during the First World War. Under current army law soldiers were liable to the death penalty if they had deserted their posts. At that date, little allowance was made for the psychological disorientation resulting from weeks in the front line. In 1916 a secret order was circulated to the effect that all men accused of cowardice were to be shot and medical evidence was not to be taken.[8] One corps commander is quoted as saying that the death penalty was instituted to make such men fear running away more than they feared the enemy. The legal safeguards were in some cases little more than a formality. The accused men rarely had an officer to mount a legal defence at the court martial.[9]

This method of ensuring military discipline was not confined to the British. During the Second World War 20 000 German servicemen were court-martialled and sentenced to death.[10]

Having surveyed very briefly the moral and psychological chaos of warfare, which is literally a vacuum of rational values, the time has now come to take a preliminary look at the Church's attitude to it and see if Christianity has made any realistic improvement to this morass. The conversion of the Empire in the fourth century provides a convenient division from a fairly simple situation to one of almost insoluble complexity. In principle the infant Church was opposed to warfare, and in the deaths of the martyrs, role models were presented to the community showing a higher form of fortitude which did not entail inflicting violence on another. The importance attached to this virtue as exemplified by the martyrs cannot be overstressed. In the first three centuries of Christian history, literally thousands of men and women endured imprisonment, torture, and savagely cruel deaths rather than betray their loyalty to Christ. It is significant that women endured the torments just as bravely as did men, showing to the ancient world an aspect of feminine psychology that the pagans had ignored. The accounts of the legal proceedings, their sufferings and places of burial were recorded with great care and provided the basis of the liturgical cult that soon arose. The festivals of the martyrs were the first feast days in the religious calendar, after the celebrations of the strictly divine interventions in salvation history like the Epiphany, Good Friday, Easter Sunday, Pentecost and the rest. Only at a later date did the Church admit to its liturgical calendar the festival days of saints whose lives were of outstanding virtue but who had not endured the martyrs' sufferings.

The most important early witness to the official attitude of the Church is the *Apostolic Tradition* of Hippolytus. This records the liturgical practices of the Roman community in the middle of the third century and by implication, their theological outlook too. In dealing with candidates for baptism, there is a detailed list of professions which are incompatible with the Christian calling and which the aspirants must abandon or else be rejected from the catechumenate. The list of forbidden occupations begins with brothel keepers, and includes gladiators and their trainers, actors and prostitutes. In this list we also find soldiers, whose status is regulated as follows:

A soldier under authority shall not kill a man. If he is ordered to, he shall not carry out the order; nor shall he take the oath. If he is unwilling, let him be rejected. He who has the power of the sword, or is a magistrate of a city who wears the purple, let him cease or be rejected. A catechumen or believer who wants to become soldiers should be rejected, because they have despised God.[11]

At the end of the section, having enumerated the most obvious categories of occupations which were considered incompatible with Christianity, the writer added: 'If we have left anything out, the facts themselves will teach you; for we all have the Spirit of God.' This is the most succinct expression of how the early Church envisaged the process of moral decision-making. It is also a perfect development of the moral programme of St Paul to which I alluded earlier in this book.

The infant Church was not totally pacifist. As with many other moral questions pluralism was the order of the day, reflecting the complexities of everyday life. The sources on the matter are principally Irenaeus (*Adversus Haereses* IV, 34, iv,) and Origen (*Contra Celsum*, V 33). The latter had to answer the difficult objection that the Christians were content to enjoy the benefits of a secure and peaceful empire, but were not prepared to defend it from attack.

At the end of the second century, Tertullian defended the Christians, declaring that they were useful citizens who could be found in all walks of life including the army.[12] Officers were required to offer sacrifices to the pagan deities or to the deified emperors. The refusal of Christians to do this led to martyrdoms, several of which are well documented.[13] Others suffered marytrdom simply from a refusal to join the army or to fight, as for instance St Maximillian of Numidia who was executed at Theveste in 295 because of his refusal to serve in the Roman army.

It seems that the development of Christian thinking on warfare was spurred on by two factors. Up to the time of Marcus Aurelius (170–80) military service was not universally compulsory,[14] and up to that time Christians had been only a small minority of the population. The second factor was the conversion of Constantine, after which Christianity soon became the majority religion of the empire. From then onwards Christians effectively had the responsibility for the defence of the empire and in that context Augustine formulated the principles of the just war. At a later date, when the Empire became officially Christian there was a complete volte-face. In 416, under Theodosius II, pagans were expelled from the army.[15]

After the conversion of Constantine and as Christians became ever more numerous in the population of the Roman Empire, various practical solutions were devised to cope with the moral problems of warfare. The theory of the just war, traceable to Augustine, was destined to be the most influential. For the individual Christian other practical measures were devised. The Council of Nicaea (325 AD) legislated for the situation of soldiers. Canon 12 decreed that if a soldier had left the army and then returned to it after becoming a Christian, he was required to do penance for 13 years before being readmitted to the Eucharist.[16] St Basil the Great declared that while a soldier must obey orders, he must do penance for three years if he should have killed a man in battle. Only at the end of that period would he be readmitted to the Eucharist.[17]

The principle of requiring canonical penance for soldiers who had killed in battle was still in force in 1066. After the battle of Hastings penances were imposed on those who were aware that they had killed an enemy soldier, and the building of the abbey at the village of Battle on the site of the original conflict was in part an act of collective penance.

The Byzantine Empire was more strongly influenced by Christian principles than its western counterpart and consistently tried to solve international disputes by diplomatic means rather than war.[18] In the West at the start of the second millenium, various limitations were imposed on warfare by Church councils, such as the prohibition against fighting on Sundays and Church Festivals. However, these measures proved to be unrealistic and in the Fourth Crusade the attack on Constantinople took place during Holy Week.

In fact the Crusades proved to be a complete betrayal of Christian principles on the part of the Church, since they were a vast military offensive, commanded, organized, and in part financed by the Church. Equally disturbing is the fact that the movement was initiated by the highest authority. The First Crusade was proclaimed by Pope Urban II at the Council of Clermont in 1095. The Second Crusade of 1147 was preached by St Bernard of Clairvaux who at that time was probably the most influential personality in the Church.

Having embarked upon the course of militarism, the Church authorities then extended the principle to further the evangelization of pagan nations and the suppression of heresy within Christendom. The military religious orders developed directly out of the crusading movement. The Knights Templar were started by Hugh de Payenes in 1118 with a view to protecting pilgrims on the journey to Jerusalem. Their rule was approved by the Council of Troyes in 1128 and over the next couple of centuries their numbers increased and their activities became more aggressively belligerent, constituting a major military contribution to the crusades.

The Teutonic Knights also originated in the period of the crusades. They were founded at Acre in 1190. Eight years later they became a military order, accepting the same rule as the Templars, which was confirmed by the papacy. Eventually their activities took them to the eastern frontier of Germany and they were engaged in fighting and evangelizing the heathen Prussians and Lithuanians. The combination of religion and politics was characteristic of Christendom at that time but even so, the deliberate use of warfare to spread the gospel must be regarded with amazement.

The principle was extended to the military campaigns against the Albigensian heretics in south-western France between 1209 and 1218 at the behest of Pope Innocent III. The same principle (that of violence and killing) underlay the practice of burning heretics. Theoretically the Church authorities kept their hands clean since, after condemnation for heresy in the ecclesiastical courts, the victims were handed over to the civil authorities who actually carried out the death sentences. The distinction was grossly artificial and the ultimate responsibility was that of the Church. It comes as something of a shock to a modern reader to see that Aquinas was among those who advocated the death penalty for heretics.[19]

With the wisdom of hindsight, it is simple to point out what went wrong. However we should be cautious in judging our predecessors' decisions because it is so difficult for us to enter into their perception of the world. Even making allowances for their being confined within the presuppositions of their own time, it is difficult to understand how the Church leaders could have departed so far from the ideals of the New Testament. 'You have learnt how it was said to our ancestors: you must not kill; and if anyone does kill he must answer for it before the court. But I say to you: anyone who is angry with his brother will answer for it before the court' (Matthew 5:21). What is equally disturbing is that those policies have not been repudiated realistically. The year 1995 passed without any disavowal of the First Crusade, although the crusading movement has done incalculable damage to relations between Christians and Muslims up to the present day, and has also constituted the principal cause of the schism between Rome and Constantinople.

There are moreover reasons to indicate that the attitude has not yet been eradicated from certain sections of the Catholic Church right up to the twentieth century. During the Second World War, in Yugoslavia, Catholic Croatians carried out a religiously motivated slaughter of Serbs belonging to the Orthodox Church. After the occupation by the Germans in 1941, they set up a puppet regime in Croatia which was elevated into an independent state, and included Bosnia-Herzegovina in its borders. Something like a fifth of the population of this small state was Orthodox, and in 1941 the ruling Ustasha party announced their policy against them, with the principle 'Convert a third, expel a third and kill a third'.

The Ustasha Minister of the Interior set the example in May 1941 by carrying out the massacre of 4000 Serbs in his native district of Bosnia-Herzegovina. A month later the wholesale massacre of the Serbs began in the region of Mostar and Caplijna. Only two Catholic priests are known to have opposed the killings. One of them was the Catholic bishop of Mostar, Aloysius Misic, who denounced the slaughter from the pulpit and wrote a formal complaint to the metropolitan, the Archbishop of Zagreb. His letter is one of the sources of information about this poorly documented incident. He supplies terrifying details, such as the fact that the victims including women and children were thrown over a cliff into a ravine. Paradoxically it took place close to the town of Medjugorje which later became a popular pilgrimage centre. One hopes that the pilgrims learn the lessons of that not too distant moral lapse.[20]

During the Middle Ages Aquinas put the just war theory into its classical form. He stipulated three conditions for a war to be morally acceptable. It must be undertaken on the authority of the king, it must be for a just cause, and it must be pursued with a rightful motive, that is the advancement of good and the repression of evil.[21] This was elaborated somewhat by the father of international law, the famous Francisco de Vittoria (died 1546), who declared that it must be waged by proper means. This was later elaborated to mean the inviolability of non-combatants, that the good to be obtained must outweigh the inevitable cruelties, and that all other methods of settling the dispute had failed.

In spite of the theoretical coherence of the just war principles, one may doubt whether they have ever exercised any practical influence on the course of politics and a government's decision about when to go to war. The Christian Churches' collective failure to protest against the tide of violence is perhaps their greatest dereliction of duty. Catholicism too must bear its full share of blame. Only one Church has pursued a consistent and realistic programme against warfare, namely the Quakers. During the course of the Civil War, George Fox could have secured his release from prison if he had accepted the offer of a captaincy in the Parliamentarian army. He declined and his refusal was symbolic of the consistent policy of that Church that their members would not take part in fighting. I do not underestimate the practical difficulties of deciding in complex political situations when warfare might or might not be morally acceptable. Christian Churches as a whole have good reason to be grateful to the Society of Friends because one Church at least has been consistent in its pursuit of peace. A further practical outcome of their principles was the important role which they played, during the First World War, in securing legislation to protect conscientious objectors.

The technicalities of modern warfare have introduced a qualitative change into the conditions of war which demand a radical reappraisal by Christians of the application of the principles of the just war. The principal new elements are universal conscription and the exponential increase in cruelty and destruction brought about by the technological development of weapons.

Prior to the establishment of conscription, it was just possible to envisage that the men of military age had made a self-selecting division into those who joined the forces because they considered that the war was just and those who refused to enlist on moral grounds. Admittedly this is an oversimplification, but when conscription for all young men came about, even that flimsy theory could not stand. Far-sighted people understood the implications. For example, when Russia introduced conscription for the whole nation in the latter part of the nineteenth century, the writer Tolstoy was horrified. He knew exactly what was involved, having served in the Russian army during the Crimean War, and he had made an extensive study of military history for the writing of *War and Peace*. In later life he became a pacifist and would go regularly to the recruiting offices in towns near his home to make vehement protests when the time of enlistment came round. He maintained that the illiterate peasants had no idea of the moral issues involved in taking the military oath. He also bitterly reproved the Orthodox priests who were in attendance to hand over the Bible and take the oath of allegiance to the Czar.

Morally speaking, the only difference between a conscript and a volunteer is that the former acts with less freedom. Neither can relinquish his own personal moral responsibility, but the volunteer and particularly the career soldier is in danger of signing a blank cheque. That is to say he has effectively undertaken to kill anyone whom the government commands him to kill, in the future too, in circumstances impossible to envisage at the time of his enlisting. That kind of relinquishing of personal responsibility is perhaps one of the worst sins that a human being can commit. Yet it is rarely adverted to in pastoral guidance. Theoretically he could and should make a fresh moral decision at the start of each new war, but in practice it is almost impossible psychologically to take such an independent line. It is at this point that the Church should have been giving carefully thought-out moral guidance but it has not done so. In reality, the only kind of moral education for this sort of scenario is the preparation of the individual to make his own decisions, having taken account of all the relevant facts. This kind of moral independence has been actively discouraged by the Catholic Church since the time of the Reformation. Catholic leaders have felt comfortable only if they can devise general rules which can be enforced by obedience. Situations like war which do not admit of such rules have been left virtually as a moral vacuum. The guidance given in the standard authors has been so generalized and remote from reality that it has resulted in no practical diminution of the horrors of war. This is a most serious reproach to the Church's moral programme.

A brief examination of the standard authors whose books were widely used in the early part of the twentieth century will illustrate the point which I am making. At the turn of the century one of the most influential Catholic moral theologians was Augustin Lehmkuhl whose *Theologia Moralis* entered its eleventh edition just before the First World War. The obligations of soldiers are enunciated as follows:

> Those who are compelled by conscription, or who are obliged by a 'contract' of service (that is, long term regulars), can wage war, as long as its injustice remains unproven. (Section 3)

> Concerning those who are obliged to obey, for most of them it is not their place to inquire into the injustice of the war. Nevertheless if circumstances give rise to serious suspicion that the war is unjust ... they are not excused from the obligation of investigating ... When inquiry is not possible nor obligatory, and while doubt remains, they are not to be prohibited from waging war (Section 4).[22]

Another equally influential moralist was Eduard Genicot, the tenth edition of whose *Theologia Moralis* was published just after the First World War. Concerning the morality of fighting he wrote:

> Conscripted soldiers and regulars who signed up before the war began are not obliged in principle to inquire about the justice of the war. They can obey their superiors as long as it is not certain that their orders are illicit. If there are grounds for suspecting that the war is not just ... they must make inquiries ... and must desist from war if they discover that it is clearly unjust. Soldiers who volunteer after it has started must inquire about its justice and may not fight until morally certain that it is just.[23]

In England, the most influential Catholic writer on moral theology was Father Henry Davis. Writing after the Second World War, his guidance on the matter was as follows:

> Soldiers who are conscripted, or those who joined before the war, may usually presume that their country is in the right: if in doubt they are bound to obey. If the war is manifestly unjust, a soldier may not lawfully inflict any damage on the enemy, though he may of course, defend his life if the enemy attack him. Soldiers who freely join up after the war has begun, must satisfy themselves that the cause is just.[24]

A careful reading of these extracts, which are thoroughly representative, indicates a number of dangerous presuppositions, which are fundamentally at variance with the outlook of the New Testament and the Church's ancient tradition. The injunctions to enquire about the justifiability of the war are soft-pedalled to the point of being impractical. There is a strong bias against making independent decisions and, given the psychological pressures on servicemen in the forces, this is the area where independence should have been strengthened by the Church's teaching. All in all, the general presumption is that the soldier must obey his government and it is similarly presumed that the government's course is morally right. Needless to say, this is exactly what the political leaders have always wanted to hear from the Churches in their domains. It goes a long way to explaining why the Catholic Church has had so little influence in curtailing the vast evil of warfare and the attendant evils that follow in its train. In contrast to the record of the Quakers, the Catholic Church's stance has, for the most part, been one of acquiescence to whatever the political leaders have wanted.

It stands as something of a reproach to the Church that in the modern period it was the civil governments and not the Churches who initiated and concluded some international measures to lessen the brutality of war, like the Conventions of Geneva (1864 and 1929) and The Hague (1899 and 1907). These agreements cover such matters as the treatment of prisoners of war and the inviolability of the ships of neutral countries. A measure of moral guidance has been given in the British legislation by the Army Acts of

1881 and 1955. For example in *The Manual of Military Law*, it is recognized that a soldier has the right to refuse to carry out an order which is illegal.[25] The matter is discussed at length in *Military Obedience* by Nico Keijzer (and others), covering legal decisions of the USA, Great Britain, France and Germany.[26]

The technological transformation of warfare came about in a significant manner during the First World War. The technical advances of engineering since the industrial revolution were applied with literally devastating effect to the weapons of that war. The appalling slaughter of the front-line soldiers has been described by countless writers. In that war the killing was still confined mainly to the men in the forces, and civilians were still spared the horrors of being directly targeted. However the scale of the slaughter and the indifference of the higher command to the sufferings of the rank and file produced an interesting change in the public perception of war.

In August 1914 the announcement that war had been declared was greeted by cheering crowds in London and Berlin. In England, men hurried to volunteer for the army, genuinely afraid that the war might be over before they were able to get into the front line. This bellicose emotion seems to have had no restraining influence from the Churches. After a number of horrifically wasteful slaughters, particularly the Battle of the Somme, the mood of the army changed to one of bitterness and disillusionment. There was deep distrust of the competence of the generals and the way in which they sent their men to their deaths. Recent research has indicated that the disastrous Passchendaele offensive was continued by Lloyd George's specific authorization for a month after he had recognized that it could not succeed.[27]

A certain number of erstwhile enthusiasts for the war underwent what can only be described as conversion. Rudyard Kipling, a typical jingoist, received notice that his only son was reported missing in action. The uncertainty about his fate left him almost demented and for the rest of his life he pursued vain enquiries in the hope of finding him alive.

General Allenby underwent a different kind of conversion. His troops gained a significant success at the Battle of Arras in April 1917, by gaining four miles in two days. With some delay the cavalry was sent in to exploit the advantage and they trotted off in a blizzard singing the Eton Boating Song. They made no impact against machine guns and barbed wire. Eventually Allenby realized that his men were exhausted. He protested formally to the commander in chief (Haig), declaring his unwillingness to send into battle 'semi-trained troops unable to use their rifles properly.'[28] Allenby was dismissed and relegated to a backwater, the Sinai Desert.

If the erstwhile enthusiasts for the war could undergo such a complete reversal of their attitudes, it is regrettable, to say the least, that the Church leaders did not. Admittedly Pope Benedict XV did try to bring about a diplomatic solution to end the conflict in 1916. It is not surprising that the governments of the nations at war ignored it. What is really disappointing is that he received so little support from the hierarchies of England and Germany. Most probably their blinkered attitude arose from their being so far removed from the realities of the war, about which I will have more to say in the final chapter.

The First World War was the occasion of another significant development in the morality of warfare in Great Britain. Conscription was not introduced until 1916 and of course posed an immediate problem for men who objected to killing on moral grounds. Under pressure from the Quakers and other enlightened pacifists, the government introduced legislation allowing for conscientious objectors to be exempted from taking up arms. The Catholic leaders were not to the fore in this movement, which is all the more depressing because a well-known atheist, Bertrand Russell, was. From a purely rationalistic standpoint he perceived the moral issues and publicly protested against the law that would compel one human being to kill others. His peers considered that he was unpatriotic and he was deprived of his fellowship at Trinity College, Cambridge. His action had all the marks of authentic witness to the truth, on account of the public nature of his protests and the fact that he was willing to suffer for his convictions. It was significantly different from generalized preaching about love of neighbour. The absence of a high Catholic profile from the movement is just one more failure of leadership in this vital area.

The Second World War saw numerous examples of unbridled cruelty, with widespread attacks on the lives of civilians and even children without any regard for morality. It is no exaggeration to say that moral restraints were brushed aside by all the main participants in that war. The Nazis have been condemned often for the slaughter of the Jews but the Americans and British were responsible for comparable cruelties. The dropping of atom bombs on Hiroshima and Nagasaki and the destruction of Dresden and many other German cities by the RAF were morally unjustifiable. In 1922 Britain had been one of the signatories of the Washington treaty which outlawed 'aerial bombardment for the purpose of terrorising the civilian population, of destroying civilian property not of a military character, or of injuring non-combatants'.[29] Early in the war the Germans were roundly criticized by British politicians for the indiscriminate bombing of cities like Warsaw and Rotterdam, where it was clear that civilians were the principal victims. Chamberlain, then Prime Minister, told the House of Commons, 'Whatever the lengths to which others may go, His Majesty's government will never resort to deliberate attacks on women and children for the purpose of mere terrorism.'[30]

However on 14 February 1942 a directive was sent to Bomber Command to attack Germany without restriction. The objective was to destroy civilian morale and especially that of industrial workers.[31] Both sides had come to realize that bombers were very vulnerable to attack by fighter aircraft in daylight, and the easiest way for bombers to operate was at night and from a very high altitude. This meant that accuracy was impossible. Bombs could not be guaranteed to land any closer than four miles from a designated target. Rather than abandoning the enterprise, the government opted for saturation bombing of whole cities, regardless of the killing of innocent non-combatants. Actually the reality was even worse than that. The British developed a technique for creating fire storms enveloping whole cities and in one such attack on Hamburg in July 1943, 40 000 civilians were killed in a single night. However the government was careful to conceal the truth from the public. Sir Archibald Sinclair, Secretary of State for Air, admitted that only by claiming that bombers kept to military targets 'could he satisfy the enquiries of the Archbishop of Canterbury, the Moderator of the Church of Scotland and other significant religious leaders, whose moral condemnation of the bombing offensive might disturb the morale of Bomber Command aircrews'.[32]

Two points are noteworthy from that admission. Firstly that protest from the religious leaders would have been effective, and secondly that the Catholic bishops were not mentioned. The realities of the situation were well known to the military chaplains. The Rev.(Squadron Leader) L.J. Collins was a chaplain at Bomber Command Headquarters. An airman, who was a member of his Christian fellowship, wrote to him after he had taken part in the bombing of Hamburg, he stated

> It was a nightmare experience looking down on the flaming city beneath. I felt sick as I thought of the women and children down there being mutilated, burned, killed, terror-stricken in that terrible inferno – and I was partly responsible. Why, Padre John, do the Churches not tell us we are doing an evil job? Why do chaplains persist in telling us that we are performing a noble task in defence of Christian civilisation?[33]

The same Padre John later became one of the founder members of CND when he was Canon John Collins of St Paul's and that was probably why he was never made a bishop.

The period which followed the end of the Second World War was characterized by two principal moral issues which are relevant to the issues of the morality of warfare. These were the development of the arms trade and the exponential increase in the destructive power of nuclear weapons, accompanied by similar developments in chemical and biological weapons. The technological aspects of both developments do not directly concern this book but the moral issues do. Generally speaking the mainstream Churches (which includes the Catholic Church) have made only token noises of disapproval, and it has been left to the Quakers principally to maintain an effective protest. It was the Quakers in the main who were responsible for the establishment of the Department of Peace Studies in the University of Bradford, which for many years was the only university in Great Britain which offered peace studies on its curriculum. It was also the Quakers who published early in the 1980s the now famous poster of a skull in a military helmet. The inscription which accompanied it read: 'The money required to provide adequate food, water, education, health and housing for everyone in the world has been estimated at $17 billion a year. It is a huge sum of money ... About as much as the world spends on arms every two weeks.'

The other post-war development in Europe and the United States was the terrifying increase in the destructive power of nuclear and chemical weapons. Towards the end of the Cold War period, there were enough nuclear weapons and long-distance rockets to carry them for the extermination of the whole human race, if all of them had been used. Even in the face of this possibility the Catholic Church was remarkably silent. During the same period Catholic Church leaders constantly spoke out against abortion in the name of the sanctity of life and did everything in their power to influence governments to criminalize the practice. The Catholic response to nuclear weapons was almost inaudible. Unfortunately this reticence was to be seen in the wider context of the peace movement in general.

The Catholic international peace movement, Pax Christi, has never really received the support and encouragement that it deserved in view of the importance of its programme. In Great Britain, for example, it has been accorded official recognition by the hierarchy, but beyond that it has been largely ignored. Funding from Church sources has been minimal and episcopal support has been lukewarn. In general all the indications are that work for peace occupies a low place in the practical priorities of Catholic pastoral strategy. One factor in the official reticence about campaigning for peace may well be the hidden agenda, about which Catholic leaders are uneasy, namely the impossibility of formulating comprehensive negative principles which would cover every eventuality. I will have more to say about this, later, in the context of the Second Vatican Council's debate about war and peace.

The Christian reaction to warfare since the Middle Ages has been a disappointing acquiescence to the widespread evil. From that time to the present, the overall consideration has been that good Christians should be loyal citizens and obedient to lawfully constituted government. In a previous chapter I pointed out that obedience is not an unconditional virtue. One can offend against it by being too obedient as well as by disobedience, and it is in the area of warfare that we see subservient obedience at its moral worst.

As if this were not bad enough, there has also been a widespread tendency for religious leaders to lend their moral influence to back up the governments' war aims with very little critical appraisal of the moral issues. A randomly chosen example is the prayer composed after Nelson's victory at the Battle of the Nile by the Bishop of Norwich 'Oh Almighty God, The Sovereign Father of all the World, in whose hand is power and might, which none is able to resist; we bless and magnify thy great and glorious name for the happy Victory which thou hast vouchsafed to the fleet of thy servant our Sovereign, in distant seas.'[34] If it be objected that the Bishop of

Norwich was an Anglican, then it is sobering for Catholics to remember that Pope Pius XI displayed the same attitude when he blessed the regimental flags of the Italian troops setting out for the invasion of Ethiopia during the 1930s. The conditions for a just war did not apply in that case. Also Cardinal Hinsley was often invited to speak on the BBC in times of crisis during the Second World War, when the nation's patriotism needed a boost.

After the Second World War a mood of much greater criticism reigned in political and ecclesiastical circles. The warlike policies of governments and the complaisant attitudes of Churches were subjected to penetrating criticism by their own followers. In that atmosphere the bishops at the Second Vatican Council, aided by their theological advisors, debated the morality of warfare in a refreshingly realistic fashion. In the document *Gaudium et Spes*, which describes the role of the Church in the modern world, we read the most satisfactory pronouncements about war and peace which have ever been stated by the teaching authority of the Catholic Church. They are so important that a number of verbatim quotations are called for.

Concerning peace, the Council stated:

> Peace is not merely the absence of war. Nor can it be reduced solely to the maintenance of a balance of power between enemies. Nor is it brought about by dictatorship. Instead it is rightly and appropriately called an enterprise of justice (Isaiah 32:7). Peace results from that harmony built into human society by its divine founder, and actualised by men as they thirst after ever greater justice.

The Council faced up to the reality of war and gave recommendations for limiting its worst excesses in the following words:

> Contemplating this melancholy state of humanity, the Council wishes to recall first of all the permanent binding force of universal natural law and its all-embracing principles. Man's conscience itself gives ever more emphatic voice to these principles. Therefore, actions which deliberately conflict with these same principles, as well as orders commanding such actions are criminal. Blind obedience cannot excuse those who yield to them. Among such must first be counted those actions designed for the methodical extermination of an entire people, nation, or ethnic minority.

The same section accepts the legitimacy of a country's defending itself, when every peaceful means of settling disputes had been exhausted. But the Council stressed the limitations on the activity:

> But it is one thing to undertake military action for the just defence of the people, and something else again to seek the subjugation of other nations. Nor does the possession of war potential make every military or political use of it lawful.

The Council next turned its attention to the modern phenomenon of total war:

With these truths in mind, this most holy Synod makes its own the condemnations of total war already pronounced by recent popes, and issues the following declaration: Any act of war aimed indiscriminately at the destruction of entire cities or of extensive areas along with their population is a crime against God and man himself. It merits unequivocal and unhesitating condemnation.

The Council also condemned the arms race.[35]

Some peace activists had hoped for a more specific condemnation of nuclear weapons but at the time there was an unresolved debate inside and outside the Council. It was generally agreed that if an enemy fleet of say 50 ships was in mid-ocean, and if the defender was acting in a morally justifiable war, then it was of no moral difference whether those ships were sunk individually by conventional bombs or all at once by one nuclear bomb. The underlying problem which haunted the whole debate was the fact that in a situation as complex as modern war, it is impossible to formulate clear general rules which could have universal application. The Council's enunciation of basic principles was good, but the only possible way for them to be translated into action must be through the personal decisions of individual soldiers. As has been noted already in this book, the Catholic Church has been unwilling to allow its members adequate freedom in the area of personal moral choice.

If we are to be realistic, we must acknowledge that in many cases neither Churches nor individuals will be able to halt a nation's going to war. In that case the duty of the Christian is to protest against it. This is incumbent on individual Christians and church communities. It is one aspect of witnessing to the truth, it is akin to martyrdom, and it is the only way of preserving moral integrity if a nation is caught up in war fever.

In addition to the pure moral protest, there is also a didactic element. This has been stressed by a Holocaust survivor, Elie Wiesel. As a youth of 15 he was in Auschwitz and he saw his mother and little sister being selected for extermination at that camp. He saw children being put into the furnaces. And he witnessed the death of his father shortly before the liberation of the camp. After he recovered a measure of normality in his own life, he began writing about the experiences. Now as an old man he insists that the dwindling number of survivors of the camps must speak out, otherwise the world cannot know what human beings are capable of doing to each other.[36]

The simple moral protest has been made by a small number of individuals. There was an interesting case in the RAF in 1922. Iraq became a British dependency when it was taken from the Turks at the end of the First World War. In 1921 the British set up a client state under King Faisal, son of the Sharif of Mecca. The regime was not popular and there were two rebellions. One was put down by the use of gas, and that of the Kurds in the north was entrusted to the RAF for subjugation. The method was of indiscriminate bombing of the Kurdish villages, where women, children, and old men were killed along with men of military age. In 1922 an experienced and much decorated veteran of the Boer War and World War One, Air Commodore Lionel Charlton was appointed Senior Air Staff Officer for the region. After a few months he resigned his post on account of his moral objection to intimidation by indiscriminate bombing. He was allowed to remain in the RAF in England, but it was the wrecking of a promising career and he was put on the retired list in 1928.[37]

Examples from the Second World War are not numerous. I will describe a couple of publicly unknown and unsung heroes. The first was a sergeant in an infantry regiment who had been conscripted and drafted to India. Towards the end of the war, there were shortages of food which provoked riots among the civilians. This man was ordered to open fire on civilians if they should break into food stores. He told his commander flatly that if the men of his platoon were attacked they would defend themselves, but he refused to fire upon the Indian civilians. Though laying himself open to serious disciplinary consequences, his courage was rewarded and he was not court-martialled. The second protester was a professional sailor who had entered the navy before the war via Dartmouth Naval College. Towards the end of the war he was the commanding officer of a submarine operating off the north coast of Australia. His ship and other submarines were ordered to sink Chinese junks because it was alleged that they were carrying munitions for the Japanese. The first sinking made it clear that it was a family boat engaged in peaceful trade. The killing of the children on board brought about this man's moral revulsion for such a task and he refused to take the submarine out again on a similar mission. The authorities tried every form of threat and pressure, but he and his fellow officers remained solid in their refusal to pursue such targets. No punitive action was taken against them. Probably the commander-in-chief was sensitive about the effect such disciplinary action would have on morale in general. However, after the war that submarine commander's career was quietly blocked.

The most famous protester of the Second World War was the Austrian Franz Jägerstatter. Having been a somewhat wild young man, he settled down to a conventional married life and underwent a profound religious conversion. When he was conscripted to serve in the German army he refused. His parish priest and the bishop both told him that it was his duty to fight under Hitler's command. He still refused, unconditionally, and pointed out that even if he were to serve in a medical unit, his doing so would simply release another man for service in the front line. He was imprisoned and suffered greatly on account of being separated from his wife and children. Eventually he was executed.

There are other examples but the instances cited above are sufficient to establish the pattern. Conscientious men made courageous and lonely decisions, but none of them received moral backing from the clergy. In Jägerstatter's case it was just the reverse.

In recent years the progress of Liberation theology and basic communities in Latin America has conscientized a considerable number of Catholics to the injustices and cruelties perpetrated in the region. This has led in turn to a number of serious protests by Catholic priests among others at the source of much of the cruelty, namely the School of the Americas (SOA), a military establishment at Fort Benning in Georgia.

Protests against the school began with a Maryknoll priest Fr Roy Bourgeois, when he witnessed the consequences of the training given there, when he was working as a missionary in Bolivia and El Salvador. In its 50-year history the SOA has trained over 60 000 troops in counter-insurgency action. Consistently the nations with the worst human rights records have sent the most soldiers to it. They came from Bolivia under General Banzer, from Nicaragua under the Somozas, from El Salvador during the bloodiest years of the civil war. Alumni of the school include Banzer himself, the dictator of Bolivia from 1971–78, General Noriega the Panamanian dictator, now in prison in the USA for drug trafficking, and Colonel Roberto D'Aubuisson, the death squad leader in El Salvador who ordered the assassination of Archbishop Romero in 1980. Other Salvadorean alumni of the SOA include three of the soldiers who raped and murdered four United States nuns and lay workers in 1980, 19 soldiers who took part in the murder of the six Jesuits in 1989, and ten of the 12 officers involved in the 1981 massacre of 900 peasants in the village of El Mozote. Alumni of the SOA have also taken part in military coups in Peru, Ecuador and Argentina, including the 'dirty' war of the 1970s in which thousands of dissidents were killed. In Argentina the numbers are uncertain because the government destroyed the records. Careful estimates vary between 11 000 and 30 000 who simply disappeared so completely that their bodies have only rarely been recovered. It is hard to think of a coup or human rights outrage which has occurred in Central or South America in the past 40 years in which SOA alumni were not involved.

Protests outside the base have been led in recent years by a Jesuit, Father William Bichsel. In September 1997 he led a first demonstration and this was a warm-up for a larger protest in November of that year in which 2000 people demonstrated and 602 were arrested. Of these, 30 were sentenced to six months in jail and also a $3000 fine. Fr Bichsel was one of those sent to prison on 23 July 1998. He has a long history of protest against the United States military, having been arrested more than a dozen times and convicted seven times. He and his friends make these protests to raise awareness of the injustices which are being perpetrated in Central and South America by the SOA.[38] In spite of it, the higher echelons of the Catholic Church in the USA have been remarkably silent.

In view of the large-scale immorality of war, it is not surprising that it brings in its train a collection of other evils. Before concluding this chapter it is relevant to emphasize one of them: lying. The mere fact that so much has to be concealed is an implied self-confession of guilt. A few examples will suffice to illustrate the point. In the autumn of 1944 as the Russian armies were advancing through Poland, the SS made strenuous efforts to obliterate the traces of the death machinery at Auschwitz. In fact the task proved to be impossible but the fact that it was attempted is significant.

The development of the atomic bomb was bedevilled by deception from its very inception. Professor Rotblat began research into the possibility of such a weapon in Liverpool in 1939 because he believed that German scientists were capable of producing one. In his view Hitler would have been prepared to use it had it been available, and this sense of urgency justified his own researches. Other scientists were encouraged to work on the project on the same assumption, although recently published evidence indicates that Japan was always the intended target. The governments of Britain and the USA feared that if the atomic bomb were dropped on Germany and failed to explode, the Germans would be presented with all the information they needed to perfect their own weapon. On the other hand, it was confidently believed that the Japanese were in no position to make their own, even if an unexploded prototype should fall into their hands.

The first planned target was to have been a Japanese fleet, but by the time the bomb was ready, no such concentration of warships remained to the Japanese. Hiroshima and Nagasaki were chosen, although they had no military potential, because they were among the few cities not already destroyed by conventional bombing. In December 1944 Professor Rotblat resigned from the project because it was clear to him that Hitler's Germany could not develop an A-bomb, and because the plea for a test explosion rather than use against people had been turned down. Professor Rotblat's integrity contrasts sharply with the deceptions of the British and US governments.[39]

The exploding of the first two A-bombs is still shrouded in secrecy and unanswered questions. The destruction of the two cities was not necessary militarily. Japan was on the verge of collapse, largely on account of the effective blockade by the US navy. Japan was entirely dependent on the oil wells of Indonesia for its fuel and not a single oil tanker had got through to the homeland in the last six months of the war. If the A-bombs were to be used to terrify the Japanese into capitulation, the effect could have been achieved by dropping them on an uninhabited island. This simple course of action was advocated by the majority of the scientists working on the development of the A-bomb. However, their moral scruples were ignored by the military authorities.[40] Was it basically to caution the Russians? All these questions remained shrouded in the secrecy that arises out of the basic shame which intense cruelty creates in even the most hardened personalities.

Events in Latin America illustrate fully the connection between injustice, cruelty and deception. The number of instances are too numerous to enumerate but a couple of examples will illustrate the point. In 1981 between 800 and 1000 unarmed peasants were slaughtered at El Mozote in the Central American republic of El Salvador; 139 of the victims were children. The killings were carried out by US-trained troops but for well over a decade the US government maintained that the incident was a creation of left-wing propagandists. In the neighbouring republic of Guatemala between 1966 and 1986 perhaps as many as 150 000 people were slaughtered after the USA had sent in experts to teach the local army 'counter-insurgency'. The CIA continued to maintain a covert assistance programme to the Guatemalan army and was only taken to task for failing to keep Congress informed after the assassination of an American citizen.

Generally speaking it is true to say that from the time of Theodosius II to World War Two, Christianity and the Catholic Church in particular has in practice adopted the purely secular outlook on war. In spite of the ideals of the New Testament and the heroism of the early martyrs, from the period when Christendom was established, Christianity made little impact on its members' activities in warfare.

However, there is hope for the future. Two things have changed in the modern period. In the first place, Vatican II has given a clear lead theologically, and secondly, this has been matched by a critical and protesting mood in the Church. In many countries, priests and committed lay people are prepared to challenge their governments over their warlike policies and even go to prison for doing so. Nothing like this has been known for hundreds of years, in fact since the days of the pre-Constantinian Roman Empire. It gives some solid hope that the Church's record in the future may be an improvement on the centuries of uncritical acquiescence to the supposed inevitability of warfare and its attendant cruelties.

Notes

1   Bourke, J. *An Intimate History of Killing*, London 1999, 30.
2   de Mann, H. *The Remaking of a Mind. A Soldier's Thoughts on War and Reconstruction*. London 1920, 198, 199.
3   Bourke, 72.
4   *Directorate of Army Psychiatry, Technical Memorandum No. 2*, 1942, quoted in Bourke, 155.
5   Bourke, 198.
6   Bourke, 75.
7   Bourke, 166.
8   Babington, A. *For the Sake of Example: Capital Courts Martial*. London 1983, 87.
9   Babington, 80, 14.
10 Grass, Gunter, in a letter quoted in *The Guardian*, 6 May 1995.
11 Hippolytus, *Apostolic Tradition*. Section 16. in *Hippolytus: A Text for Students*. ed. G.J. Cumming, Nottingham 1984, 16.
12 Tertullian, *Apologia*, 37:4, MPL vol. 1, col. 525.
13 Cf. Ruyter, K.W. (1982), 'Pacifism and Military Service in the Early Church' in *Cross Currents*, vol. 32 (1) 59.
14 Ruyter, 56.
15 Ruyter, 62.
16 ACOD, 12.
17 St Basil, Letter 188, MPG, vol. 32, col. 681.
18 Runciman, S. *A History of the Crusades*, London 1951, vol. 1, 83.
19 *ST*, II–II, q. 11, a.3.

20 *The Guardian*, 20 August 1992.
21 *ST*, II–II, q. 40; cf. also Jenny Teichmann, *Pacifism and the Just War*, Oxford 1986, 46–62.
22 Lemkuhl, A. *Theologia Moralis*, 11th. edn, Freiburg 1910, vol. 1, 573.
23 Genicot, E. *Theologia Moralis*, 10th ed. Bruxelles 1922, vol. 1, 315.
24 Davis, H. *Moral and Pastoral Theology*, London 1949, vol. 2, 149.
25 *Manual of Military Law*, HMSO, London 1914, Chap. III section 9 and 10, p. 17.
26 Keijzer, N. *Military Obedience*, Alphen aan den Rijn 1978, 135–210.
27 Cecil, H. and Liddle, P. (eds), *Facing Armageddon*, London 1996, reviewed in *The Observer*, 11 August 1996.
28 James, L. *Imperial Warrior: the Life and Times of Field Marshall Viscount Allenby 1861–1936*. London 1993, reviewed in *The Guardian*, 13 April 1993.
29 *The Guardian*, 24 July 1993.
30 *The Guardian*, 24 July 1993.
31 Webster, C. and Frankland, N. *Strategic Air Offensive against Germany 1939–1945*. London 1961, vol. 4, 143–5.
32 *The Guardian*, 24 July 1993.
33 Quoted in the journal *CND Today*, Spring 1993, p. 135.
34 Pocock, T. *Horatio Nelson*, Oxford 1987, 183.
35 *Gaudium et Spes*, sections 78–81, DV II, 290–95.
36 *The Observer*, Sunday Review, 9 June 1996.
37 *The Observer*, 10 February 1991.
38 The information comes from an article by Rev. G.W. Hughes SJ, in *The Tablet*, 5 September 1998.
39 *The Guardian*, 19 April 1995.
40 This fact became common knowledge with the publication of the misgivings shared by Einstein and the Hungarian physicist Leo Szilard in *The Guardian*, 12 August 2000.

Chapter 10

Healthy Restraint

Temperance seems to be the most boring of all virtues because it is carica-
tured as a joyless negation of attractive pleasures and emotional fulfilment.
Several Churches have overreacted in their espousal of its beneficent potential. Methodists who saw the evils of alcoholic abuse opted for total abstinence from all intoxicating drinks. The Catholic Church has crusaded against
sex in all but its strictly reproductive aspect. It required the arrival of the
financial crises of the 1990s to illustrate the positive potential of moral
restraint. In the last years of that decade we perceived just how much can go
wrong when pecuniary greed gets out of hand. The class of 1998 has had
good reason to wish that temperance might have curtailed the moneymaking
ambitions of a minority before they caused damage not only to individuals
but to national economies too.

Among Catholics a negative attitude to sex has been traced as far back as
St Augustine and his influence could be felt throughout the Middle Ages
and beyond. At the end of the seventeenth century when Pope Innocent XI
gave the first encouragement for frequent communion, his directive to confessors urged them to recommend to married couples that they should
abstain from sex before receiving the eucharist. It was said to be a suitable
preparation in view of the reverence that is owed to this sacrament.[1] This
attitude remained in force until the twentieth century. Some years ago I
knew, indirectly, of a married couple who wished to become daily commu-
nicants in the days before Pope Pius X gave the practice his complete
encouragement. They were given permission by their bishop on condition
that they both took vows of chastity.

The pessimistic attitude to sex still bedevils the policies of the Catholic
Church, be it in the realm of clerical celibacy or marriage. One significant
change has taken place in recent years. The volte-face on masturbation has
been mentioned in the Introduction and, for that at least, let us be grateful.
Future generations will not be guilt-ridden and haunted by the fear of
eternal punishment. A similar conversion about family planning is taking
longer to achieve.

When the possibility of contraception arose in the latter part of the
nineteenth century, there was considerable opposition to the practice in
society in general. In England, for example, in 1878 Charles Bradlaugh
and Annie Besant who wrote about it were charged with publishing an
obscene book. In fact they were acquitted, but in 1886 a doctor was struck
off the medical register for publishing a book on contraception. Marie

Stopes felt that it was unwise to open her family planning clinic in London until 1921.

The Lambeth Conference of 1930 (Resolution 15) gave its approval to the practice. In 1931 Pope Pius XI condemned it in his encyclical letter entitled *Casti Connubii.*[2] One cannot help reflecting on how much that decision was influenced by the widespread aesthetic distaste about contraception which was prevalent in middle-class and working-class families in Europe at the time. There may also have been annoyance at the Anglican bishops' decision of the previous year.

For the next few decades Catholic theologians and textbooks were consistent in their opposition to the practice. The arguments were few, clear and simple. The sin of Onan (Gen. 38:8–10) was alleged as the scriptural evidence. Rationally it was condemned on the basis of the subordination of purposes in marriage, namely the primary being the procreation of children and the secondary variously described as the assuaging of lust or the expression of love. It was alleged that to secure the second and prevent the primary purpose artificially was immoral. Although this line of thought was able to invoke St Thomas Aquinas among its supporters, the reasoning was not in line with the consistent tradition of the Church. Fertility was never regarded as the essence of marriage, but intercourse was.

As far as the Canon Law was concerned, a marriage could be declared null if the parties were incapable of intercourse, but its validity was never challenged on the basis of there being no offspring. In this perspective it would have been more accurate to say that the primary purpose of marriage was sexual intercourse, and the secondary end was procreation. On this, the practice of the Church courts has been consistent and it is also in line with the Church's tradition of never forbidding intercourse during pregnancy and after the menopause. In antiquity both of these activities were forbidden by the Stoics, and against that pessimistic background the Church elaborated its more lenient attitude.

The word 'artificially' portended problems. The restriction of sexual relations to times of natural infertility had received cautious approval from the Vatican in 1880.[3] In the 1920s the independent researches of Ogino in Japan and Knaus in Austria put the matter on a scientific basis whereby it was reasonably predictable and it became widely used. However, caution ruled the day, the matter was hushed up as far as possible, and confessors were forbidden to suggest it to married couples. Their counsel was restricted to supplying information if asked. This discipline was still in force in the 1950s until Pope Pius XII's address to a meeting of Italian midwives brought the matter into the open (within the Catholic Church). He gave his circumspect approval to the use of the infertile period, on a permanent basis, as a means of limiting the size of a family.[4]

From that time onwards the question was out in the open and was in crisis. The papal approval of the safe period had effectively sold the pass. Many people realized that if conception had been ruled out by deliberate choice and action, why should not the pope also approve of artificial means to achieve the same result. The 1950s were a time of great anguish for the parochial clergy trying to uphold a discipline that they could not justify convincingly.

A couple of examples will illustrate the agonies. In one parish in which I worked a poorly paid family with five children under the age of ten lived in a four-bedroom council house. They also had living with them the husband's elderly parents, both of whom were alcoholics. Both parents had to work and even so, they could scarcely make ends meet. Their main strength and consolation in a difficult life was their tender love for each other, but the safe period did not work for them. When the wife found herself pregnant for the sixth time she was in despair and her husband attempted suicide. Fortunately he survived it. In another parish there was a young couple who were told by the doctor that after two children the woman's heart could not sustain any further pregnancies. They tried the safe period without success, and with four children under the age of seven the wife's heart condition became so serious that she was allowed to go upstairs only once a day. Shortly after I left the parish she died leaving her husband overwhelmed by grief and with four young children to bring up on his own. Admittedly hard cases make bad law but equally, if the rules are going to result in such tragedies, then they must be rooted in absolute certainty. The arguments against contraception were, even then, anything but certain.

Implied in all the discussion about family planning among Catholic theologians at that period, was the unquestioned assumption that sexual pleasure was not intrinsically good and therefore needed some other justification for its enjoyment. The commonest justification was the intention to conceive a child, and after that the need to defuse sexual tension, which was held to be a reasonable interpretation of St Paul.

The Second Vatican Council effectively wrecked these presuppositions. Marriage was dealt with in the document *Gaudium et Spes*, which spelt out the Church's relationship to the modern world. In a deceptively simple statement about marriage the document stated 'By their very nature, the institution of matrimony itself and conjugal love are ordained for the procreation and education of children, and find in them their ultimate crown.'[5] The simplicity of that statement is important because it sedulously avoided the well-established distinction between primary and secondary purposes. In the context, that must be regarded as a significant omission and an indication of the deliberate intention of the bishops to chart a new path in the theology of marriage.

This became apparent in their delicate treatment of sexual love. In section 49 the text reads: 'This love is uniquely expressed and perfected through the marital act. The actions within marriage by which the couple are united intimately and chastely are noble and worthy ones.' In other words, sex was good. Most people would have taken it for granted and regarded such a statement as unnecessary. Within the Catholic Church it was extremely significant because it was the first time that the goodness of sex had ever been proclaimed by the Church's magisterium.

Planning the size of the family was dealt with in two sections of the document. In section 87 it stated: 'For in view of the inalienable right to marry and beget children, the question of how many children should be born belongs to the honest judgement of parents.' The same message is found in section 50 in slightly different words. Having spoken of material, social, and spiritual considerations about the size and spacing of a family, the document stated:

> The parents themselves should ultimately make this judgement, in the sight of God. But in their manner of acting spouses should be aware that they cannot proceed arbitrarily. They must always be governed according to a conscience dutifully conformed to the divine law itself, and should be submissive toward the Church's teaching office, which authentically interprets that law in the light of the gospel.[6]

With prudence and wisdom, the Council went no further than that. It would have been equally wise to allow free debate within the Church for a reasonable period of time about what methods of birth control were in keeping with the law of God. Pope Paul VI kept that matter off the agenda of the Council's final stages and appointed a commission to examine the precise question of contraception. After months of frank and open discussion, which the subject had not hitherto received, the members of that commission underwent an interesting collective conversion. After careful deliberations the overwhelming majority (more than 60) came to the view that artificial methods were morally acceptable. They were opposed by a minority of four who admitted that they could not justify their opposition to contraception by reasons of theology or ethics, but only by an appeal to Church authority.[7] It would have been intellectually healthy if two reports had been published, a majority and a minority report, just as is done by British parliamentary commissions of enquiry. Instead the results were kept in secret and the document was hijacked by the conservatives in the Roman Curia, who were determined that the teaching of Pius XI against contraception must be upheld.[8]

In July 1968 the encyclical *Humanae Vitae* was published renewing the condemnation of artificial methods of birth control. When the argumentation of the document came to be studied it was seen to be seriously defective. There was no attempt to appeal to Scripture because on this matter the Bible is silent. This is not surprising since it was a problem that the sacred writers did not face. It was agreed on all sides that the sin of Onan was an offence against generosity with regard to children who would be heirs of his dead brother rather than himself. It was not an offence against sexual purity. The same applies to Tradition. Although the Church Fathers were clear in their opposition to abortion, they had nothing to say specifically about contraception. Their outlook was entirely governed by the prevailing bio-logical theory of the ancient world that the father provided the whole human being in his semen and the mother merely contributed the suitable environ-ment for its development in her uterus. The exact process of conception (the fertilization of the ovum by the sperm) was established scientifically only in the nineteenth century.

The only area left for the opponents of contraception to prove their case was in the realm of rational ethics and this is what was attempted in *Humanae Vitae*. There was no attempt to resurrect the old distinction between primary and secondary purposes: the members of the commission were aware that it had been omitted deliberately by the Second Vatican Council. The authori-ties were left with nothing to appeal to but authority: in effect an appeal to loyalty, in the sense that Pius XI's decision must be upheld for the sake of discipline, for the reputation of the papacy and so on. Finally it must be remembered that very soon after the publication of the encyclical, the offi-cial spokesman of the Vatican, Mgr Lambruschini stated explicitly that it was not an infallible document.[9]

The admission that the decision was not infallible is extremely important. After the definition of papal infallibility in the First Vatican Council of 1870, theologians, parish priests, and teachers had all insisted that it was a limited power. Laypeople in the parish and pupils in Catholic schools were taught constantly that the pope was not always infallible in everything that he said (his sermons for example). It was agreed too that if he were talking about matters outside the narrow limits of revealed doctrine, as specified by the Council, he could make a mistake. In spite of this healthy attitude, there was a parallel cast of mind that developed alongside it saying, in effect: 'Since the pope can sometimes speak infallibly, it would be respectful and prudent to treat all his public utterances as if they might be infallible.' This was the beginning of what came to be called creeping infallibility.

In practice, all papal encyclicals were treated with the sort of unquestion-ing respect that would be given to the decrees of General Councils. It was an unhealthy tendency because it was based on a particular emotional attitude towards the papal office rather than on serious theological principles. In 1968 the bubble was burst and Catholics had to come to terms with a situation which they had provided for at the theoretical level but not yet in practical realities, namely a mistake by a pope in an area which was not covered by the gift of infallibility. Fortunately it was a relatively clear issue on the periphery of moral behaviour and clearly in the realm of merely rational ethics. Central doctrinal tenets like the Incarnation or the economy of grace were not under even the most remote indirect threat. In spite of all that, it was reassuring that Mgr Lambruschini stated quite openly that infal-libility was not at stake. It showed that Pope Paul VI and his advisors were under no false illusions about it.

One is left with the serious question: what line of ethical reasoning could be invoked to justify the ban on contraception? The basic argument put forward in the encyclical was that the procreative and unitive aspects of sex must never be separated artificially.

The precise wording of the prohibition deserves to be examined in detail. The crux of the prohibition is contained in section 11 of the encyclical: 'None the less the Church, calling men back to the observance of the norms of the natural law, as interpreted by her constant doctrine, teaches that each and every marriage act (*quilibet matrimonii usus*) must remain open to the transmission of life.' The reason for that command was not given in that paragraph; the ban remains as a simple statement. One is left wondering what is the exact meaning of 'open to the transmission of life'. In the context, only one intelligible interpretation is possible, it must mean 'not impeded artificially'. This interpretation is confirmed by the simple reflection that the Catholic Church has never forbidden sex after the menopause nor during pregnancy. The phrase 'open to the transmission of life' can only mean that intercourse is not impeded artificially.

The reason for this ban is given, supposedly, in section 12: 'That teaching, often set forth by the magisterium, is grounded upon the inseparable connection, willed by God and unable to be broken by man on his own initiative, between the two meanings of the conjugal act: the unitive meaning and the procreative meaning.' That statement is ambiguous. Taken on its own, it condemns the use of the safe period. Since *Humanae Vitae* expressly allows the use of the infertile period as a method of birth control (section 11), the words 'unable to be broken by man' (in section 12), must mean the artificial separation of unitive and procreative meanings.

We are left with a dilemma. The rather opaque wording of sections 11 and 12 are either two simple statements of the prohibition presented in slightly different wording. Alternatively they mask an unacknowledged tautology whose essence is as follows: The artificial separation of the procreative from the unitive meanings of sex is wrong because the act of intercourse must remain open to the transmission of life. What is the meaning of 'open'? It means that the procreative and unitive aspects must not be separated artificially.

To make the point clearer, one could say that in section 11 the word 'open' means 'not impeded artificially', and in section 12 the words 'unable to be broken' mean 'not impeded artificially'. In other words, sexual intercourse must not be impeded artificially because its unitive and procreative aspects must not be impeded artificially.

In addition to that tautology the argumentation of the encyclical is flawed by another unstated presupposition, the concept of artificiality. On a number of moral issues, Catholic textbooks of moral theology rely upon a line of reasoning which amounts to this: if an activity is artificial it is unnatural, and if it is unnatural it is immoral. A few minutes' reflection will indicate that this is an invalid line of reasoning and it has never been applied consistently, even by its most devoted supporters. To cite one straightforward example, one only has to look back to the 1930s to remember how tuberculosis was treated.

Sufferers from that disease were taken out of big cities where the air was polluted by the smoke and fumes of coal fires and industrial processes. They were housed in sanatoriums situated in rural areas where the air was known to be pure. There, with a regime of rest, good food and clean air their lungs sometimes recovered from the fatal disease. This could be described as the natural method of curing tuberculosis. In modern times, drugs have been developed which cure it rapidly and without the lengthy period in the country. This latter could be described as the artificial method. Never has it been suggested that Catholics are obliged to go to a rural sanatorium for their treatment and refuse the cure by drugs. On reflection it is clear that the whole of modern surgery is artificial and so is most of medical treatment. The Catholic practice of invoking the criterion of artificiality is applied only to activities related to sex, such as contraception or IVF. The kindest thing that one can say about it is that it constitutes special pleading. It does not constitute a rational argument against contraception.

The unsatisfactory reasons given by the encyclical on such a vital matter caused an outcry when the document was published. There were many private and public protests. A number of priests who voiced opposition were suspended or dismissed from teaching posts. This was foreseeable and the handful who were disciplined acted as a warning to others who understood the rules. From the start, the matter was treated as a disciplinary issue and no satisfactory theological justification of the ban has ever been produced. Eventually a sullen silence settled down over the Church. From that time onwards large numbers of priests resigned from the clergy and far greater numbers of laity left the Church altogether. Among those who remained a measure of cynicism prevailed.

Laypeople know that morality is not based on arbitrary rules. Since no coherent reasons were ever given for the ban on contraception, increasing numbers of practising Catholics ignored it. The parochial clergy were well aware of this and continued to give them Holy Communion acquiescing to their silent rebellion. The bishops have made no serious attempt to enforce the encyclical, except by the oaths which are required of candidates for major orders. It is a situation where truth has been banished, an unhealthy silence reigns, and it puts an increasing strain on priests who are men of integrity. Needless to say, this kind of approach commands practically no confidence in the laity. For decades, opinion polls have indicated that the encyclical is widely disregarded. A recent report issued by the National Family Planning Association in Scotland claimed that only 2 per cent of Catholics were following the Vatican's teaching on birth control. The accuracy of this conclusion was accepted by the Catholic Bishop of Motherwell, John Devine.[10]

In spite of this, obedience to *Humanae Vitae* is one of the conditions specifically required in candidates for the episcopate. From time to time certain priests and laypeople receive a questionnaire from the Vatican via the local Papal Nuncio asking their opinion as to the suitability of a named priest for promotion to the episcopate. Thirteen specific questions are asked about the individual and his aptitudes. Question six is about his orthodoxy in belief. Does he show true loyalty to the teaching and the teaching authority of the Church? There is particular reference to documents from the Holy See concerning the ordination of women, marriage and the family, sexual ethics (with particular reference to the transmission of life in conformity with the teaching of the encyclical *Humanae Vitae* and the Apostolic Letter *Familiaris Consortio*) and to matters of social justice. The recipients of such enquiries are instructed to keep the whole matter secret but the full text was published in an Austrian periodical.[11] Needless to say, the presence of this requirement in the selection of bishops gives the maintenance of the discipline on birth control a widespread power base.

A similar compulsion is exercised by the Vatican through the profession of faith which must be taken by all candidates for the priesthood and ecclesiastical office. Statements of belief of this kind have been in use for a long time and in principle their use is perfectly reasonable, granted that unity of belief is one of the cardinal elements of the Church's unity. However the formula of the profession of faith which was introduced in 1983 by the Congregation of the Faith contained an unusual novelty. In addition to accepting the decisions of General Councils (which is perfectly reasonable) it includes acquiescence to doctrine definitively declared by the magisterium and submission to non-definitively intended official pronouncements. It would be hard to find a precedent in Christian history, Eastern or Western, for such a presentation of a profession of faith.[12] It implies that acceptance is required of matters which are not necessarily revealed but which have the authority of the magisterium. The document should more correctly be entitled a Profession of Intellectual Submission, rather than Faith. In view of the date and the preceding controversies it is difficult to escape the conclusion that it was framed in this way to ensure that future priests obey the teaching of *Humanae Vitae*.

Like the requirements for candidates for the episcopate, it strengthens the grip of the Vatican over the clergy's acceptance of the ban on birth control, but it does nothing to engender conviction in the laity or the priests for that matter. The resulting situation is an almost universal double standard which is demoralizing for the Church and has damaged the authority of the papacy more seriously than anything in recent history.

When the ban on contraceptives is pushed to its logical conclusions, then the full impact of its falsity is seen. I refer to the AIDS crisis. It is most serious in Africa where its ravages have been accelerated by the widespread employment of migrant labour and where the culture has been hostile to condoms for reasons that have nothing to do with the theology of the Catholic Church. If a man, living away from home for six months out of every year, should contract the disease, what should he do when he returns home? Assuming that his wife is not yet infected, only one course of action is feasible. If they refrain from sexual intimacy their marriage is in real danger of breaking up. If they do not use condoms, the wife is effectively condemned to death. The clergy have no right to demand total sexual abstinence of such couples unless their moral argumentation is faultless and this, as I have shown above, is definitely not the case. The callousness with which the Church authorities consign people to their deaths through AIDS is beyond belief. It is one more depressing instance of how the Catholic Church's moral practice alienates well-intentioned people, and erodes its credibility.

The Vatican returned to the subject of contraception in 1997 with the publication of *The Morality of Conjugal Life: Handbook for Confessors.*[13] Almost three decades of quiet resistance have borne fruit. The document is poor on theological reasoning but stronger on its appeal to authority and obedience. Section 4 repeats the central message of *Humanae Vitae* but in stronger terms: 'The Church has always taught the intrinsic evil of contraception, that is, of every marital act intentionally rendered unfruitful. This teaching is to be held as definitive and irreformable.'

There are several serious objections that must be raised against those sentences. Firstly the choice of words is misleading, to say the least, because the phrase 'intentionally rendered unfruitful' applies to the use of the infertile period to avoid conception. The writers of that document must have been aware that birth regulation by the safe period was approved by Vatican II and by *Humanae Vitae*. Secondly they claim that the Church has always opposed contraception. This cannot be true since contraception has been understood and biologically possible only since the nineteenth century when the process of human conception was understood scientifically. Abortion has always been opposed by the Church and the attempt to equate the two is a sort of theological sleight of hand. In reality it serves as an indication that opposition to contraception lacks a coherent theological argument, so the authorities try to associate it with abortion. Finally the adjectives *definitive* and *irreformable* are now invoked. The first Vatican Council used the term *irreformable* for statements of revealed doctrine which had been defined by the Church's infallible authority. It is inadmissible to change the scope of that term and apply it to matters of ethics which have not been dealt with by the infallible magisterium. As I noted above, when the encyclical was published in 1968, it was explicitly stated in Rome that the pope did not claim infallibility for the document. It is difficult to escape the conclusion that in the absence of any serious theological justification over the years, the document has had to be propped up by firmer discipline.

Therein lies the sad paradox of this whole unedifying episode. The final lesson to be learnt from this dispute is that truth cannot be abused with impunity. In 1968 the hardline minority in Paul VI's birth control commission sought to retain the ban on contraception to maintain consistency with the prohibition of Pius XI and thus safeguard papal authority. The result has been just the opposite. Having acted untruthfully, the pope's moral authority has been damaged more severely than in any other incident in recent history.

The Lust for Money

Whereas the papacy has expended great efforts to limit the pleasures of sex, the popes would have employed their energies better had they sought to curtail financial greed, which is clearly doing immense damage to human society, particularly since the 1990s.

In the Middle Ages both theologians and the magisterium maintained a concerted opposition against lending money at high rates of interest, technically known as usury. Official pronouncements on the matter provide a rare example of General Councils defining a moral issue. The First Vatican Council, when dealing with the Church's infallibility, spoke of its sphere being faith and morals. It is clear from the context that they meant morality as revealed in Scripture, not ethics. The mediaeval Councils' pronouncements against usury provide a classical illustration of Conciliar authority addressing an issue of revealed morality.

As I pointed out in Chapter One half a dozen General Councils in the Middle Ages condemned usury, always basing their decisions on the authority of the Scriptures.[14] The biblical authorities to which they were alluding were most probably Exodus 22:25, Deuteronomy 23:19 and Matthew 5:42. What is of prime importance theologically is the link between the Bible and Conciliar authority. There was no attempt to justify the ban on principles derived from the rational science of ethics. It was a question of clarifying the content of revelation, in other words what the Scriptures had to say about the practice.

The determining moral issues at stake were exploitation and lack of generosity. It is useful to reflect that the Old Testament prohibitions were formulated first of all when the Israelites were living in the era prior to the use of coined money. The writers probably had in mind a system of bartering. Since the majority of the population were small farmers and, let it be remembered, subsistence farmers operating close to starvation, a failed harvest could be a disaster. A typical scenario would be crop failure and the imperative necessity of having or borrowing seed corn for the next year's harvest. If a farmer working on poor soil suffered the failure of his harvest owing to drought, he would have to borrow seed corn from a neighbour, possibly from one who might have had more fertile land. It was then considered morally correct to seek the return of only the same quantity of grain as had been lent. To lend two bags of seed corn and demand three in return was clearly exploiting a poor farmer whose plight was due to causes outside his control. The element of exploitation should be borne in mind in the later history of this practice. At a later date the same principles were extrapolated to the exploitation of people's debts in a cash economy and not one of bartering.

In the mediaeval period, commerce had become more sophisticated and the theologians had identified the very crux of this problem, namely the quest for unlimited profit, and the operative word is unlimited.

In the fifteenth and sixteenth centuries commerce flourished in many parts of Europe. In the cities of Florence, Antwerp and Munich vast sums of money were lent by bankers whose operations were on such a large scale that kings and emperors were able to make use of their services to finance costly projects such as wars. But these operations were still not the same as modern capitalism. Ingenious efforts were made to circumvent the mediaeval Councils' prohibitions of usury, such as the pretence that they were seeking compensation from the debtor for money that the creditor was prevented from spending on himself. Nevertheless, public opinion, backed up by the Church, still had considerable influence in opposing unlimited profits and interest rates. One of the most important contributions of Tawney's classical study, *Religion and the Rise of Capitalism*, was his identification of the concept of unlimited profit as the great divider between mediaeval and modern commerce. To quote his own words: 'The mediaeval theorist condemned as a sin precisely that effort to achieve a continuous and *unlimited increase* in material wealth which modern societies applaud as meritorious, and the vices for which he reserved his most merciless denunciations were the more refined and subtle of the economic virtues.'[15]

The significant change came with Calvin. To his credit he perceived that the Old Testament prohibitions were formulated in a society which was totally different from Renaissance Europe. The expansion of trade, particularly after the discovery of sea routes to the Far East, meant that interest on a loan did not mean taking advantage of someone's misfortune but sharing in his opportunities. If for example a merchant had paid a tenth share in the purchase of a ship, a tenth share of its profits might eventually far exceed the sum advanced. He argued that gaining interest on capital was no more unreasonable than taking rent on land. However the religious constraints on greed were still powerful and Calvin insisted that interest rates must be reasonable and that loans to the poor must be free of interest.[16]

In spite of Calvin's insistence on moral restraint, this was the thin end of the wedge. With the passage of time and the diminution of the Churches' influence on commerce the restraints gradually evaporated. The technological advances of the industrial revolution and the computer revolution of the latter part of the twentieth century both increased the creation of wealth and the opportunities for individual profit. By the end of the twentieth century, the logic of capitalism was inescapable. The pursuit of unlimited profit was almost universal and the consequences were plain for all to see.

The most striking feature of that period has been the incredible disparity between rich and poor, not only within any given country but among nations on the international scene. Examples could be multiplied indefinitely. The following instances must suffice.

In the 1970s a number of events converged to upset the relative stability of international finance, the most influential of which was the increase in oil prices. In 1970 the price of oil had been $1.80 per barrel. This went up to $2.90 per barrel in mid 1973. In October that year at a meeting in Kuwait

City the leaders of the oil cartel OPEC raised the price to $5.12, and by the end of that year it had gone up again to $11.65 per barrel, which was a fourfold increase in less than three months.[17] This left the oil producers with billions of dollars looking for employment. It is significant that none of it was given in aid like the Marshall Aid at the end of the Second World War. It was lent to developing countries in the Third World at what were considered to be realistic rates of interest. In fact moral and financial restraints were set aside. As one writer has put it, 'The rules of prudent banking were cast aside in the rush to lend. Banks overextended themselves to a greater extent than ever before. By 1982 the nine biggest US banks had lent nearly three times their total capital to the Third World.'[18]

The repayment of those debts has reduced the said countries to misery. In 1989 the United Nations Childrens' Fund published a report indicating the devastating effects of poverty on children in the developing world. Since the early 1980s living standards in Africa and Latin America fell by between 10 and 25 per cent. For one-sixth of the human race, 900 million people, the march of progress had become a retreat and it was showing itself principally in the health of children. For example in Mali, Mozambique and Sierra Leone, 30 per cent of children did not survive until the age of five. In 1989 the World Bank issued figures showing that the capital outflow from the Third World to the rich nations was running at $43 billion annually.[19] Since then matters have got worse.

In 1993 *The Guardian* printed an eye-catching headline title page bearing the words: 'Question: What's the difference between Tanzania and Goldman Sachs? Answer: One is an African country that makes $2.2 billion a year and shares it among 25 million people. The other is an investment bank that makes $2.6 billion … and shares most of it between 161 people.'[20] It needs no comment. The gap between rich and poor continues to widen. About the middle of the 1990s really rich people were no longer called millionaires but were referred to, accurately, as billionaires. In 1996 the United Nations Human Development Report stated that the total wealth of the world's richest people, 358 billionaires, equalled the combined incomes of the poorest 45 per cent of the world's population, namely 2.3 billion people. Once again, the figures are so startling and clear that any comment would be superfluous.

Neither the passage of time, bringing with it the knowledge of these problems, nor natural disasters have ameliorated the inexorable demands of the financial powers for repayment by the poorest communities. The devastating hurricane 'Mitch' which hit central America in 1998 caused havoc in the poorest countries of that region. Honduras is a typical example. In 1997 their debt to international financial organizations and banks stood at $4.45 billion. In the preceding decade they had paid $4.39 billion in servicing the loans. Yet the annual repayment in 1997 was still $564 million. The tragedy could be expressed in another way: namely the debt per capita in 1997 was $767, whereas the Gross Domestic Product per capita in 1996 was $657.[21] They are caught in a poverty trap from which there is no escape as long as the powerful international financial institutions maintain their present policies.

In the half century which followed the Second World War, the Catholic Church mobilized its energies to be the champion against communism. Surely the time has now come for the Church to summon up similar energies in a worldwide crusade against capitalism.

Parallel to the realization that the Third World is being exploited financially is the awareness that the planet and its material resources are being plundered in a similarly irresponsible manner. Until comparatively recently human transformation of the environment was considered a necessary and creative activity. In the post-war period it was realized that there were limits to this process.[22]

The alarm was raised in the 1970s by a seminal study entitled *The Limits to Growth*. In that decade many people were seriously concerned by the realization that the world's population had just about doubled within living memory. It was equally apparent that this rate of progress was unsustainable in view of the necessary concomitants like food production and the consumption of fuels. The authors' message can be epitomized in a couple of sentences: 'If the present growth trends in world population, industrialisation, pollution, food production and resource depletion continue unchanged, the limits to growth on this planet will be reached sometime within the next hundred years.'[23] There has been some dispute about the timescale which was predicted but the main conclusions have been widely accepted.

Further widely researched studies and reports followed broadly confirming the prognosis that humanity is pursuing an unsustainable exploitation of the planet's resources. This was the conclusion of the Brandt Report in 1980,[24] and later of the Brundtland Report in 1987. To their credit various United Nations Agencies became involved in the task of transforming those scientific findings into practical guidelines for the world's policy-makers. The first result of this heightened awareness was the Montreal Protocol of 1987 which was a first attempt to limit emissions into the atmosphere of carbon dioxide and other harmful gases. By the last decade of that century it was clear that the ozone layer was being damaged seriously, in addition to other dangers such as acid rain.

Towards the end of the twentieth century, some of the predictions sounded apocalyptic in their forecasts, for example, the 1992 World Development report stated: 'The coming generation presents unprecedented challenges and opportunities. Between 1990 and 2030 as the world's population grows by 3.7 billion, food production will need to double, and industrial output and energy use will probably triple world-wide.'[25]

What is the answer to these staggering challenges? At the most fundamental level there is a moral problem to be faced. The equitable redistribution of the world's limited resources will not be achieved without a general perception that there is a moral obligation for the richer nations to share their wealth with the poorer countries. This sharing goes beyond money and comprises skills, educational programmes and trade agreements. In the 1970s there was the first mention of rich nations giving 1 per cent of Gross National Product in overseas aid.[26] As the century drew to a close even that modest figure proved too difficult to achieve. Clearly it was a matter of motivation. Human greed was seen to be impervious to the unanswerable findings of the scientists, because the basic moral problem had not been solved.

Where are we to find a solution? Clearly Christians are best placed to give a lead on this matter. All Churches believe that the universe was created by a benevolent deity and that the human race has been entrusted with the stewardship of this planet. Our mandate is not to destroy it by selfish exploitation but to enhance it by the equitable distribution of its resources. Wealthy societies must learn restraint in their own consumption and practise generosity in sharing their resources with poorer nations. The Catholic Church is compromised in this crusade because the papal policy on birth control is an aggravating cause in the world's accelerating birth rate. One can only wish that the efforts made by Vatican diplomats at world population conferences had been directed instead to encouraging governments to pursue the paths of material restraint and generosity. In 2001 when the newly elected President Bush repudiated the Kyoto agreement on the restriction of greenhouse gases, the US Catholic bishops indicated their support.[27]

The financial and environmental factors have been widely known for several decades. A vast literature exists on the subject.[28] More information is not necessary; what is lacking is the political and moral will to change the situation. As the preparations for celebrating the millennium gathered momentum, there was a concerted attempt by various pressure groups and development agencies in Great Britain and other countries to persuade governments to put pressure on the banks to wipe out the Third World Debt absolutely. To their credit Pope John Paul II, the Catholic bishops and the leaders of all the mainstream Churches in Britain and elsewhere supported the initiative.

At the end of 1999 the British government announced that it would cancel the debts of several of the poorest nations, and for that all honest people should be thankful. However the mechanisms which created the debt are still in place and working as before. There is no guarantee that the impoverished nations will be secure in the future. The whole rapacious process could start again. What is needed is a structural reform of the world's financial systems incorporating on the international scene something analogous to the British concept of the limited liability company. The Churches should continue to press for such reforms for as long as it takes. This is an aspect of Christian witness where we must proclaim the truth publicly even when no practical success seems likely. As far as the Catholic Church is concerned, our leaders would be well advised to stop their campaign against condoms and direct their efforts towards the abolition of Third World poverty. The basic causes are matters of motivation and moral principles and not the normal interplay of market forces.

In conclusion, it is worth noting that the mediaeval hostility to usury and commercial profit which seemed so quaint and out of date, even as recently as the 1940s, has proved surprisingly prescient. As far as the Catholic Church is concerned, one cannot but lament that the energies that have been expended against particular forms of birth control have not been directed against the lust for money. In short, the virtue of temperance has been aimed at the wrong target and the credibility of the Church has suffered as a result.

Postscript   A lamentable change of policy about money took place within the Catholic community in England shortly after the end of World War Two. In a way it was rather pathetic but as it was symptomatic of a desertion of principle it has to be mentioned. Hitherto, when Catholics were mostly poor, vast sums of money were given to build churches and schools in the century roughly between 1845 and 1945. I repeat that the money was given. In the 1940s and 1950s parishes came to rely more and more on gambling to raise money, in a largely unnoticed change of attitude. In the wake of the 1944 Education Act, a vast programme of school building had to be undertaken. The financial resources available to the Catholic community were considerably larger than those of previous generations when the first wave of parish schools had been built in the latter part of the nineteenth century. The characteristic financial gimmick of the late 1940s was the local football pool. In the 1950s practically every parish had one. As a result the majority of the parishes' money was then coming from gambling and not from freewill offerings. It was a significant shift of principle and many of the clergy seemed unaware of its moral implications. In those days the announcements in Sunday mass followed immediately after the second reading of the gospel (in English). Even when the gospel had been the famous 'lilies of the field' text, the results of the week's football pool were not infrequently read out in almost the same breath.

Notes

1   DS 2092.
2   DS 3716.
3   Decision of the Sacred Penitentiary, 16 June 1880, DS 3148.
4   Noonan, J.T. *Contraception*, New York 1967, 530.
5   *Gaudium et Spes*, section 48, DV II, 250.
6   *Gaudium et Spes*, sections 87 and 50, DV ii, 250, 253, 302, 254.
7   This astonishing admission was revealed by one of the commission members, Prof. J. Marshall, in a letter to *The Times*, 3 August 1968, quoted in Mahoney, J. *The Making of Moral Theology*, Oxford 1987, 266. It has since become common knowledge, cf. Fagan, S. *Does Morality Change?* Dublin, 1997, 150.

8   The unedifying story is related in detail in the book by Robert Blair-Kaiser. *The Encyclical that Never Was*, London 1995.

9   Mahoney, 271.

10 *The Observer*, 14 March 1993.

11 *Kirche Intern*, February 1994.

12 Orsy, L. writing in *The Tablet*, 16 January 1999.

13 Published by the Pontifical Council for the Family, English translation, published by the Catholic Truth Society, London 1997, p.16.

14 The Councils in question were: II Lateran of 1139, canon 13 [ACOD 200], III Lateran of 1179, canon 25 [ACOD 223], IV Lateran of 1215, chapter 67 [ACOD 265], I Lyons of 1245, part 2, section 1, [ACOD 293], II Lyons of 1279, canon 26 [ACOD 328], Vienne of 1311, canon 29 [ACOD 384], V Lateran of 1512–1517, session 10 [ACOD 626].

15 Tawney, R.H. *Religion and the Rise of Capitalism*, Harmondsworth 1972, 48. On this point I follow Tawney in preference to Noonan, whose comprehensive study of usury seems not to have adverted to this precise moral consideration of unlimited, as opposed to normal, profit. Cf. Noonan, J.T., *The Scholastic Analysis of Usury*, Cambridge, Mass., 1957, pp. 32, 365, 396.

16 Tawney, 116, Troeltsch, E. *The Social Teaching of the Christian Churches*, London, 1931 vol. 2, 643.

17 *The Guardian*, 17 October 1998.

18 Jackson, B. *Poverty and the Planet*, Harmondsworth 1990, p.102.

19 *The Guardian*, 21 December 1989.

20 *The Guardian*, 10 December 1993.

21 *The Guardian*, 23 February 1999.

22 Woodhouse, P. 'Environmental Depradation', p. 97 in *Poverty and Development in the 1990s*, eds Tim Allen and Alan Thomas, Oxford 1992.

23 Meadows, D.H. ed. *The Limits to Growth*. London 1972, 98.

24 *North South: A Programme for Survival*, edited by a committee under the chairman Willy Brandt, London 1980.

25 *World Development Report 1992*, eds Andrew Steer, Laurence H. Summers et al., Oxford 1992, p.2.

26 Ward, B. and Dubois, R. *Only One Earth*, Harmondsworth 1972, 198.

27 *The Tablet*, 30 June 2001.

28 In addition to the works already cited, one further book of exceptional value deserves to be mentioned, namely Geoffrey Lean, *Rich World, Poor World*, London 1978.

Chapter 11

Epilogue

The previous chapters have revealed a depressing record of moral failures in the practice more than in the theory of the Catholic Church's moral programme. They fall roughly into four categories. The first derives from a failure to recognize the complexity of the real world and responding to its moral dilemmas with oversimplification. This produces the quest for quick uncomplicated solutions (like demanding obedience to clear regulations, even in situations for which it is impossible to devise comprehensive rules). Secondly, and leading directly from the first, is the practice of acquiescence to the demands of political authorities as well as to the pressures of social and commercial interests. Thirdly, the failures to live up to the clear demands of the New Testament, such as the systematic neglect of truth, and activities like the Crusades. Fourthly, the relatively rare instances of theoretical error (like the condemnation of artificial birth control).

One is bound to ask how a Church endowed with so many natural advantages and supernatural gifts could have got itself enmeshed in such difficulties and ill-conceived policies. All human enterprises are fraught with limitations but, in the case of the Church, I think that there are two distinctive weaknesses that set it apart from the errors and blunders of secular organizations like failing businesses. The first is the phenomenon of clerical privilege and remoteness. The second is the absence of an effective dialogue with the laity. Defective channels of two-way communication have meant that the clergy do not listen to lay people properly and consequently cannot educate them, in the sense of sharing with them relevant guidelines for life.

I shall consider the first for the moment. All the official teaching and decision-making is reserved to the clergy who constitute a privileged class and whose effectiveness is diminished by the degree of artificiality in their lives. They are cut off from everyday realities like earning their living and raising a family. This removal from reality inevitably undermines their effectiveness in perceiving moral issues and offering relevant guidance on them. As responsibilities increase in the upper echelons of the hierarchy, so does the degree of privilege and remoteness from ordinary life. This isolation of the teachers and decision-makers is compounded by the fact that they are not answerable for their activities in any realistic sense either to their superiors, their peers, or to their subordinates. Theoretically a bishop is in overall charge of all the parishes in his diocese but since there may be 500 of them, any effective oversight is out of the question. The parish priests have extensive powers and are not answerable to their parishioners. Similarly bishops are under the jurisdiction of the pope, but as there are more than 3000 dioceses in the Church, once again effective oversight is impracticable. Bishops, being even more removed from the laity, are even less accountable to the people of the diocese. Finally the pope is answerable to no one, cannot be voted out of office, and can remain in power till his death, even if his last years might be so plagued by ill health that one might doubt his clarity of judgement.

The artificiality of the leaders' lives begins when young men enter seminaries to commence their training. Until the Second World War, the majority of the secular clergy entered junior seminaries which would receive them as early as the age of 14 and sometimes even younger. It is worth bearing in mind that they had put themselves forward. They had not been invited to assume spiritual leadership, which was the Church's ancient practice and which defined the meaning of the word vocation. Having entered these institutions the adolescent was placed on a conveyor belt which would lead him to ordination and beyond, without a single further serious decision. This may sound like an exaggeration but it is not. Admittedly seminarians had to make a specific application to receive minor and major orders, but the dynamics of the system were such that the momentum of the process would lead the young man forward. At any given stage it would have required a greater expenditure of psychic energy to leave rather than to stay inside. Other systems have displayed the same characteristics. It is said of the Nazis' SS battalions that fair-minded young men would enlist unaware of the tasks which they would later be called upon to perform. In the course of their training the unpleasant side of their duties would gradually become apparent but by that time the *esprit de corps* had bound them into the system, making it easier to stay inside rather than taking the hard decision to resign. It is difficult to overestimate the power of internal dynamics in a closed community. It is compounded of group expectations and an implied sense of moral failure if a man had put his hand to the plough and then turned back.

To this subtle process must be added the consideration that there are no absolute criteria for entry to seminaries. Unlike universities there are no clear examination qualifications for acceptance of students. A young man of goodwill who is not obviously stupid will be taken on if he has a good character reference from his parish priest. Since the Second Vatican Council there have been attempts to tighten up the admissions process by selection conferences and psychological screening yet it still lacks the precision and rigour of the systems for entry into university or officer training school.

Having entered the seminaries the students are effectively isolated from the realities of everyday life. They do not have to pay for their tuition; someone else does. From that moment onwards they will not have to work for their living in the sense that other people do. Ordination is irrevocable in the theology of the Catholic Church and no amount of inefficiency will cause them to be dismissed. Even if they should become alcoholics or child abusers the remedy was usually a transfer to another parish, though on that latter problem public pressure has caused the bishops to adopt a more realistic policy in recent years. In the seminaries the students were never required to do any cooking or cleaning; usually it was done by nuns or domestic servants. And so it went on. At the most impressionable period of their lives, they never had to look for work, find lodgings, cook a meal or catch the bus for work. After they were sent to their first curacy by the instructions of the bishop, they knew that they would always have a roof over their heads and would never stand in a dole queue. In this sort of situation conscientious men would make use of the freedom from material cares to devote themselves heart and soul to the work of the apostolate. Yet not every priest displayed that degree of zeal. The whole system from seminary to parish provided a secure haven for those whom one could perhaps describe as 'easy-going' or immature personalities.

To those who have not been through the system, it is difficult to convey just how insidious is the process of building the cocoon and insulating the man from reality. A couple of examples may serve to reinforce what I have said. In the immediate aftermath of the Second World War, I was studying in a seminary where about half the students had come from the armed forces, some of them having been on active service for about six years. No attempt was made by the teaching staff to integrate their vast experience into the formation for the priesthood. Some of them had faced life and death, sailed the seven seas, escaped from prisoner of war camps, and lived in cultures totally different from Britain. All of this was ignored as if it were irrelevant. Some years later I was teaching in a seminary for late vocations. All those students had come from years of ordinary work and some from very responsible posts. Once again there was no attempt to integrate their richly varied experiences into their training for the priesthood. The artificial world of the clerical caste had no place for anything so authentic.

One final consideration about the artificiality of the training of the priests is to contrast it with that of university students. To enter university they must pass the very demanding A-level exams. Usually the university will arrange a room in hall for their first year. After that they have to fend for themselves, finding flats or lodgings in crowded cities in competition with other would-be tenants. Having found somewhere to live, they have to feed themselves, doing the shopping and cooking in addition to fitting in their studies. Most university students are short of money and many have to supplement their grants or loans by finding work in the vacations. That pattern of life is totally healthy, normal, and provides a satisfactory environment in which young people mature quickly. The contrast with the training for the clergy could not be more depressing. The latter are being prepared for life in a privileged class. It has an attraction for inadequate and immature personalities who have never really outgrown the atmosphere of the sacristy that they got to know as altar servers.

As I have indicated above, the artificiality does not end with ordination but gets worse. There is no other walk of life where payment bears no relation to efficiency. Moreover the Catholic clergy have the additional isolation of being unmarried. Once again the conscientious men and those to whom God has given the gift of celibacy will use the freedom for greater commitment to their pastoral work. Not all clergy utilize the detachment so creatively. For the majority of the human race the most effective way of maturing the personality, engendering generosity, and experiencing creative happiness is to bring up children. If God has bestowed the special grace of celibacy they will not suffer, but if that rare gift is absent then the absence of marriage merely compounds the unreal atmosphere of their lives.

In antiquity, when wiser counsels prevailed, the parochial clergy were both married and worked at ordinary jobs. A number of provincial councils of the fourth and fifth centuries afford glimpses of how the parochial clergy earned their living and supported their wives and children. The fourth century Council of Elvira in Spain stated in its 18th. canon: 'Bishops, priests and deacons shall not depart from their districts for the sake of business; nor shall they follow up profitable business deals going round the provinces. For earning their living let them send a son, a freed man or a servant or a friend, or anyone: and if they wish to negotiate business, let them do so within the province.'[1] Clearly it was not the principle of commerce that was frowned upon but the scale of the operation which would take the clergy away from the scene of their pastoral work. It is also an admirable example of restraint. The clergy had to be content with not maximizing the profits and opportunities but had to be content with an income which was sufficient.

A similar picture emerges from a document known as the *Statuta Ecclesiae Antiquae* which was thought to have been a collection of Canons of several councils at Carthage in north Africa at the end of the fourth century. It is more likely to have come from southern Gaul in the second half of the fifth century. Canon 51 stated: 'Even the learned clergy shall earn their living by a trade (*artificium*)'. Canon 52 declared: 'The clerics shall gain their food and clothing by a trade or by agriculture, without prejudice to their office.' Canon 53 stated: 'All clerics who are capable of work shall learn a trade besides their regular duties.'[2]

The picture is clear. If the priest were a carpenter, for example, he could put down the hammer and chisel and go to the church to join in the singing of vespers or to conduct a funeral. They were directed to avoid occupations that would deny them that degree of freedom with the disposal of their time.

As with other areas of the early Church's practices, there was a healthy pluralism. After the conversion of Constantine a number of provisions were made for the payment of the clergy from public funds so that they did not need to work like other people. It was all part of the process that led to the creation of a privileged class which has so seriously separated the clergy from the harsh realities of the lives of their parishioners. It has also made bishops and priests unduly deferential to the wishes of governments. It is an attitude that has become so entrenched over the centuries that it has persisted even in the modern world where the separation of Church and State has become a reality. The habit of mind shows itself in the reluctance to criticize or confront the government, of which there are countless examples, that of Nazism in Germany being the most notorious. It may be relevant to bear in mind that Germany is one of the few countries in the modern world where the clergy of all Churches are paid a salary by the state. It puts them on a par with civil servants and school teachers.

The importance of work was brought home to me through the activities of a parish in a prosperous part of southern England in the 1980s. The parish had a hall but it was pulled down and rebuilt in grander style at the cost of £100 000. The parish priest was an exceptionally conscientious and hard-working man. It seems not to have occurred to that community that the money might have been spent better in other ways. Granted that they were able to raise £100 000 without any apparent difficulty, they could have built a block of four modest maisonettes and invited four families to move there from the workless north-east of England. The new arrivals could have found work without any difficulty in that part of the south and, having brought some neighbours with them, they would not have suffered too much from being uprooted from home. The value that is to be attached to work was the unspoken but defining consideration as to how that large sum of money was to be spent.

Special clothing has been another source and symptom of the unreal state of the clergy's way of life. In the Middle Ages many men wore the livery of their lord or employer. Since the French Revolution and the perception that all people are equal, such distinguishing marks of dress have vanished from society in all but the most necessary cases like policemen. Doctors, school-teachers, and social workers, who have vital roles in society, do not wear distinctive clothing so why do the clergy? Quite simply because they are still living as a privileged class and the clerical collar reinforces the isolation from reality. Admittedly Great Britain was not as bad as mainland Europe. In the decades after the Second World War the French clergy generally wore the 'soup-plate' hat and cassock in the street (which necessitated a lady's bicycle too). Yet as late as the 1950s some of the parochial clergy in England still wore buckled shoes and cloaks over their cassocks.

It is interesting and depressing to reflect that in antiquity a pope expressly forbade the secular clergy to dress differently from the laity. In 428 Pope Celestine I reproved Honoratus the bishop of Arles because he had intro-duced for his clergy the tunic and belt as worn by the monks. He also wrote to the bishops of Narbonne, with the message: 'We should be distinguished from other men, not by our dress, but by our knowledge, by our outlook on life, not by our style of life.'[3]

All these factors have tended to isolate the parish clergy from the realities of everyday life. In relation to the average lay member of the Church, it is the parish clergy who make all the decisions and impart nearly all the teaching about religion. The separation from reality shows itself in the poor quality of most sermons and the neglect of moral education in the really crucial areas of life. These are the factors which have deprived the Catholic Church of the ability to give a convincing lead in a troubled society, and indirectly these same factors could well contribute to the massive departure of so many adults who had once been baptized into the Church.

The situation of bishops is even worse than that of priests. They live in larger houses, they can surround themselves with a comfortable group of hand-picked chaplains and secretaries. In that club-like atmosphere they are more removed from reality than are the priests in parishes. They at least meet lapsed Catholics regularly, the bishops do not. What is really strange is that there is no specialized training for a bishop. In the army, officers of ability are sent to staff colleges, before being promoted to really high rank. The same applies to large-scale commercial enterprises which have their own training establishments for those destined for higher responsibility. In the Catholic Church nothing is done to prepare a priest for the task of being a bishop. It is almost true to say that just the reverse happens. In order to rule out ambition, no man is allowed to apply for the post. The consultation to fill a vacant diocese is conducted in secrecy and then the decision is sprung upon the chosen candidate without any prior warning, preparation, or training.

Until recently the bishops were surrounded and psychologically debilitated by the remnants of eighteenth-century social conventions. They wear a ring as a sign of authority and, before the Second Vatican Council it was customary for Catholics, on meeting bishops, to genuflect before them and kiss the ring. They were always addressed as My Lord, or Your Grace (for an archbishop). The clothes too are more elaborate and artificial. Few people would object to special vestments for the liturgy but it is peculiar, to say the least, to see a bishop at his desk wearing a cassock with red buttons, a red sash, a pectoral cross, and a red skull cap. At one level it could be looked upon as a harmless eccentricity but a more sober view cannot but regard it as a component of the scenario of artificiality.

The quest for special clothing as a mark of privilege has a long but not distinguished history in the Catholic Church. As far back as the early Middle Ages the popes were accustomed to grant to Benedictine abbots the privilege of wearing a mitre and carrying a crozier. For centuries these had been the badges of episcopal authority. Eventually every Benedictine abbot enjoyed the privilege. As far as the popes were concerned it enhanced their power as the bestowers of privilege, and enriched their coffers too.[4] It is sad to think that so many monks desired such marks of privilege.

The right to wear red or purple garments is no longer confined to the bishops. They are also the distinguishing badges of canons and those who enjoyed the honorific title of monsignor. These worthy gentlemen and the honorary canons too are allowed to wear purple socks and, depending upon the grade of monsignor, purple cassocks too. In the days when birettas were common, there was also the privilege of wearing a black biretta with a purple tassel on the top. It is almost inconceivable that some grown men really do enjoy these so-called privileges. It can only be because their lives are deprived of the simple but authentic joys of real life, like seeing one's children learn to read, swim, and ride a bicycle. And also because they are simply cut off from reality.

Once again, parallels with the French court of the *ancien régime* come to mind. When the court of Louis XV moved from place to place, the courtiers had rooms assigned to them in the various palaces. Their rooms were designated by the major-domo who went round with a piece of chalk writing their names on the doors, such as 'Duke of Orleans'. The king devised a particular category for special favourites, the order of *pour* (that is 'for'). Beneficiaries of this degree of play-acting saw written in chalk on their doors the blessed designation not just 'The Count of Acquitaine' but *'for* the Count of Acquitaine'. Apparently the privilege caused great jealousy among those who did not receive it.

What is clear to the modern world is that such a system of meaningless privileges could only operate within a group that was permeated with artificiality. It is sad that the bishops, canons, and monsignors of the Catholic Church still indulge in such infantile badges of privilege. It is an indicator of how far removed they are from the realities of everyday life. Viewed in this context, Cardinal Bourne's notorious judgement on the General Strike is not so surprising. It is unlikely that he would have designated the participants as being in sin if he had been the father of six children and had to contemplate a cut in his unemployment benefit.

In all fairness to the Catholic bishops, it should be remembered that the Anglican bishops too are surrounded by factors of artificiality which are almost as debilitating, but most of them are married. People who have the joys and responsibilities of bringing up children can never be quite so isolated from real life as are the Catholic bishops.

One final factor must be borne in mind too and that is the absence of any support structure for the bishops. In the course of their work they have some really difficult problems to cope with, such as what to do with elderly priests who may be burnt out psychologically. Most dioceses do not have any pension scheme for their clergy and alcoholism is not unknown. All of this has a very draining effect upon a bishop, and there is no structure to support him. A few years ago, one of the bishops in Ireland admitted that the isolation of his work had made him an alcoholic. He was very humble and honest about it and sought professional treatment.[5] A similar personal crisis occurred in the life a of Swiss bishop who resigned after becoming the father of a child.[6] What is really sad is the situation which allows these personal crises to arise.

All these factors do not prevent the bishops from understanding the Church's dogmatic tradition and indeed in the Second Vatican Council some remarkably fine documents were hammered out. The collective solidarity of that council may well have given them a sense of support which they had never before experienced in their work. However, in practical matters, where the moral choices arise, it does weaken the value of their judgement on moral issues because they have never experienced the realities at first hand, in the trenches, in the factories, or in families, like ordinary people.

At the highest level of decision-making, the Roman curia, the artificiality and the isolation from normal reality reach staggering proportions.

First of all, the process of recruitment gives rise to several disturbing questions. If a man wishes to be a priest, he might well exercise that ministry in a parish or the foreign missions, possibly as a monk or in some form of intellectual apostolate as do the Jesuits and Dominicans. If he desires none of these, but seeks the bureaucratic work of the Roman curia, one is forced to ask why he requires ordination. There is no care of souls in the conventional sense, no community for whom he would celebrate the Eucharist and bestow sacraments. In short, the tasks could be carried out by lay people. In the past, many of the entrants to the curia studied for the priesthood in Rome in a special seminary named the *Accademia dei Nobili Ecclesiastici*. No great knowledge of Italian is needed to understand what it signified. Not even the most snobbish of the ancient Oxbridge colleges ever presumed to label themselves so pretentiously. It does not amount to anything significant in the class war but such a title is a sure indicator of the realm of unreality.

Whereas the clothes of bishops are seriously anachronistic, the robes and garments to be seen around the Roman curia are literally out of this world. There is no denying the exquisite beauty of the uniforms which Michelangelo designed for the Swiss Guards, but does the Church of God really need this kind of pageantry? Equally the palace of the Vatican is one of the world's masterpieces of Renaissance art and the whole human race must be thankful to the sixteenth-century popes who were such generous patrons of the arts. Yet their practical impact upon the modern Church is a subtle reinforcement of the atmosphere of unreality. The personal titles are even more exalted: Your Eminence, Your Excellency, and so on.

Until very recently the popes were carried into St Peter's for spectacular ceremonies on the *Sedia Gestatoria*. It was a throne on a platform with horizontal poles and was carried literally on the shoulders of footmen in gorgeous costumes. It is simply staggering to reflect on the psychology that would approve of one man being treated in this fashion, no matter how important his office might be. It becomes intelligible only in the context of a group of people who are fundamentally out of touch with normal life. There is no shortage of anecdotes which illustrate this air of unreality in the activities of the Roman curia. Here just one must suffice. In the time of Pius XII officials receiving telephone calls from the pope were expected to conduct their part of the conversation on their knees.[7]

The largest section of the curia's personnel are in the diplomatic service. When the Papal States functioned as a nation-state, comparable in size and importance with other Italian states or the smaller nations of Europe like England and Portugal, a diplomatic service could be justified. With the abolition of the Papal States in 1870 when the Kingdom of Italy was reunited, it would have been logical to dispense with ambassadors. Quite the reverse happened and the number of ambassadors from the pope to heads of states has increased steadily over the last century. In 1978 there were 89 nunciatures and 21 apostolic delegations. In 1998 the number had risen to 167 representatives to governments and 18 special delegations attached to international bodies like the United Nations and its agencies.

Several serious questions have to be asked. Firstly, if the Pope wishes to communicate with the British government, for example, can it not be done through the Archbishop of Westminster? The local man will have the advantage of understanding the nation in which he grew up. A subordinate question is to theorize on how rare are the occasions when the pope and the British government have any business that requires consultation. The next question is why such ambassadors (papal nuncios) should be in holy orders and indeed archbishops? Clearly the whole institution is a relic of the past which has not been rationally phased out with the total change of circumstances in the modern world. Some theologians have questioned the validity of such episcopal ordinations since the Council of Chalcedon declared that absolute ordinations were invalid (that is not linked to a specific diocese).[8] Be that as it may, the existence of this unnecessary but extensive network of bureaucrats in holy orders is yet another element contributing to the overall atmosphere of artificiality of the Roman curia. The personnel are so far removed from the normal conditions of life that their decisions are bound to be lacking in realism.

The Catholic Church is thus governed by decision-makers who at every level from parish to Roman curia are structurally isolated from the realities of ordinary life. They cannot be voted out of office and in practice they are answerable to no one. In some respects they resemble the British House of Lords at the end of the twentieth century just as the Labour government was planning its demise. No other country in the world has so outmoded an organ of government. It was a total anachronism. But let it be remembered that over the last few centuries its real powers had been so pared down that it did not constitute a serious obstacle to the efficient running of the state. The Catholic system has undergone no such pruning and even after the Second Vatican Council the clergy still hold all the effective power of decision-making and official teaching.

In addition to the artificiality of their lives and isolation from everyday realities, the decision-makers do not have to suffer from errors in their decisions. It is rather like the classical argument against referendums. Namely there is something inherently unsatisfactory in giving the power to make a far-reaching political decision to people who will not have to implement its practicalities, nor will they have to bear the bear the responsibility for what might go wrong. In short, it can easily lead to irresponsibility. This is precisely the framework within which the Catholic clergy make their decisions. For example, if the parish priest overspends on extravagant decoration of the presbytery, a building society will not repossess the house. In one diocese of England a church was almost burnt to the ground though an accidental fire and it was found afterwards that the parish priest had forgotten to renew the fire insurance. He did not have to rebuild the church at his own expense nor was he disciplined. In the end, the parishioners had to find the money. In any other walk of life, this degree of irresponsibility would never be tolerated, quite simply because businesses would go bankrupt and armies would be defeated.

Apart from particular errors like the example cited above, the Catholic decision-makers do not have to live with the consequences of their commands. This has been most strikingly apparent in the matter of contraception. It can hardly be a coincidence that the only major body in the world which condemns the practice is the only one whose senior decision-makers are all elderly celibate men. The Anglican bishops who began their ecclesiastical careers usually as poorly paid curates when their children were young have been sufficiently in touch with the realities of family life to have avoided such a mistake.

Two other important areas of human experience which have also received too little attention from the Catholic leadership are those of warfare and the exploitation of workers. One cannot help feeling that the Catholic authorities would have addressed these issues with a greater sense of urgency had they been for years in dangerous mines or trenches. Yet for centuries the clergy of all grades have been provided for financially and exempt from military service. There is one exception to that statement, namely modern France. Since the anti-clerical governments of the late nineteenth century, French priests were conscripted and indeed several thousand of them were killed in the First World War. In that country too the clergy were the poorest in Europe, public funding having been withdrawn and the laity being unaccustomed to supporting their pastors. Paradoxically it was from France that the most important pastoral and theological initiatives came in the 1940s and 1950s. Possibly there is a connection. One is reminded too that the Methodist Church exercised its most effective influence on the English nation at a time when its clergy were for the most part lay preachers who worked in mines and factories for six days a week and preached sermons on Sundays.

Although the privileged status of the clergy is the main cause for the ineffectuality of the Church's moral programme, the complementary cause must not be overlooked, namely the absence of a satisfactory method of education for the laity. The effective communication of ideas, particularly those which are to influence personal conduct, must entail dialogue and listening. Indeed it has been said that people learn more when they are talking than when they are passively hearing information.

Although free speech has been allowed since Vatican II, the organs of free dialogue have so far been largely ineffectual and the structures which do exist are often no more than talking shops. The National Conference of Priests in England and Wales is a depressing example.

The Laity had reasons for optimism in the immediate post-Conciliar period, but the euphoria was destined to be short-lived. Three international congresses of the Lay Apostolate were held, but that of 1967 proved to be the last. In that year the Vatican set up a body known as the *Consilium de Laicis* all of whose officers were clerics. In England the Laity Commission was set up in the early 1970s but it was disbanded in 1982, the year of the Pope's visit to England. It was replaced by three new departments, composed of bishops which would call on lay experts as needed. Very rarely have they been needed, and as a result there is in practice no satisfactory institution to enable laypeople to participate in the policy-making of the Church in England and Wales. The experience and competence of the laity is once again effectively absent from ecclesiastical decision-making: all the power is in the hands of the bishops. As a result, great quantities of suggestions come from books, journals and newspapers (being the only surviving avenue of one-way communication), very little of it is taken up by the authorities. The resulting situation is one of bitterness and frustration. As a result, important decisions are made on the basis of inadequate knowledge and limited experience, and governed by an outlook which is simply out of touch with reality. Two centuries ago there was a notorious and much publicized dialogue between the French Queen Marie-Antoinette and her chief minister: 'Madam, the people have no bread'. Reply: 'Let them eat cake'. In the Catholic Church, things are not quite as bad as that but basically the same factors are at work, isolating from harsh realities the people who have the exclusive power to make the decisions.

The principles for a more satisfactory structure of decision-making and dialogue were outlined by Vatican II principally in advancing the role of laypeople, enhancing the collegial responsibilities of the episcopate, and endorsing the principle of subsidiarity. It would have been reasonable to expect the detailed implementation of these principles in the decades following the Council. Unfortunately the reverse has been the case. In the pontificate of John Paul II the Church has tended to revert to the pattern of centralized government and decision-making which was current in the time of Pius XII. One cannot but hope that in future pontificates the Council's vision will be implemented. Only a pope can do it, and if these issues are not resolved satisfactorily it can only result in further marginalization of the Church from the important issues of life and further abandonment of Catholicism by increasing numbers of conscientious people.

As a consequence of the factors outlined above, no structure has been devised for education based on dialogue. The Church is left with basically two methods of transmitting its moral programme: schools and sermons. Both have serious limitations.

Pupils in Catholic schools may hear about the sacrament of matrimony, for example, when they are simply too young to see it as relevant to their lives. The same applies to nearly all the significant areas of moral behaviour like warfare, economic exploitation and the resistance of organized labour, relationships, sex, marriage and the Christian upbringing of children. They may hear the words but even at the age of 18 they are not sufficiently experienced in the realities of life for the Church's teaching to make a realistic impression on them.

In this context it is worth mentioning that no realistic evaluation of the success or failure of Catholic schools has ever been undertaken. Although the schools' programme is one of the largest consumers of the Church's resources (both financial and human), no one knows how well the enterprise functions. To the simple question 'Does it succeed?' no one can give an answer because no systematic evaluation has ever been undertaken. Some of the clergy maintain that invisible realities like spiritual progress cannot be measured and so evade the issue. This is false since the problem is not essentially different from other forms of evaluating the educational process. The inspection of schools and the publication of league tables can tell us only a certain amount about education. 'Do these children have an appreciation of beauty?' is a question that cannot really be fathomed. Nevertheless reliable indicators about the effectiveness of education can be devised and monitoring of religious convictions is perfectly feasible, if one keeps in mind some limitations of the exercise.

In the 1980s one group of educationalists was determined to remedy the defect; they were the university chaplains. For years they had observed the end-products of Catholic schools. In their dealings with students they had become increasingly aware that the majority of young people seemed to abandon all religious practice when they left school and not infrequently beforehand. As a preliminary step to measuring how far the objective of Catholic education was attained, they devoted considerable care to defining what that objective was. Official sources and current literature were, surprisingly, silent on the matter. At the conference of Catholic chaplains in 1981 the following definition was agreed: 'The aim of Catholic education is the establishment of a relationship of trust with the institutional Church, in the context of which the young person will renew, or make for the first time, his or her definitive commitment to Christ.' Unfortunately the moving spirits behind this initiative were soon moved on to other posts and the matter was never pursued further. It means that the apparent ineffectuality of Catholic schooling is compounded by the fact that its effectiveness has never been evaluated.

Having left a Catholic school, the only vehicle of communication for the vast majority of practising Catholics is the sermon at Sunday mass. This is the most impractical method that one could envisage. Research has shown that when people are totally passive listeners, with no possibility of questions or dialogue (like party political broadcasts on television), the communication of conviction is insignificant. The sermon has the added disadvantages that the message is addressed to perhaps 300 people of both sexes, all ages, and every degree of intelligence. The possibility of conveying a realistic message is minimal.

A totally different method was devised by the movement known as the Young Christian Workers with the 'See, Judge and Act' process. Small groups of about half a dozen people would discuss an event in their lives that demanded a Christian solution and, having analysed the problem in the light of the gospel, would make a joint decision and agree on how to act upon it. This is an eminently satisfactory method of educating people and relaying Christian morality to everyday life. Unfortunately, only a tiny minority of all Catholics, in England certainly, have benefited from this methodology.

One other educational enterprise had a brief period of success around the time of the Second Vatican Council, namely residential centres for adult education. The pioneers were the Grail community in Middlesex and the Dominicans' house at Spode in Staffordshire. In these centres small groups of laypeople attended intensive courses on every aspect of theology. Their work received a great impetus after the Council and several more such centres were opened. The essence of their method was dialogue, discussion, and shared experience. Many people who took their courses were enabled to rethink the whole of their religious and moral principles to the great enhancement of their Christian commitment. Unfortunately the outreach was to a relatively restricted segment of the articulate middle class, and as the hopes engendered by Vatican II gradually evaporated so too did the dynamism of this movement. The closure of Spode House in the 1980s was both sad and symbolic. As a form of education it did not reach to the masses who have been left with the unproductive agencies of Church schools and sermons on Sundays.

As a consequence of the factors discussed in this chapter, even the best moral principles remain so often within the pages of books, encyclicals, and archives, rarely applied to reality, and in many cases unread. This failure of effective communication is yet one more factor that accounts for the ineffectuality of the Catholic moral programme, together with the many other causes discussed in the preceding chapters. Bearing in mind all these failings, can we really be surprised if thousands of well-intentioned Catholics have simply despaired of the Church's moral programme and quietly walked out?

Lest this chapter should end on a totally negative note, let me add a few constructive ideas. It lies outside the scope of this book to plan detailed remedies for decision-making and the communication of moral principles. However a few general ideas can be put forward as to how improvements might be planned. The guiding principle must be to seek some checks on the absolute autocracy of the pope and Vatican, without undermining the pope's legitimate authority within the Church.

I will start with the clergy, since they now have a monopoly of power. So, to begin with, no one should be admitted to the priesthood until he is mature. This means that he must have been earning his living like other people and be accustomed to the exercise of responsibility which would normally entail the responsibility for bringing up his own children. Laypeople must be given some sort of realistic voice in deciding which priests are sent to their parishes. The old system by which the bishop commanded a particular priest to work in a particular parish without consulting either party must cease. The structure which was used to choose the pastor could also join him in decision-making once he is installed as parish priest.

In a similar way, bishops ought to be elected locally. The details of how to assign voting rights to clergy and laity need not detain us here. It is not an insuperable problem. It was done thus in antiquity, as was the consecration of the candidate by neighbouring bishops of the region which would ensure that though he was chosen by vote his authority derived from the apostles via the other bishops. If bishops are to be removed from office, it must be through a proper legal process, conducted openly and with due respect for human rights. The present system of removal by administrative decision following secret enquiries must cease. The same applies to the treatment of theologians whose ideas are thought to be at variance with the Church's traditional doctrines.

In the normal day-to-day running of parishes and dioceses the principle of subsidiarity must be observed. There must be a reversal of the present tendencies whereby the Roman curia reserves to itself so many small decisions. Needless to say, all of this would require fairly extensive revision of the Code of Canon Law. All these suggestions are consistent with the authentic practice and theology of the Church, as can be seen by the way in which the ecclesiastical organizations have functioned in the past.

Although this book has contained many instances of misguided policies in the faulty transmission of the New Testament's moral programme, I wish to finish on a note of optimism. For about half a century a healthy climate of free speech has prevailed in the Church. Scholars, committed laypeople and clergy have no wish to remain in a ghetto. The principles for realizing an effective moral programme have been safeguarded in the documents of the Second Vatican Council, where they are locked away safe from the depredations of ideological betrayal. All that is now needed is for someone to take the key and unlock their transforming potential for the enrichment of the world at large.

Notes

1   Hefele , K. and Leclercq, J., *Histoire des Conciles*, Paris 1908–49, vol. 1, 191.
2   Hefele and Leclercq, vol. 2, 414.
3   Quoted by Congar, M.J. *Problems of Authority*, ed. J.M. Todd, London 1961, 135 .
4   Southern, R.W. *Church and Western Society in the Middle Ages*, London 1970, 113.
5   *The Guardian*, 29 February 1996.
6   *The Tablet*, 24 June 1995.
7   Duffy, E. *Saints and Sinners: A History of the Popes*, Yale 1997, 263.
8   Canon 6, ACOD, 90.

Bibliography

Allen, T. and Thomas, A. (eds) (1992), *Poverty and Development in the 1990's*, Oxford, Oxford University Press.

Aristotle, *Ethics*, (1953) (ed.) J.A.R. Thompson, Harmondsworth: Penguin Classics.

Auer, A. (1977), 'Freedom to be Autonomous or Freedom to Obey' in *Concilium: Moral Formation and Christianity*, Dec. 1977.

Augustine, P.C. (1923), *Commentary on the Code of Canon Law*, St. Louis: Herder.

Babington, A. (1983), *For the Sake of Example*, London: Paladin.

Bilio, A. (ed.) (1868), *Bullarum Diplomatum et Privilegium S. Romanorum Pontificum*, Turin: A. Vecco.

Blair-Kaiser, R. (1995), *The Encyclical That Never Was*, London: Sheed and Ward.

Boff, L. (1993), *The Path to Hope*, New York: Orbis Books.

Bourke, J. (1999), *An Intimate History of Killing*, London: Granta Books.

Brading, D. (1992), *The First America: The Spanish Monarchy, Creole Patriots and the Liberal State 1492–1867*, Cambridge: Cambridge University Press.

Brandt, W. (1980), *North South: A Programme for Survival*, London: Pan Books.

Browning, C.R. (1993), *Ordinary Men: Police Reserve Battalion 101 and the Final Solution in Poland*, New York: Harper.

Bruns, H. (1839), *Canones Apostolorum et Conciliorum Saec. IV – VII* (2 vols.), Berlin: G. Reimer; reprinted in 1959, Turin.

Byrnes, T.A. (1991), *Catholic Bishops and American Politics*, Princeton: Princeton University Press.

Carlen, C. (ed.) (1981), *The Papal Encyclicals 1958–1981*, New York: McGrath Publishing Company.

Casaldaliga, P. (1978), *I Believe in Justice and Hope*, Notre Dame, Indiana: Fides/Claretian.

Catechism of the Catholic Church, (1994), London: Geoffrey Chapman.

Cecil, H. and Liddle, P. (eds) (1969), *Facing Armageddon*, London: Leo Cooper.

Chadwick, O. (1975), *The Secularisation of the European Mind in the Nineteenth Century*, Cambridge: Cambridge University Press.

Cochini, C. (1992), *Apostolic Origins of Priestly Celibacy*, San Francisco: Ignatius Press.

Congar, Y.M.J. (1953), *Vrai et Fausse Reforme dans L'Eglise*, Paris, Editions du Cerf.

Congar, Y.M.J.(1964), *Power and Poverty in the Church*, London: Sheed and Ward.

Corley, F. (1993), 'The Secret Clergy in Communist Czechoslovakia', *Religion, State and Society*, 21 (ii).

Corpus Iuris Canonici, (1879), Leipzig: Bernhard Tauchnitz.

Curran, C.E. (1999), *The Catholic Moral Tradition Today, A Synthesis*, Washington: Catholic University Press.

Davis, C. (1967), *A Question of Conscience*, London: Hodder and Stoughton.

Davis, H. (1949), *Moral and Pastoral Theology* (3 vols), London: Sheed and Ward.

de Man, H. (1920), *The Remaking of a Mind. A Soldier's Thoughts on War and Reconstruction*, London: George Allen & Unwin.

d'Entrèves, A.P. (1970), *Natural Law*, London: Hutchinson.

Denzler, G. and Fabricius, V. (1984), *Die Kirchen im Dritten Reich*, Frankfurt: Fischer.

Dublanchy, E. (1922), 'Infallibilité du Pape', *Dictionnaire de Théologie Catholique*, Paris: Letouzy et Ané, Vol. 7 cols. 1638–1717.

Duffy, E. (1997), *Saints and Sinners: A History of the Popes*, New Haven: Yale University Press.

Fagan, S. (1997), *Does Morality Change?* Dublin: Gill and Macmillan.

Fessler, J. (1871), *Die Wahre und falsche Unfehlbarkeit der Papste*, Vienna: Grav und Pest.

Friedburg, A. (ed.) (1879), *Corpus Iuris Canonici*, 2 vols. Leipzig, Bernhardt Tauchnitz.

Genicot, E. (1922), *Theologia Moralis* (10th edn, 2 vols), Bruxelles: A.Dewit.

Gryson, R. (1970), *Les Origines du Célibat Ecclésiastique*, Gembloux: Duclot.

Goldhagen, D.J. (1996), *Hitler's Willing Executioners*, London: Abacus.

Graham, D. (1972), *Moral Learning and Development: Theory and Research*, London: Batsford.

Gurwin, L. (1983), *The Calvi Affair*, London: Pan Books.

Guttierez, G. (1971), *A Theology of Liberation*, London: SCM Press.

Guttierez, G. (1993), *In Search of the Poor of Jesus Christ*, New York, Maryknoll Orbis Books.

Hanicq, H.J. (ed.) (1826), *Sanctissimi Domini Nostri Benedicti Papae XIV, Bullarium*, Malines: Celsiss.

Haring, B. (1963), *The Law of Christ* (3 vols), Cork: Mercier Press.

Harris, P. (1970), 'The Church and Moral Decisions', *New Blackfriars*, (51) November, 518–27.

Hastings, A. (ed.) (1977), *Bishops and Writers*, Wheathampstead: A. Clarke.

Hastings, A. (1986), *A History of English Christianity, 1920–1985*, Oxford: Oxford University Press.

Hefele, K. and Leclercq, J. (1908–1949), *Histoire des Conciles*, Paris: Letouzy et Ané.

Helmreich, E.C. (1979), *The German Churches under Hitler*, Detroit: Wayne State University Press.

Hippolytus, (1984), 'Apostolic Tradition' in Cumming, G.J. (ed.), *Hippolytus: A Text for Students*, Nottingham: Grove Books.

Hornsby-Smith, MP. (1978), *Catholic Education: The Unobtrusive Partner*, London, Sheed and Ward.

Hughes, G.J. (1986), 'Totality, Principle of' in Childress, J.F. and McQuarrie, J. (eds), *New Dictionary of Christian Ethics*, London: SCM Press.

Hughes, G.J. (1998), 'Absolute Norms' in Hoose, B. (ed.), *Christian Ethics, An Introduction*, London: Geoffrey Chapman.

Jackson, B. (1990), *Poverty and the Planet*, Harmondsworth: Penguin.

James, L. (1993), *Imperial Warrior: The Life and Times of Field Marshall Viscount Allenby 1861–1936*, London: Weidenfeld and Nicholson.

Justin Martyr (1996), *Apologia*, Ante-Nicene fathers, vol. I, Edinburgh: T&T Clark.

Keijzer, N. (1978), *Military Obedience*, Alpen ann den Rijn: Sijthoff and Nordhoff.

Kelly, K. (1992), *New Directions in Moral Theology*, London: Geoffrey Chapman.

Kelly, K. (1998), *New Directions in Sexual Ethics*, London: Geoffrey Chapman.

Kuhner, H. (1960), *Lexikon der Papste*, Frankfurt, Fischer Bucherei.

Küng, H. (1990), *Global Responsibility*, London: SCM Press.

Lampe, G. (1961), *A Patristic Greek Lexicon*, Oxford, Oxford University Press.

Lean, G. (1978), *Rich World, Poor World*, London: George Allen and Unwin.

Lean, G. (1980), *God's Politician*, London, Darton Longman and Todd.

Lemkuhl, A . (1910), *Theologia Moralis* (11th edn, 3 vols), Freiburg: Herder.

Lessing, D. (1994), *Under My Skin*, London, Harper Collins.

Liguori, A. (1911), *Theologia Moralis*, (2 vols), Rome: Cuggiani.

Litvinoff, B. (1988), *The Burning Bush: Anti-Semitism in World History*, London: Collins.

Logie, D. (1992), 'The State of the World's Children', UNICEF Report, in *The British Medical Journal*, 30 May 1992.

Lora, E. and Simionati, R. (eds) (1996), *Enchiridion delle Encichliche*, Bologna: Edizione Dehoniane.

Mahoney, J. (1987), *The Making of Moral Theology*, Oxford: Oxford University Press.

Mansi, G. (1927), *Amplissima Collectio Conciliorum*, Arnhem and Leipzig: H.Welter.

Manual of Military Law, (1914), London: HMSO.

Marx, K. (1976) 'Theses on Feuerbach' in *Karl Marx and Frederick Engels: Collected Works*, London: Lawrence and Wishart.

Meadows, D.H. (ed.) (1972), *Limits to Growth*, London: Pan Books.

Milgram, S. (1969), *Obedience to Authority*, New York: Pinter and Mann.

Moltmann J. (1967), *Theology of Hope*, London: SCM Press.

Morrissey, F. (1986), 'Is the New Code an Improvement for the Law of Catholic Church?', *Concilium*, June 1986.

Murphy-O'Connor, J. (1978), *Becoming Human Together*, Dublin: Veritas Publications.

Murphy-O'Connor, J. (1997), *Paul: A Critical Biography*, Oxford: Oxford University Press.

Nédoncelle, M. (1946), *La Réciprocité des Consciences*, Paris: Aubier.

Noldin, H. (1951), *Summa Theologia Moralis*, (4 vols), Innsbruck: Herder.

Noonan, T.J. (1957) *The Scholastic Analysis of Usury*, Cambridge, Mass.: Harvard University Press.

Noonan, J.T. (1967), *Contraception*, New York: The New American Library.

O'Connell, J. (2001), 'The Discernment of Morality, Distinguishing Grounds, Guidelines and Laws', *Theology*, May/June, 173–83.

O'Connell, M. (1994), *Critics on Trial: An Introduction to the Catholic Modernist Crisis*, Washington: Catholic University of America Press.

Oldmeadow, E. (1943), *Francis Cardinal Bourne*, (2 vols), London: Burns & Oates.

Paton, H.J. (1951), *The Moral Law*, London: Hutchinson.

Peters, R.S. (1981), *Moral Development and Moral Education*, London: Allen and Unwin.

Piaget, J. and Inhalder, B. (1969), *The Psychology of the Child*, London: Routledge and Kegan Paul.

Pocock, T. (1987), *Horatio Nelson*, Oxford: Oxford University Press.

Pontifical Council for the Family (eds) (1997), *The Morality of Conjugal Life: Handbook for Confessors*, English translation, London: Catholic Truth Society.

Ponting, C. (1985), *The Right to Know*, London: Sphere Books.

Ranke-Heinemann, U. (1990), *Eunuchs for the Kingdom of Heaven*, London: A. Deutsch.

Runciman, S. (1951), *A History of the Crusades*, (3 vols), Harmondsworth: Penguin.

Ruyter, K.W. (1982), 'Pacifism and Military Service in the Early Church', *Cross Currents*, 32 (1), 54–70.

Salmon, P. (1959), *L'Office Divin*, Paris: Editions de Cerf.

Schillebeeckx, E. (1965), *Marriage: Secular Reality and Saving Mystery*, (2 vols), London: Sheed and Ward.

Simpson, J. and Bennett, J. (1985), *The Disappeared*, London: Sphere Books.

Sipe, A.W.R. (1995), *Sex, Priests and Power: An Anatomy of Crisis*, London: Cassell.

Socrates (1874), *Ecclesiastical History*, London, George Bell.

Southern, R.W. (1970), *Western Society and the Church in the Middle Ages*, Harmondsworth: Penguin.

Spicq, C. (1965), *La Théologie Morale du Nouveau Testament* (2 vols), Paris: Librarie Lecoffre.

Steer, A. (ed.) (1992), *World Development Report 1992*, Oxford: Oxford University Press.

Stolfuss, N. (1996), *Resistance of the Heart*, New York: Norton.

Strauss, H.A. and Kampe, N. (eds) (1988), *Anti-Semitismus*, Frankfurt: Campus Verlag.

Sweeney, G. (1977), 'The wound in the right foot, unhealed' in Hastings, A. (ed.), *Bishops and Writers*, Wheathampstead: A. Clarke, 207–34.

Tawney, R.H. (1972), *Religion and the Rise of Capitalism*, Harmondsworth: Penguin.

Teichmann, J. (1986), *Pacifism and the Just War*, Oxford: Blackwell.

Theolbald, M. (and Schwäger, R. Hilpert, K., Kremer, P. and Schlegel, H.) (1995), 'Gehorsam', in *Lexikon für Theologie und Kirche*, Freiburg: Herder, vol.4, 358–63.

Thomas, H. (1996), *The Slave Trade*, London: Picador.

Tillard, J.M. (1982), ' Obeissance' in *Dictionnaire de Spiritualité*, Paris: Beauchesne, vol.11, cols. 535–63.

Todd, J.M. (ed.) (1961), *Problems of Authority*, London: Darton, Longman and Todd.

Truchlar, K.V. (1967), 'Obedience' in *New Catholic Encyclopedia*, New York: McGraw-Hill, vol.10, 602–6.

Vallely, P. (ed.) (1998), *The New Politics: Catholic Social Teaching for the Twenty-First Century*, London: SCM Press.

Vatican Congregation for the Clergy (eds) (1994), *Directory on the Ministry and Life of Priests*, London: Catholic Truth Society.

Vbra, R. and Bestic, A. (1964), *I Cannot Forgive*, London: Transworld Publishers.

Vogels, H.-J., trans. G.A. Kon (1992), *Celibacy: Gift or Law*, Tunbridge Wells: Burns Oates, English Translation of *Priester dürfen Hieraten* (1992) Bonn, Kollen Verlag.

von Böckle, F. (1980), *Fundamental Moral Theology*, Dublin: Gill and Macmillan.

Ward, B. and Dubois, R. (1972), *Only One Earth*, Harmondsworth: Penguin.

Warnock, M. (2001), *An Intelligent Person's Guide to Ethics*, London: Duckworth.

Webster, C. and Frankland, N. (1961), *Strategic Air Offensive against Germany 1939–1945*, London: HMSO.

Wills, G. (2000), *Papal Sin: Structures of Deceit*, London: Darton, Longman and Todd.

Wistrich, R.S. (1991), *Anti-Semitism*, London: Methuen.

Woodhouse, P. (1992), 'Environmental Depredation' in Allen, T. and Thomas, H. (eds), *Poverty and Development in the 1990s*, Oxford: Oxford University Press.

Index